PRAISE FOR INDIGEN

MW00779888

"Indigen is a thought-provoking book by Khadijat Quadri. Khadijat is an expert in the captivating exploration of spiritual psychology that intertwines spirituality with personal growth. This book is a profound journey that delves into the complexities of the human mind and spirit, offering readers valuable insights into personal development and self-awareness.

Khadijat's expertise as a practitioner of spiritual psychology is evident throughout the book. Khadijat's skills as a practitioner, combined with her empathetic communication and practical applications, make this book a valuable resource for anyone seeking personal growth and a deeper understanding of spirituality.."

~ Gwen Foster, Owner of NuVision

"INDIGEN reads deceptively easily. But when you pause for a minute, you realize that every paragraph warrants a chapter, and every chapter warrants an entire book. The writing is so rich. You will have to reread this quite a few times to get everything out of it, each time going a layer deeper. One can have admiration for how Khadijat Quadri has survived her childhood and adult life ordeals, both physically and mentally. They have been described in a matter-of-factly way, so that you might easily miss the depth and pain of them. But one cannot avoid being in huge awe for how Khadijat Quadri has been able to turn these adversities into something so powerful and positive.

She shows us what true healing is, away from hacks and quotes, away from compromise. She shows us that healing is hard work, on a slow and painful process, with many ordeals and indeed unfortunately a lot of uncertainty and loneliness. You will leave many people behind if you truly heal. This book carries the weight of 20 years of collected experiences: being abused, betrayed and let down, stumbling and getting up again, searching, learning, and healing. It shows us what integrity is and what being true to yourself is. Some readers may take offense, since Khadijat Quadri does carry her heart on her sleeve. She has no patience for anything superficial and quick, nor for anything other than autonomous and authentic. If you do take offence, you know you have work to do. She is the real deal. "

~ Verele Vorstman MSc, GMBPsS.

"Even in the darkest of dark, Khadijat Quadri sees God's light. She is fearlessly resilient and a leader, especially for those who are lost. Khadijat is an inspiration to say YES to His mission, just as Mary did."

~ **Denise P. Krohn Ph.D**

"Khadijat became a healer by divine 'intervention.' Her life, particularly her childhood and upbringing, organically brought her to this place where she can be a psychotherapist who is able to connect with the light. The suffering she experienced as a young girl would have derailed most people's path to enlightenment. Khadijat had the divine ability to transform these awful experiences into powerful awareness and overcome and improve herself, so she can help others in similar situations. Her personal experience and ability to disengage from negative energy allowed her to not become victimized, but to become a psychotherapist with a deep spiritual and cosmic awareness. She draws from all spiritual human realms to help people in emotional and spiritual distress. From the Holy Spirit to incarnation, she connects the universe to the individual's soul.

Reading INDIGEN gave me goosebumps. Khadijat has an ability to describe deeply emotional and psychological processes with a natural ease and surprising clarity. INDIGEN was not only helpful for me as a healer, but simply moving to the core with the countless human experiences she touches on in this book. Both personal and through many clients' stories she even brings all this in context with societal phenomenon.

If you or a loved one had to navigate any kind of emotional or psychological crisis, you could only dream of finding a psychotherapist with the depth of consciousness, connection to the universal energy and ability to connect to the light like Khadijat."

~ **Dr. Bernard Straile, developer of The SHOW Method, an epigenetic healing method.**

INDIGEN

Journeys of A Wounded Healer

Healers should not be measured by their tools but by the measure of light within them. The light is what makes any tool effective. Just as a bad farmer with good tools cannot yield a good harvest, a healer not in the light cannot wield healing. God chooses His healers—they are the ones assigned to carry the light.

INDIGEN

Journeys of A Wounded Healer

A Spiritual & Multicultural Guide
For Psychotherapists & Healers

KHADIJAT OMOBOLANLE QUADRI

KUADRA PUBLISHING
San Antonio, TX

Copyright © 2024 by Kuadra

All Rights Reserved.

Published 2024 by Kuadra
4100 East Piedras Drive
San Antonio, TX 78228

Without limiting the rights under copyrights reserved above, no part of this publication may be reproduced, stored in or transmitted in any form or by any means without the written consent of the copyright owner and the above publisher of this book, except by a reviewer who wishes to quote brief passages in connection with a review for a website, magazine, etc.

Neither the publisher nor the author is engaged in rendering professional advice or services to the individual reader. The ideas, procedures, and suggestions contained in this book are not intended as a substitute for consulting with a physician. All matters regarding your health require medical supervision. Neither the author nor the publisher shall be liable or responsible for any loss or damage allegedly arising from any information or suggestion in this book. While the author has made every effort to provide accurate telephone numbers and Internet addresses at the time of publication, neither the publisher nor the author assumes any responsibility for errors, or for changes that occur after publication. Further, the publisher does not have any control over and does not assume any responsibility for author or third-party websites or their content.

Indigen: Journeys of A Wounded Healer
A Spiritual & Multicultural Guide for Psychotherapists and Healers
By Khadijat Omobolanle Quadri

ISBN:

Paperback: 979-8-9905388-0-1
EPub Ebook: 979-8-9905388-1-8
PDF Ebook: 979-8-9905388-2-5

LCCN: 2024911971

Contact The Author at
www.kuadracs.com

Book Design and Layout:
Eddie Egesi, Apricot Branding

For my beloved son, Rilwan Olatubosun Quadri (09/10/1999-08/13/2023).
Like a rose that springs from the soil, it is within the deepest drudges of pain has our love risen and will it forever abide in the love and light of God. For my children Aminah, Rahman, and Kafaya.

The popular Yoruba song "Ja Funmi" (Fight for Me)-King Sunny Ade: Narration -Translation
To all those who have faith in the forces controlling fate and destiny and their determination to persevere, I offer an invocation for spiritual enlightenment as we walk the treacherous path of humankind. This plea is contextualized in the Yoruba cosmological paradigm of the spiritual and supernatural realm ("Eleda") and the earthly one ("Ori"). "Ori," meaning "head," is a metaphysical concept in Yoruba, referring to a person's intellectual abilities, spiritual intuition, and Soul destiny.

To all my friends and clients who have contributed their healing journeys to this book, I owe a depth of gratitude. Your presence in my life is healing for me, and I pray it has been for you as well.

Special thanks to my editor, Alice Heiserman of WriteBooksRight, contributor Grayham Forscutt https://galacticastrologyacademy.com/, Gwen Foster, ND of http://gwenfoster.com, Laralee List, www.historyinretrograde.com, Dr. Denise Krohn, Dr. Monica Hernandez, Eddie Egesi of www.apricotbranding.com and Maureen Galindo for supporting the birth of my book and providing me with valuable insights.

Most importantly, I thank the Supreme Creator, Holy Spirit, and all Divine Emissaries who walk in and with the light of truth and wisdom for their unconditional love and continued support for me at all stages of my journey, and for their dedication to the healing and advancement of the universe and all sentient beings.

CONTENTS

FOREWORD

I was thrilled to meet Khadijat Quadri in person when she presented her work at a conference in Bangkok Thailand, where I was also scheduled to speak. Khadijat invites you to a soul-to-soul contact; you can take it or leave it. Before reading this book, know that Khadijat generates discomfort. She bothers us by bringing cruelty and effort before us. She leads us to the depths, urging us to stand at the bottom and propel ourselves upward instead of procrastinating about facing her message.

Indigen's message unveils unpleasant truths, challenging the comfort cultured to recognize the value of deep internal work, reminding us of our power to swim against the stream and participate in building a better society. Such a proclamation crashes against the inertia of a long way down from heaven to earth. Although history shows countless examples of the need to broaden our consciousness and willingly project our light impulses out to heal the world, too often, we remain passive, letting ourselves go where society takes us.

The listening Khadijat requires is not passive but a call to action. Faced with the appeal to break free from our buried pain, I can honestly cry: "I am completely overwhelmed by daily life. I have no energy to attend to more demands. I am doing my best, and yet, it is not enough!" Who is willing to become conscious despite such a frustrating perspective in times of selfishness? Anyone who has such willingness should check this book out. You will discover that no further effort is required, but you will be confronted with questioning the cultural bias of running away from pain. Likewise, with the guidance of a reliable professional, you should easily be able to make gold out of the lead. One might need to overcome the harshest internal battlefields to master spiritual healing. Possibly, the depths Khadijat had to face seemed to have distilled the essence of pain, resulting in wisdom.

She comes to show us how liberating it may be to leave the pain behind instead of sweeping it under the rug. She outlines her story to encourage us to redirect our forces to light and love, setting us free from the heaviest weight. What you will find in these pages might be briefly described as a genuine perspective conveyed through retelling the path that led the author to her certainty—and even further, to a certainty of health that surpasses our humanity.

Like Khadijat, I am also a spiritual healer, a dance therapist, a member of the International Dance Council and UNESCO, and an Orientalist at El Salvador University in Buenos Aires (where I reside). Later, as a counselor, I specialized in neurophysiological-based trauma reprocessing techniques such as eye movement desensitization and reprocessing (EMDR), one eye at a time, hemispheric glasses, pain-erasing techniques, and chromotherapy. Additionally, I am an astrologist, channelizer, medium, and an Akashic Records reader. I am also a flower remedies therapist and practitioner in energetic healing techniques, including bio quantum medicine, touch for health, Pranic healing, Tesla healing, emotional freedom technique, and TREE.

Besides, I had the honor of accompanying my Hindu teacher, José Bullaude, who for eighteen years supervised the research that resulted in the progressive development of the Dynamic Integration Method (DIM) for expanding our consciousness. Building DIM foundations on proven experiences took me twenty years of trial and error to ensure the safety and effectiveness of the method. Only then could I develop its variations like DIM Dance, DIM Flower Remedies, and DIM Therapy and create a spiritual healing center with three branches. All this dedicated work has allowed me to travel the world sharing my experience.

In my travel, I had my striking encounter with Khadijat Quadri. She introduced a Psychology and Spirituality conference by opening her deep, huge heart, even though not everyone felt like embracing her message. However, she cannot deny her gift. She speaks loudly from her treasure: truth.

My immediate reaction was reverential. But I soon realized that we might not always be in the right mood to face an honest answer when we are challenged to rise to the occasion. I needed to step forward and be courageous enough to accept the invitation to allow Khadijat's truth to enter my soul. When I did that, it became clear that I was witnessing how an actual light warrior fights!

We should be aware of the temptation to dismiss the diversity of styles and keep in mind that Khadijat expresses herself in a universal language despite using catholic terms that might be charged with personal affection for many. She presents faith as a state of mind that works as a door to personal and universal improvement, one anchored in the light of the superior loving power. It does not necessarily depend on a specific religion. Let us be driven to the core of the message. Allowing a greater consciousness to act through us brings about greater changes in the world.

Khadijat's scope is the profound universal truth. We need just a little effort to overcome our defenses and open ourselves to reach enlightenment so that the journey of a wounded healer can spread. She partners an odyssey not only to her soul but also to our own. In my experience, it is more about letting go than striving. But we must walk our own way to find our glorious destination.

As the book progresses, you will be immersed in the author's sacred world: her experience, and if you are courageous enough to face your roots, you will then be able to resurge to the depths of clarity.

Continually, you will be presented with the deployment of her healing instruments. Every tool here is a step of worldly wisdom to cover along an internal peregrination. You will be lovingly guided to discover a way back to heaven. Khadijat offers a manual on conquering inertia and driving our consciousness back to the supreme light. The only condition to get on board is trust, not in the author but in the Highest that guides her. If you surrender and persist, you can be sure that on the way, and find yourself building a new identity—a sacred, healthy, and loving one.

Visualizing the overall picture formed by the different elements presented in consecutive chapters may be a grueling challenge until you grasp how they are integrated into clinical cases. Only then may you grasp how the mosaic of spiritual therapy practice can be comprehended—which is where we should pay close attention as the practice determines a therapist's authority.

To illustrate the author's expertise before you get to the "juicy part of the book," let us go back to my personal experience. I decided to have a session with Khadijat as soon as I met her, and I realized why at the moment she received me. I could feel the energy flowing through my body like a wild river. It seemed as if stones in my energetic field would be turning into fluid light and as if a hundred pounds of debris would be removed from me. It felt like my whole system was being transformed, like dough in a baker's hands.

By the end of my initial session, I had regained a long-forgotten sensation—the vitality I had fifteen years ago! I was healthier, lighter, younger, freer, and definitely more myself. The change kept going deeper every long-distance session I had.

Therefore, it is a great honor for me, and I am profoundly thankful for my humble contribution to the overwhelming lightstorm of *Indigen's* message.

Khadijat offers us numerous clues about the healthy state of being we get when aligning ourselves with our higher purpose. "We took on the labor of love to incarnate on this planet to assist in the healing and restoration of the collective human Soul and move it along its natural God-given developmental process."

She delves into our essence, explaining that "Anyone whose mind is open to the inflows of divine wisdom and whose heart emanates love that comes from God is a Healer."

We might wonder: Why aren't we all healers? The author explains that we are not all healers, probably because we fear facing our shadows. I radically support her, as office experience crowds me every day with examples of how we wrongly believe that we are not going to be able to overcome pain. I think it is worth noticing that humanity would possibly have been extinguished long ago if we were not stronger than we think.

Such an idea is far from being a kind of collective flummery but arises from genuine reasons to believe we are unable to live our lives fully. Trauma is an experience doted with such a massive emotional charge that we are, at that moment, unable to process it healthily. When our perceptive apparatus refers certain information to our brain, we feel overwhelmed, overmatched and, therefore, unable to integrate the notions of time, language, and resources into our understanding of the traumatic event.

As time remains remote from the experience, our underground sensation is that we will remain trapped in this extremely vulnerable situation forever. Without professional intervention, we do not see how to overcome previously deemed insurmountable obstacles.

However, it is essential to be aware that facing spiritual healing far exceeds addressing trauma. This therapy delves deep into the transcendental origin of problems, undeniably releasing them. Reaching the enlightening experience of spiritual healing is never an intellectual matter. It is more about opening our hearts and consciously contacting our souls than about closing our ideas to rational meanings.

My final suggestion for better understanding the quantum transformation journey is to avoid attempting to comprehend it as it broadly surpasses our rational understanding. Becoming healthy instruments of light requires recognizing our true finite nature and the perception of a bigger dimension. We need to quit our control impulse and surrender to transcendental truth.

Thus, it seems worthwhile to take the risk of immersing ourselves in spiritual healing and becoming aware of our luminous essence. On the journey we are being invited to take, our personal and universal meaning will be deeply pondered, potentially unveiling a new harmonious self.

Professor María Lucila Belluscio
Director, Dynamic Integration Center
El Salvador University, Buenos Aires

PREFACE

For the last decade, I have been seeing 11:11 everyday and so have my friends and clients. We contemplated the sacred numbers and why so many people have been drawn to uncovering its hidden message. Some spiritualists have deduced that it must be a message from the universe. It later came to me that the message is directing us back to the bible in Isaiah 11:11 which states: "On that day, the Lord will extend His hand a second time to recover the remnants of His people from Assyria, Egypt, Pathros, Cush, Elam, Shinar, Hamath, and the islands of the sea." Could this be the re-gathering of God's chosen ones? So many of us have been hungry for a truly spiritual community on earth, a loving community whose sole purpose is the development of unconditional love and service to one another.

For many nights, I have dreamt that I was gathering crowds of people. I did not know what this meant. Now, it is all coming together: how I drew people to me and what I must do. If God assigns me to the role, I will gladly accept with great honor to serve in the capacity of Ensign, the international person who will send out the call (the voice) and gather God's children.

In 2021, I had a vision. I was standing on a huge stage behind an elderly-looking man in a white robe seated in front of me. I could see a sea of people all resonating in different Soul colors representing their different energies and various skillsets. My demeanor was one of victory! Many clients over the years have fondly told me that I remind them of the oracle in the movie *The Matrix*, the voice, the flag that gathers the people. I hope you will join me on this great journey to materialize a heaven on earth.

INTRODUCTION

I am an Angel sent by God and there are millions like me incarnated on the planet upon the commission set by God. Our true nature as angels is a birthright and a natural developmental process. Just as caterpillars turn into butterflies and eggs become birds, humans become angels. Our mindset is one of true service and a joy for doing what is good for the sake of good. We cut across race, gender, ethnicity, geographical locations, countries of origin, age, and more. We are in the healing professions: from doctors, psychotherapists, healers, religious leaders, teachers, accountants, parents, children, friends, classmates, caregivers, and others. We took on the labor of love to incarnate on this planet to assist in the healing and restoration of the collective human Soul and to move it along its natural God-given developmental process. In taking this journey upon the request from the universe for volunteers, we understood we would temporarily give up our identity to be in a human body and undertake a journey towards igniting collective healing.

Angelic Souls represent the Christ Consciousness; our role is to destroy the Control System from within and bring the world back into rightful harmonization with the Universe.

Entering via the womb and being confined to a human body, we forget who we are and accept the shackles of mental and spiritual retardation and get raised by unevolved parents and families.

Underneath, we still retain our innate sense of wisdom, freedom, and spiritual intelligence that puts us outside societal norms. We learn to overcome social programming and work steadfastly towards our God given mission. Upon our spiritual awakening, we begin our inner and outer journey towards our divine mission and adopt thoughts, speech and ideas that are in accordance with higher wisdom, but which society cannot comprehend. We learn to endure ridicule and persecution for refusing to fall in line with the rest of the society.

By taking on aspects of the guilt and shame of humanity, we heal ourselves and simultaneously map the path for healing others. Anyone in possession of the Light of God within is a healer.

Anyone whose mind is open to the inflow of divine wisdom and whose heart emanates the love that comes from God is a healer. We act upon the knowing that there is no love but God and like a river flowing downstream, love flows from God to us and out into the world. Like a fire that dissolves matter, our mind is home to the flame of Christ consciousness, ready to dissolve all the delusions of this world. We lean not upon our own understanding but open our mind to receive the wisdom that comes from God. We understand that all healing comes from divine light, and we are but vessels for extending that light. For love is light and darkness is devoid of light, both are existing on the planet as a learning ground for us to grow out of the dark and into the light.

All Angelic Beings were humans at one time and the same can be said of Demons. Our earthly life is a time spent on clarifying what we desire the most and which direction we will go after this life. Just as a fifth grader is preparing for sixth grade and high school prepares us for adult life, our entire earthly life prepares us for the eternal spiritual afterlife. If we fail, we can get a redo and, in some circumstances, eternal devolution is the result. God is an equal opportunity employer and earth school is self-paced, we can take as many lifetimes as possible, but we will not be admitted into the heavens if we do not qualify for it.

INTRODUCTION

Earth school is a place where we learn multiple spiritual lessons such as love, wisdom, forgiveness, overcoming pride, manifestation, Jealousy, and enlightenment to name a few. The plan of the universe is that we graduate earth school and accept the requirements for participating in the greater universe. If we choose not to work towards the greater plan and prefer to seat on the sidelines, we will find ourselves on the other side looking like a rock, or a piece of dried log on its way to devolution. Our report cards are carefully tabulated to the last grain, including our desires, intentions and actions and we will look exactly like a compilation of all our activities. These days, people are preoccupied with their physical bodies, obsessing about it, patching it, and dressing it up like an easter egg that is shallow within. They live in fear of its inevitable demise and all the while no attention is paid to the forever body they will acquire after this life.

Spiritual psychotherapy is a place to clarify our inner desires, the feelings that come from those desires, and to work on refining our desires with the expectation of developing good intentions while taking daily actions towards them. Initiates of Spiritual Psychotherapy are trained to understand the importance of processing emotional and mental traumas, just as the body digests food, the emotional and mental body must process and digest life experiences and transmute trauma into true spiritual convictions. This is why we are here on the planet. We came for experiences not for material gain. Our material earning do nothing for our Soul, not unless the gains are used in service of others. What we will take with us beyond our material life is our experiences and the earnings of enlightenment.

Our true self is the Soul, and our Spirit is the eternal part of us that comes from the Light of God and Spirit of God. Enlightenment occurs when the Spirit of God joins with the Soul of the man or woman while the mortal body is still alive. The Spirit of God holds the mind of God and can merge with the Human Soul if the vibration of the Soul is in alignment with Spirit and Spirit wishes to engage the Soul's activities. This results in a type of metamorphosis or transformation of the Soul. When an illumined Spirit joins with the Soul and the Soul engages the material body, such a person becomes an Angelic being because they are an enlightened Soul.

Through meditation and past life regression therapy, I discovered that I have walked the earth thousands of years ago and learned all the required spiritual lessons, so my current life challenges were easy to overcome. I also learned that I come around every thousand years for specific missions and I have taken on my current incarnation to aid in this new developmental process of humanity. My earth name is Khadijat Omobolanle. I am one of three hundred million Angelic Souls sent by God. Our development is a natural organic evolution to realize the Christ consciousness and illuminate the Soul. I am one of those whom God has sent to return to earth to carry the light into the depths of darkness, engaging all manner of traumas and human atrocities for transmutation, transformation, and resurrection.

My journeys have been painful and audacious, for they did not recognize me and saw me as a threat that could expose their evil thoughts and deeds. I knew I was special, not in the way humans regard being special, but for me, it was a quiet integration of all ideas in the world with divine truths. I was in it, but not of it, and from the age of four, I faced spiritual warfare which I regard today as rites of passage to integrate all levels of the mind and become more whole.

I was born with a heightened sixth sense. My intuition was essential for survival and through these abilities, I could discern what was to come, and it showed me the decisions I must make and the path to take. At the age of five, I had multiple experiences of the light of God and in other instances encountered demonic influences and pledged to serve the good and resist all evil. For this reason, family and friends could not understand my resistance to things they found good, but I believed were connected to darkness. There was no technology in the 1970's growing up in Nigeria, but many social and economic issues shook the country at the time and to this day. Nigeria has long been a free-for-all child kidnapping enterprise, with many rough and harsh terrains and extreme forms of violence; my clairvoyance and intuition and absolute trust and solace in the divine were my only saving Grace.

By the age of ten, I could recall my five past lives, all of which were violent, abusive, and in extreme poverty. This current life has been my best life despite my difficulties. It hast paled in comparison with what I have seen of my past lives. I saw different lives where I was a persecuted Christian, betrayed and thrown to the lions in a Roman Coliseum, other lives where I had lived as a monk in Tibet, a medicine woman in India, a warrior in Mongolia, and a sex slave in Africa. Each one barred me from the opportunity to fully develop my potential as a healer. I recalled that in each life, my hands were always raised in absolute faith and trust in the divine, and through my previous lives, I established my energy on the planet and worked through major spiritual lessons. My previous lives would be a testament to the strength I gathered for this moment in time to face new challenges and opportunities for spiritual growth. When it comes to the universe, growth is infinite, and all good angels and beings of light are ever learning and expanding their light.

By the age of thirteen, I had two near-death experiences resulting from disease and extreme sensitivity to my environment and seeing ghosts and entities became a norm for me. My mother called me an idiot and a fool far more than she called me by my name. She flogged and assaulted me almost daily until I was married off at the age of twenty-two and ended up in the United States. I was frequently ostracized and bullied by classmates in secondary school, and college offered me no peace being one of the most dangerous gang-ridden universities in Nigeria.

After being married off to a man I did not even know and made it to the shores of America, I thought I would get some solace and safety but not long after my arrival, I was met with the brutal realities of racism, culture shock, problems with assimilation, and spiritual confusion.

With my emotional traumas, I educated myself as a therapist and worked with organizations dedicated to helping abused children. Through the process of helping others heal, I healed my traumas as well. My biggest catalyst for healing was to remember who and what I was and why I was on this planet. At the age of five, I had a distinct sense that earth was not my home, and I could recall episodes of dissociation which left me with a feeling that

I was in some type of dream state, and nothing was real. Differentiating my waking state from my dream state was difficult up until the age of eight when I encountered multiple experiences with Divine light. It was important to me to connect the puzzle pieces to recollect what I was and to create tools that supplied plausible clues for others without clairvoyant abilities. Deep down inside, I knew I was different. I could not explain my sights or my telepathic abilities. The challenge was to find a way to manage these differences in the practical world. People often say one thing but mean something else, especially in the corporate world. I had to be careful not to respond to people's thoughts but rather their words and somehow, in the process, find a way not to lose my authenticity. In my mind and heart, the consistent questions were —who am I, why am I here, and where am I going? Upon reflection and analyzing the puzzle pieces of my childhood in Ijebu-Ode, Nigeria, my clairvoyant, spiritual, and dream experiences, as well as the traumatic history of my past and present lives, I have determined that I am an angel sent by God. All angels were human at one time, and so were all demons. The Angelic Spirit is the natural evolution of all Human Souls.

This book is an account of my journey to healing traumas and the tools I used in assisting others who chose to embark on their intimate spiritual journey. It is a quest to find the right map and clues for uncovering our paths and unique configurations to bring about a successful incarnation so we may ascend to luminous heights.

I attended mental health programs with a desire to find out how I can make meaning of my traumas, but quickly found several challenges with the traditional approaches for treating childhood traumas. The first issue was that as with all other professions in the United States, practically all theories and healing techniques were created by white men, and I could not reconcile any of their techniques with my spiritual and cultural beliefs. The other issue I found was that except for Christian counseling, spirituality was completely avoided because there were no evidence-based theories for students to learn from. Anything that bordered on the supernatural could easily be attributed to psychosis, schizophrenia, or dissociation. I knew that I did not fit any of these diagnoses because I also happened to be reflective and logical. I had the ability to use both sides of my brain hemisphere whereas most people leaned heavily towards one or the other.

Based on the left-brain, right-brain dominance theory, the left side of the brain is adept at tasks that are considered logical, rational, and calculating. By contrast, the right side of the brain is best at artistic, creative, and spontaneous tasks (Corballis, 2014). Mental health programs often laid more emphasis on research, logic, and analysis and less on exploring activities of creativity, imagination, and intuition that the right brain offers.

Additionally, coming from a culture much like other collectivist countries around the world that did not view mental health separate and apart from spiritual health, it explained why people of indigenous cultures, Buddhist and Muslim religions viewed western traditional forms of mental health with cynicism.

My healing journey went beyond traditional psychotherapy, where I began to weave spiritual tools and insights with practical mental health theories—something I was able to do for myself and now also employ with my clients. Using grounded theory, my approach to psychotherapy is integrative and creative and gives a space for people of different faiths and cultures to engage their mental health and validate spiritual experiences.

In the West, the idea of focusing on the past is often met with disdain. Multiple new-age teachings advise people to forget the past and focus on the now, misquoting the teachings of the Buddha, which did not advocate forgetting the past but carefully contemplate our inheritance, including our traditions and belief systems. The reality is that we do not just carry our ancestral DNA but also mannerisms, behaviors, and traumas programmed into us from birth. As in the words of the Vietnamese monk Thich Nhat Han, "We are the continuation of our ancestors." The challenge humanity faces today, is the willful disregard for its past evils and a failure to confront and address them. They pretend that the past is the past and then continue to commit the same evils generation after generation. So, we have new generations carrying transgenerational traumas and with each generation, does the vibration of the children become denser with increasing challenges and karma.

In the future, the world will be led by philosophers and great thinkers, not politicians, billionaires, and the military. Our leaders must be people whose spirits are tuned to the luminous heights, those who have developed themselves spiritually, leaders who have taken the time to advance themselves by developing a deep connection with their Spirit and the Cosmos.

If we do not recognize ourselves as Spiritual Beings first, if we do not listen to our Spirit, our entire collective will not ascend. Our future leaders must be people of open minds and hearts who carry divine light and not simply clever politicians. As a collective, we need to assess the energy behind the energy correctly- in other words the Soul inside the body.

Following great teachers and adopting their beliefs will never be enough without vetting them against our own experiences and deeply contemplating spiritual truths so that these truths can move beyond the cognitive mind and into the subconscious mind which govern behavior, from here we open the Christ consciousness within. Despite millions of motivational books, the world still suffers from delusions and lacks practical steps to self-discovery. We must each take our own journey and trust our stories. Many authors have given sound messages, and many of us choose to live vicariously through them. A seed cannot grow by focusing on other seeds; likewise, all human Souls must focus on their individual growth. We are all together in the great garden of earth. We must work collaboratively to keep our environment in harmony so that the Soul of humanity can grow and thrive.

Spiritual psychotherapy offers the healing space for healers to take their journeys to self-realization and develop critical contemplation while receiving academic training in undergraduate and graduate studies. In spiritual psychotherapy, we integrate tools that heal at the emotional, psychological, and spiritual levels and empower clients to embrace their own unique Journey.

This book attempts to integrate the ancient and the new frontiers of science and quantum healing. It combines western, eastern, and indigenous practices for healing each unique individual and the collective consciousness of the planet at the same time. I explore spiritual complexes in therapy using them as puzzle pieces towards greater understanding and insights.

INTRODUCTION

The important components to healing in any profession and with any instrument are as follows: first, the healer accepts the inflow of the light of God and carries the light; second, the healer's mind is open to the inflow of divine wisdom; and third, the healer's heart is open to the inflow of divine love.

We must begin to identify ourselves as vessels of light. Because we are born into the natural world a blank slate by design so that the light of God can house in us but instead, we are given various artificial labels, inheriting the evils from our parents and their parents. We must clean ourselves up physically, mentally, and spiritually so that we do not pass on evils and traumas to the next generations.

Anyone can claim that they are an angel, but are they good? Are they practicing and acting like wise and loving angels and what is the measure of light in them? The human eye may be blind to ethereal energies but people are not so easily fooled. A person can be very clever with words, but it does not mean that their heart is open to divine love. Consequently, they may be quite knowledgeable, but their mind is not open to wisdom. Still yet, they may accept divine truths but use them for evil gains. Then there are those with dark and evil Souls pretending to be healers, doctors, therapists, and so on. And still yet many are demonic Souls who should not be on this earth plane and walk among us.

The path to healing is the path to integration. Integration requires new ways of thinking and seeing things from a more holistic and divine perspective. When we connect the dots and integrate all thoughts, whether good, bad, or ugly and especially the dark thoughts, we will have a more open view of life, and more likely to connect with the higher consciousness of wisdom and enlightenment. This highest state of consciousness is personified by Vairocana Buddha, the embodiment of luminosity and all that is required for spiritual evolution. Integration of spiritual truths brings wholeness, and wholeness brings unity, and unity is love, which is the entrance to God and the universe.

The collective unconscious mind of the race of human Souls on this planet seems more adapted toward destructiveness, as seen in all schools of thought, culture, religion, and science. Complicated names separate plants, human body parts are given different names, people are assigned different roles, and life is taken apart piece by piece by science. While people recognize one planet, strenuous efforts are made to divide it from the cosmos by claiming that there is no life outside of it, so dividing the world from the infinite universe.

Our destructive nature has taken on a new and dangerous territory, with people attempting to destroy the Soul within humans. To counter this threat, many highly evolved beings of light have taken on an incarnation into a physical body to heal the disconnected mind of humanity. A wholesome mind is a peaceful and healthy mind, and the physical body will naturally tune itself towards wholeness because the body is only a function of the mind. A simple example of this would be false pregnancy, clinically termed pseudocyesis—when a woman believes that she is expecting a baby when she is not really carrying a child. People with pseudocyesis experience symptoms of pregnancy—except for an actual fetus.

Some men experience a related phenomenon known as couvade or sympathetic pregnancy and will develop many of the same symptoms as their pregnant partners, including weight gain, nausea, and backache, clearly indicating that the body responds to the mind's deepest desires, whether good or bad.

Disease is the disintegration of the body by a diseased mind. When the mind is truly in a state of emptiness and open to the inflow of divine truths, the mind will have integrated all thought and become enlightened. The body will become more beautiful, younger, and more luminous. Thus, we identify the sages—not by their fancy words but by the totality of their appearance, for the body is simply a result of the mind.

The future of healthcare must be about the integration of science, spirituality, philosophy, ideas, and cultures, not about forcing people to accept other cultures by wearing their regalia or joining their festivities; it is about accepting other people's ideas and integrating these ideas with spiritual truths so there is no dualism or split mind.

The journey of the wounded healer involves healing the mind by taking responsibility for our traumas, including collective traumas, so humanity can be made whole.

CHAPTER 1
Origins of Indigen

Icome from an ancient tribe in Nigeria called the *Jebu*, short for Jebusites, who live in the remote kingdom of Ijebu-Ode in the Western Hemisphere of Nigeria. The Jebus can be traced back to the Old Testament in the bible. Very little historical data or information is available about the Jebusites. Alice C. Linsley (2020), in "Biblical Anthropology," writes that the Jebusites were a well-entrenched "Canaanite" population with two main branches. One branch lived in the Gilead region and the other around Jerusalem, a Jebusite stronghold before David's time. 1 Chronicles 11:4 – "David and all Israel marched to Jerusalem, that is Jebus, where the Jebusites were, the inhabitants of the land." David purchased a threshing floor from the Jebusite chief, Araunah, and on the site erected an altar to God. Threshing floors were sacred places among many biblical populations.

The two Canaanite groups of Jebusites maintained their solidarity, giving military aid to each other when needed. They were never defeated or driven out of Canaan by the Israelites. Jebusites served in David's army and court. 1 Kings 9:20-21 makes it clear that Jebusites also served in Solomon's kingdom (Linsley, 2020).

Linsley explains that the Jebusites are very ancient people who spread into Canaan and westward from the Nile Valley into Nigeria, where they are known as "Ijebu." As with the Canaanite Jebusites, the Ijebu are divided into two groups: the Nago-Jebu and the Ketu-Jebu. Both divisions take the serpent as their totem. Ketu and Naga are two ancient words for serpent. In ancient Egyptian literature, the cosmic serpent is called RahuKetu. The term "Jebusite" is derived from Yebu, which designated sacred shrines such as the one on Elephantine Island (Yebu) on the Nile. Jerusalem was originally called Yebu/Jebu. Today, the two IJebu provinces are called Jebu Remu and Jebu Ode, and the title of their high king is "Awujali." The IJebu are classified as Yoruba, but the term 'Yoruba' was applied to related tribal groups only after the 18th century.

The people greeted Jesus as he entered Jerusalem with palm branches as a king to be crowned John 12:12-13. The ceremonial installation of rulers with palms was an ancient tradition and possibly emanated from when Jerusalem was a Jebusite city. Even today, fresh palm tree fronds are used ceremonially at the installation of Ijebu rulers. Jude Adebo Adeleye Ogunade writes in his memoir about growing up in Ijebu. He was warned not to touch the leaves of the Igi-Ose tree because, as his Mama Eleni explained, "That tree is the tree whose leaves are used to install Chiefs and Kings of Ijebu and as your grandfather was a custodian of the rites of chieftaincy and kingship you must not play with its leaves."

Naming Ceremony

Customarily, in Ijebu traditions, the spiritual life of a child is divined eight days after birth. During this time, the child receives a name based on the information uncovered about the destiny of the Soul. Mine was not special except for the story that unfolded during the naming ceremony.

As the prayers commenced, the Babalawos (wise healers of the Yoruba people) and Imams seated in a circle began their incantations. After a display of the cowries and more chants, the head Baba emoted! The others turned to him, and they had an animated conversation that bordered on argument. My father interjected, "Baba, what do you see? Is there something wrong with our daughter?"

The Baba gazed at my father with a serious look on his face. "Ah! This child will abandon you! She is not of the world; she came from beyond the universe. She came for the world; she is the teacher for all Babas!" They then gave me the name Khadijat (the name of the prophetess and wife of the Prophet Mohammed, an influential woman in the Islamic world) and Omobolanle (the child who meets the path of God and the one who brings love home).

This reading was unsettling for my parents. Colonialism had gained ground in Nigeria, and western education was touted as the only sure way to a good quality of life. The last thing my father wanted was a child who joined the native Babalawos in the village. He wanted his children to be educated in the colonialist's ways.

My mother, on the other hand, took to heart the part about the child abandoning her. Why, she asked, would I waste my time with a child who would abandon me? And this set the stage for a tumultuous relationship. My mother did not feel the need to bond with me.

Birth Omens

In the West, when a woman is pregnant, the attention of doctors and nurses is on the child's biological well-being. The Jebus place importance on the natural events unfolding at the time of conception leading to birth, such as if a child is born feet first or breached or facing backward or moving upward instead of moving down through the birth canal. Corrective care is taken but such events are taken seriously. The time of day is said to influence the child's overall energy and motivation, as well as the position of the stars and any environmental anomalies like the harvest that year, financial successes, other deaths occurring during the time of the child's birth and so on.

All these happenings are considered significant, along with the divination of the destiny of the Soul. These events are puzzle pieces of the spiritual composition and destiny of the child, called oriki. *Ori* means head. *Oriki* alludes to the spiritual destiny of the child.

Children receive special names based on the unique events that occur when they are born. When a child is given a name, it is the result of the signs and divination of the child. When I was born, my mother was in labor for a long time. I was born *ige* (breach) and *aina* (feet first). The spiritual significance of aina, feet first, is that the child is very powerful because they landed with their feet on Earth, the first sign of the spirit of the child—displaying spiritual strength as they enter the world. The community views the *ige* child with reverence and gives them a special oriki.

Divination is an ancient tradition practiced by a trained Babalawo who is clairvoyant and experienced in the spiritual realm. The Babalawo is a revered person in this village. *Baba* means father, and *awo* means secrets, or hidden principles that explain the mystery of creation and evolution. Babalawos attend to vision quests and have contemplated the wisdoms of human life, devoting their lives to spiritual practices and carefully applying spiritual understanding with everyday life for healing.

The divination process involves purification practices, mental and emotional focus, and meditation prior to going into a transcendental state. They then move between dimensions, accessing the past, present, and future, and communing with *orunmila* (the heavens) to obtain solutions to problems. They can exorcise evil spirits, use herbs for wellness, and support the material success of individuals. They can connect with positive, supportive spirits to receive guidance, information, and healing.

Because the Babalowo (also known as spiritual healers) are charged with connecting with a child's spiritual history, divination must be done with precision. Many people in my culture have names connecting them to past incarnations, which helps their Soul integrate its past, present, and future. For example, Babatunde means the father has returned. Iyabo is a name given to a child believed to be an incarnation of an ancestor. Names are also prayers and affirmations which have an energetic impact on the child's life.

At my naming ceremony, the Babalawo divined that I was likely to abandon my parents because I came for the world and that I was an angel. This divination was not well received. At the time, Christianity had gained a foothold on Nigeria. Traditional religions were being demonized as evil. Western medicine and education were gaining popularity. Babalawos live very austere lives, like the curanderos in Mexico and the shamans of Peru. My father thought, "Why would I want my daughter to be a babalowo?" He wanted me to be educated in the western ways and receive a sound Western education, not to become a Babalawo living in the jungle.

My mother, on the other hand, had a different reaction. She had some jealousy and wanted power for herself, she asked herself, "Why am I being entrusted with someone more powerful than me? Why would I bond with a child who will abandon me in the future?"

Based on these reactions, my childhood was very difficult from the beginning. My parents did not accept what the divination told them. My father looked towards the future and success of western principles, even though he continued to practice traditional religious rites to advance in his material life.

My parents ruled their household with an iron fist and reigned fear and terror in the hearts of their children, housekeepers, and extended family members. Except for a few favorites, no one else was saved from an erratic daily life of the most egregious forms of emotional, psychological, and physical abuse. With my father's loud, baritone voice, his words cut into me much deeper than the tree branches and whips my parents used for daily beatings.

My father, a successful businessman, was the first in the kingdom to attend college at Fourah Bay College in Sierra Leone, where he studied

English. He came from a long line of successful traders and learned the art of negotiation at an early age. After college, my father managed international manufacturing companies with affiliates in the United Kingdom and owned private businesses in mining and in the manufacturing of household products. Owing to his success, we lived a life equivalent to a middle-class American. My parents had a tumultuous relationship filled with adultery. My father was married to his first wife, and had two children when he met my mother. My parents began an adulterous relationship, which eventually resulted in my stepmother leaving. My mother moved into the home and was then responsible for caring for my stepsiblings. Mother had much jealousy towards my father's relationship with his children, resulting in years of fighting, passive-aggressive cruelty toward my stepsiblings, and rivalry among the women.

Although they were considered a common-law marriage, my father did not officially divorce his first wife, which left my mother with quite a few insecurities and an obsession with keeping her status. Clinging onto my father was her sole purpose, and she was ready to do anything to keep other women away. Her obsessions kept her revolving from one Babalawo to another, and her need for power became stronger. Babalawos will make love potions, protective spells, and rituals to curse and bring down competitors. She was an indomitable force that nobody dared to challenge. She loved attention, adorning the best clothing, and she always made her presence felt wherever she went. People seemed to worship the ground she walked on, and she hated anyone who did not give her this reverence.

My father had an insatiable obsession with sex and preyed on almost anything in a skirt. From the housekeepers to the neighbors, employees, and even my mother's sister, he was a philanderer par excellence. On many occasions, we heard about how he and his friends would pass women onto each other and engage in sexual orgies at the house. Considering that my father was a Muslim and entitled to four wives, he used this religious clause as an excuse for his sexual deviance, which left my mother often angry and frustrated, and she took out her anger on certain children.

Narcissistic Parents and the Truth Teller

As with all narcissistic mothers, my parents had their favorites, and I was the truth teller who quickly became the black sheep. As with all family roles in narcissistic families such as the golden child, the enabler, the brainwashed, and the scape goat, I took on the role as the truth teller and understood what was going on. I could see the games, lies and manipulative tactics of my parents. I was one who called out these lies especially the ones my mother told about my stepsiblings, grandmother, and uncles and because of this, I quickly became hated by her. I would challenge her fake meltdowns to spread lies about my stepsiblings and even when I knew I was risking severe abuse, I chose to uphold my integrity. I could sense early on that mother had a plan to destroy anyone she deemed a threat to her financial stability and future. Even though I couldn't put words to what was going on around me, I was already asking the Holy Spirit questions about why anyone could become so wicked and manipulative. It was very difficult for me to defend, engage or explain her behavior. Later in life, I learned to spot narcissistic behaviors in therapy and maintain strong boundaries. Until we were well into adulthood, none of my siblings could see how severely their personalities, outlook in life and mental health had been impacted by the slow and corrosive poison of narcissism.

Nobody was strong enough to stand up to mother and daily life was unpredictable as it revolved around her shifting mood. If we dared set the dinnerware wrong or the China plate was not properly cleaned, or we added too much or too few servings, ate their leftovers without permission, or left a speck of dust on the table, we could receive several strokes of cane cut from long tree branches, made to face the wall and raise our hands for several hours, or even have the food we served thrown in our face. As years went by, the tree branches got bigger, longer, and better designed to leave welts and bruises and, on many occasions, broke the skin and caused serious injuries. As they both aged, they began to employ the guards to hold the hands and feet of their children while they flogged them naked. Once, my oldest brother met such a fate for playing my father's 1980's music records, and I received a similar punishment for making an international call to a high school boyfriend when I was sixteen.

I am not writing this background story to demonize my parents, and I am not looking for a pity party or playing the blame game. I am writing my story for the reader to understand the wounds inflicted on my body, mind, and spirit and to follow the story of my journey into the psyche to heal my buried traumas and discover the truth about who and what I am.

Reviewing research studies on parental bonds, I long knew that my life was beyond typical. And my relationship with my parents was devoid of any sort of tenderness except for them providing food, clothing, and bringing us up in an affluent home while ninety percent of the country lived in poverty. Far from a healthy bond, my mother's voice would strike the children with the most heart-wrenching fear. The sound of her car horn signaling to the guards to open the gates, announcing her return home, brought the worst frenzy, dread, and panic attacks.

My five younger brothers and sisters would begin to cry, and I would often vomit from my heart beating so fast that it felt like it would jump out of my body at any moment. We would frantically clean the house and set the pot on the stove to cook her dinner. I learned to cook in the kitchen and serve food to my siblings by the age of seven. We had daily chores along with the housekeepers, who often ran away after being severely abused or got fired for not doing a satisfactory job, so the children had to fill in with extra chores until new help came from the village.

CHAPTER 1

When my mother would arrive and park the car, my job was to run out and kneel on the ground. "Welcome, Mommy." I grabbed her bag and raced upstairs to open her bedroom door. I had to move fast; any sign of being lax would be met with floggings. I then went into her room to change her bedsheets, make her bed, sweep, and wipe down the furniture. She would leave her dirty underwear on the floor, which I would pick up to wash. Depending on her mood, I would be subjected to flogging for not making up the bed right or washing her underwear clean enough. If she brought anything home for the children, she would throw it on the floor, and we had to kneel to pick it up. On some occasions, she would punch me so hard in the stomach that I would pass out. Beatings happened for any minor infraction, such as not spelling a word correctly, not bringing her food to her fast enough, not arriving quickly enough when called, or not washing the dishes clean enough.

I was the oldest of six children and had two older stepsiblings. We were not encouraged to love or show any form of empathy toward one another. My mother made sure she instilled a divide-and-conquer rule, so sibling rivalry and jealousy was common. Since Mother had her favorites and I was the scapegoat, siblings distanced themselves, and relationships became strained. They knew that so long as Mother projected her anger on one child, they were saved from it—when it was me, then it was not them.

My parents were members of elite occult groups in Lagos, Nigeria. The rich and powerful of Nigeria are largely members of this group, and many rites and rituals occur regularly. My maternal grandfather was a Babalawo (translated as the father of secrets, diviners, or priests and custodians of spiritual wisdom), and rightfully, he must pass down these secrets and practices to his chosen child. In the late 60's to early 70's, traditional religious cults like the Ogboni secret society and elite political groups began to merge with international humanitarian organizations. They ran orphanages for abandoned children and provided them with vaccinations. In the 70's many children became permanently disabled and died from western pharmaceutical companies' vaccination trials and imported contaminated baby foods.

Customarily, in the occult, parents would sacrifice their firstborn child, and being my mother's first born, she thought that I would be dead by age ten. Therefore, I was neglected, and suffered various illnesses, from sores and allergic reactions to boils and blisters all over my body. Suicidal ideations would constantly run through my mind.

My mother was a classic textbook narcissist, sociopathic type who seemed to enjoy inflicting pain on others. But there was another twist and turn to this disorder, which I observed growing up. As a sensitive person, I could see that spiritual possessions brought about this narcissistic condition. The demonic possessions of anger, sexual deviance, and their insatiable taste for power and admiration led my parents deeper into occultic practices. Narcissists share similar characteristics as demonic forces. They are selfish, belligerent, manipulative, controlling and sadistic. Narcissists are on a tract to joining evil forces and are very much surrounded by them. These forces embolden them as their insatiable appetite for power and control grows.

My mother visited many Babalawo high priests and engaged in various rituals to keep her marriage intact and deter the beady eyes of women who wanted to take her place. Mother kept her position at all costs, and in the process, she got more entangled in contracts and agreements of an evil and insidious nature. Some of these contracts with evil entities involved making sacrifices to gods and demigods in exchange for power, and, in one instance, she even offered me, her firstborn child, in exchange for the accumulation of more power. When this happened, my childhood took a turn for the worst. In the Yoruba traditional cultures, all power and wealth are accumulated through spiritual processes and appeals to gods and entities. My parents' obsession with wealth and power led them to seek Babalawos who promised rituals in exchange for my life.

I mentally distanced myself from my entire family as a means of self-protection and even though life felt lonely as a child, I had a rich inner world. I could see the energies of trees and plants and had profound premonitions that came true the next day or next week. I would wake up the next day and pray to God to prevent my nightmares of beatings from coming to pass. Like a tape recorder and movie playing, the events of abuse occurred exactly as my dreams had predicted. I would even dream of places I have never been and people I had never met only to meet them soon after and they would be wearing the same exact clothing and saying the same things they communicated in my dream.

I was mostly disappointed when I couldn't prevent bad things from happening to me and I asked God why he didn't answer my prayers to avert these mishaps. I then received a vision from the Holy Spirit showing me a book and turning the pages. I got an impression that I had a Soul destiny, and I was being shown what was going to happen, and not to attempt to change it, but to prepare for it. I then thought to myself, well, if this was the case, then I can ask for my future to be revealed to me. My dreams after that revealed an incredible life filled with God's love, and of helping and healing people, teaching and leading them and supporting their highest potential. I saw my light and my love, and this gave me peace to carry on and not allow the darkness to enter my being. I also saw that as an angelic being, I did not have free-will but rather a soul destiny. In order words, my soul plan was set in stone and I had very little wiggle room to change direction as others can. For this reason, I knew from an early age, to trust in God's plan for my lifetime.

Today, as a holistic psychotherapist trained in past-life regression therapy, I realized that many of my childhood dreams were past-life dreams. I could see the energies around people and had experiences of the pristine light. Seeing the evil entities around my family made me seek the light for safety and comfort. When there was no electricity, which was always in short supply, I would light a candle and pray to God to aid in my escape from my parents. I promised God that if he helped me escape, I would be forever grateful and serve him with all my heart and Soul.

During my early years, my mother had a niece she adored and cared for—better than her own children. Her niece was older than me, and her father had died suddenly and mysteriously. My mother took a strong liking to her and bought her clothing, paid her school fees, and gave her special attention.

One night, at the age of ten, when the time came that I should have had my last breath squeezed out of me, as the occult called for the spirit of my mother's firstborn, I was spared, and instead, my cousin was taken instead of me. It seemed I was protected because my mother treated my cousin like her firstborn. I watched my mother wail over the death of her beloved niece, crying to the occult that they had taken the wrong one. "It was not supposed to be her," she said. At the time, I did not understand why she said that. My cousin had died in her sleep with no apparent cause. From that moment on, Mother treated me with even more disdain.

By the age of sixteen, I had experienced two near-death experiences and miraculously escaped each. Despite all of Mother's efforts, she failed to remove me from the planet. God had plans for my life, and Mother could not put these plans asunder. My naivety and lack of self-worth made me think that my still being alive was simply my luck. My mother consistently told me that I was useless and worthless, and I believed her. After several failed attempts to have me killed, she arranged for me to be married to a man in the United States to get rid of me.

I do not blame my parents or anyone else for anything. Again, this book is not a journey of projecting anger, resentment, or rage but one of understanding and showing others that they, too, can learn to heal themselves, and we must do this with love and forgiveness for ourselves and our parents. I do not believe in playing victim. Instead, I am thankful for the life they gave me, which set me on my spiritual journey.

To be healthy, we must be accountable for our own lives and feelings. I, first, had to understand what I experienced as a daughter of two narcissistic parents, and then I could move forward in psychological and spiritual recovery. Without understanding what my parent's narcissism did to me, it would have been impossible to recover. I also recognized at an early age the spiritual implications of my relationship with my parents. Since they loved worldly material things and seemed to want to steer me in that same direction through abuse and manipulation, I saw how I could become corrupted if I bonded with them. People who have formed loving bonds with one another and their families in this life find it incredibly difficult to break them in the hereafter.

A bond between a parent and a child cannot be pulled apart because they are like branches that have been merged onto other branches. Even if one of them is good but the other is bad, they will continue to be stuck together much like a deer to a lion and a mouse stuck with a cat as predator and prey. The one who is bad will always arouse negative impulses in the one who is good but the one that is good almost never ignites positive impulses from the bad. I could see how the branches looked like snakes extending from the negative and dominant parent as it wraps around innocent and unsuspecting children and weaker people. It looked like an octopus with tentacles latched onto the brains and ethereal bodies of the children, sucking their lifeforce and igniting feelings of fear, jealousy, and hate. It became apparent to me how easy it is for good people to end up in hell due these types of relationships. By the time the weak and unsuspecting wake up to their ethereal cords it is too late as they continue to suffer in the hands of the negatively dominant one in hellish realms after death. Therefore, it became important for me not to form close bonds with my family.

Out-of-Body Experiences

"Bolanle! Bolanle! Bolanle!" My mother screamed my name at the top of her lungs. Sheer terror ran down my veins. When she called, my spine always hardened and felt inflexible. My heart would beat so fast I felt it would leap out of my chest cavity and onto the floor in front of me.

"Yes, Ma!" I responded almost immediately as I hurried down the stairs, any delayed response would earn me extra strokes of the cane. With tears running down my face, I asked myself, 'What have I done now?'

My mother stared me down with a look of anger etched on her face. "Go to my room and fetch me my brown slippers."

"Yes, Ma."

I ran back upstairs to her room, panicking in fear. As looked around the room and saw five pairs of brown slippers lined together, I panicked at this point because I did not know which pair she wanted. Which one is it? I asked myself. I cannot get it wrong, I thought, as my heart skipped several beats. Finally, I decided on one pair, picked up the slippers, and hurriedly ran downstairs. I handed Mother the slippers she requested, but they were not the right ones.

She looked at me scornfully as she held the slippers in her hand, "That is not what I asked you to get! You fool, you idiot! You cannot even follow simple instructions!"

I kept apologizing as she continued hitting me with the tree branches, which were kept hanging on the wall behind her and within arm's reach. I dared not run because I knew from experience that running would only result in more beatings. I crouched down on my knees and prepared myself mentally for what would come. I asked God to take me away from this place, so I did not feel the pain anymore.

In such moments, I would leave my body and watch my physical body repeatedly being beaten. As time passed, I became even better at taking flight out of my body during these beatings. I knew just when to return to my body, usually right after my mother's hands were tired and the demon that possessed her had fed and satiated itself with her rage. When I leaped back into my body and looked at her, she would become even more terrified and angry that she was unable to break my Soul. As far as she was concerned, I had no remorse for what I did.

Despite the abuse, my childhood was not entirely fearful. When my parents were gone for the day, and after school, my siblings and I had time to run out to play. We could put aside our anxiety and fear and simply be children while my parents were away at work. After school, we had two hours of playtime before hearing my mother's car horn.

Our family lived in a large compound with many mangoes and fruit trees to climb. For fun, my siblings and I would run with the dogs, play hide-and-seek, or catch tadpoles after it rained. I found safety in the quarters of a few housekeepers who stayed longer than most and, from them, learned how to plant beans, tomatoes, and peppers. A huge lake across the street from our home became a dumping ground, but as children with big imaginations, we loved to pretend that we were taking a walk to the seaside to catch some fish.

Alongside traditional religions taught by the Babalawos, my father was Muslim. My mother came from a Christian background, and I attended a private Christian school. Much of my early life was spent studying the Bible alongside the Quran, and despite the seeming contradiction, I found more commonalities in the religious texts than differences. I always wondered why they fought against each other; surely, they must know that they share the basic tenets of love. Christian hymns, Muslim songs, and prayers were part of my daily life and these I really enjoyed. Later in life, I studied Buddhism and travelled to countries like Bhutan, Thailand, and India. Engaging in different ways of life and teachings was something I truly appreciated because I could transcend the earthly meanings of these religions and sense their spiritual and heavenly qualities.

We had a black and white tv that was turned on at 4 p.m. daily, and for one hour, we would watch the television show 'Tales by Moonlight' about Kunkuru, the wise tortoise, and the animal's stories from the village.

When my paternal grandmother visited, life was sweeter. As me and my siblings stood behind the curtains waiting for Mama to arrive from the village. We would scream with excitement as we took turns jumping and hugging Mama. Mama always had the most infectious belly laugh as she opens her old rusty bag to hand us her famous Eja Agbodo (dried fish), African walnuts and dried peanuts from the village. The children will all seat on the floor and listen to songs of our forefathers.

Mama! Tell us about Grandpa, the children will ask excitedly. We have heard Mama tell this story a thousand times and each time, Mama's voice felt like fresh morning dew to the skin.

Mama will smile, "he was a very tall man and his father's father founded Ijebu land." Then Mama belts our favorite song:

Ijebu-Ode ni won bi wa si O,

Ijebu-Ode ni won bi wa si.

Babawa pheluwon loni le,

Ijebu-ode, yeho, Ijebu-Ode ni won bi wa si.

Translation: We are born in Ijebu-Ode, our forefathers own the lands, this is our birth land.

The girls will take turns as we sat between Mama's legs to have our hair braided.

Ouch! We could hear each other react in discomfort as Mama worked on our hair. Mama, would smile and say, "you will soon look beautiful." Mama took hours as her hands were frail, laughing and telling stories about the village. She would sing and dance as we watch her talking to herself and pictures of Grandpa.

Everyone benefitted from Mama loving energy including my father whose demeanor would change when Mama was around. He laughed more and endearingly call his daughters "Miss Nigeria", referring to us as beauty queens. Dad loved music and adventure and he never hesitated to take his children on trips to Ghana, Benin and Togo. Eventually, my mother would insight quarrels and attacks that drove Mama from the house and kept her away.

I loved to spend many a day dancing to Diana Ross's "Upside Down" and Donna Summers' "Unconditional Love." I would tie a scarf to my head, pretend to have long and flowing hair, turn on the fan, and sing and dance. In those instances, I would see orbs of light surround me, healing my wounds and energy field.

My happy demeanor always seemed to perplex my mother as she could not understand why she was unable to break my spirit. As we got older, quarrels and animosity grew even more among the siblings. I developed jealousy and anger for the seeming favoritism my siblings had with my mother. They were convinced that I was bad, and they all distanced themselves from me. As part of my mother's divide-and-conquer rule, she gave no favors to my stepsiblings and, on some occasions, refused to feed them. I was treated with the same aggression, except that I cooked most of the meals for my siblings, and some of them could not stand to eat certain foods my mother insisted we eat. Once, she caught my younger sister throwing food in the toilet and made her remove the food and eat it. My mother always cooked my father's meals. He had separate menus and separate dinnerware; no one was allowed to sit at the table with him.

My School, Gboko

In the summer of 1984, the political climate in Nigeria was filled with military coups and counter coups, civil wars, and oil booms. It was a time of economic prosperity and corruption. Ethnic inequality became a dominant feature in the geo-political landscape. The government announced a quota system for education—a type of social engineering to move children from the south and western regions of the Yoruba, Igbo, and Efik tribes to the northern parts of the country which were inhabited by the Hausas and Fulanis.

By eleven years old, I was assigned to attend a boarding school in Gboko Benue State, Nigeria. Neither parent had any information nor sought to find out about the school I was to attend. My father made sure that my stepsiblings did not fall into the quota system. He had connections and kept them close to home, but he did little to nothing to assist me or my other siblings and made no effort to prevent my eventual departure to boarding school.

If anything, my mother encouraged my departure despite grave concerns about my health and well-being at Gboko. She knew that it was highly unlikely that I would survive the harsh physical and mental conditions of its rough terrain. It was not a safe place for children as rumor had it that girls were often kidnapped and married off. There was no healthcare system in Gboko; food was in short supply, and children went without adequate nutrition. Even her trusted Babalawo advised her not to send me there, but she had made a pact with the occult to capture my Soul by sending me to my demise.

At eleven years old, never having left home, I was now moving to a remote town 500 miles away. The school was situated at the bottom of Mkar Hill and had a spectacular formation of two distinct peaks, rising to 2,600-3,200 feet above sea level. The rough terrain had a thick, deep forest with a highly wooded natural trench at Tse Mker, a natural habitat for pythons, lions, hyenas, and exotic birds. Gboko had a tropical climate with extreme weather conditions and only two seasons, wet and dry. The wet season was generally filled with torrential rain, hail, floods, and monsoons. In the dry season, temperatures of over 100 degrees were common, along with dust winds.

On the day of my departure, as I was carted off to the airport, my mother left me a parting gift by beating me mercilessly, punching and slapping me in the middle of the busy airport. Nobody attempted to stop her.

Other students and their family preparing to leave, observed this spectacle, and potential friends immediately began to distance themselves from me. Many years later, I would run into old classmates who reported observational traumas from watching this assault. Lonely and bruised, I arrived at Makurdi Airport after a four-hour flight, and then the other students and I took public transport for three hours to Gboko. With a small bag of clothes and provisions, I began my life as a student at Gboko. Not long after I got there, my body could not withstand the harsh conditions.

For the first few weeks, I cried uncontrollably. Despite the beatings and antagonisms, I was terribly homesick, as I was stuck in a remote place where I knew no one. The dormitories were in the worst squalor. Twenty girls were in a small room with ten bunk beds. We lacked water and students had to walk up a hill for five miles to fetch water to drink and bathe. The dorms had broken windows and makeshift doors, making them unsafe since hyenas and snakes frequented the grounds.

Students often became sick from malaria, typhoid fever, and cholera, and a few died from a lack of medical attention. To survive a night of being eaten senselessly by mosquitos, we had to use mosquito nets as well as repellents, which did not seem to work. Due to lack of water, the toilets and bathrooms would fill up with feces, and most of the girls would resort to bathing in the open field. Swamps filled with flies, bees, and wasps surrounded the school, and owing to my sensitivities, I soon developed boils and skin infections.

At night, students would huddle together for fear of snakes. On top of fighting the elements, new students in form one, equivalent to sixth grade, were subject to bullying by older students. If a student did not have a school mother (a senior), she was likely to be mistreated by the older students. I was assigned a school mother, and although she was very kind and empathetic towards me, she could not keep the seniors from bullying me.

The food was absolutely disgusting—we had dry bread and lemongrass tea during school days and rice and beans for lunch. Bugs crawling out of the plates were not unusual. Snakes were often found in the dining hall. Despite this, girls fought over getting their fair share. On weekends, we would get a plate of yams and tomatoes and might be lucky to get some sardines. We had fifteen minutes to finish eating, so I learned to eat fast. We then had to take turns getting water from a tank to drink.

When the school bell rang, we had thirty minutes to get to the assembly line, where teachers inspected students for dress code violations. The children at the boarding school came from all over the country- from Port Harcourt, Enugu, Lagos, Abeokuta, Imo, Kaduna, Kano, Benue, and Benin. Girls quickly formed cliques, and I had a difficult time making friends or assimilating into boarding school life. I was sick most of the time, and when I wasn't, I was bullied and had my provisions stolen.

Not long after I arrived, I was told to cut my long hair because it was a violation. Seniors showed up at an assembly to shave my head. As an eleven-year-old child, I could not understand why this was happening to me. However, I would remind myself that anywhere was better than home with my parents. Never losing sight of my future visions, my mind stayed in a constant state of presence and inner peace.

The classrooms had no windows, and the ceilings would leak during the torrential rains. Two students sat at each desk, and textbooks were in short supply. Learning was almost impossible as there were not enough chairs or desks.

One day during physical education, my classmates and I began our warm-up by jogging around what looked like a barely constructed field. The bush had been cleared, and white lines were drawn so students knew what direction to go. Not long after we began running, I made a sharp bend and fell, rolling several feet down a slope, receiving lacerations and a broken leg and rushed to the sick bay for first aid.

The sick bay looked and smelled like death. There were not enough beds for the hundreds of sick children, and many laid on the floor. There was only one nurse available care for the entire clinic, and she barely had any medicines except for chloroquine injections to treat malaria. Nobody could avoid swarms of insects, and I doubted that the entire clinic had ever been cleaned. The nurse looked at my leg and cleaned the wounds but did not bother to check if my leg was broken. She sent me back to the dormitory, where my pain and illness progressed rapidly.

I could no longer walk on my broken leg, and it began to swell considerably. Soon after, I developed a high fever as days went by. I was completely ignored and left with my illness. The other students went about their day as the morning bell rang; students would rush to get out of bed and run to get their buckets of water to bathe out in the open. They each had their chores, from sweeping the dormitory to dusting cobwebs. Nobody liked toilet and bathroom duty, and there was the frontage and backyard grass that needed to be cut low and raked.

Two weeks after my fall, I was unable to get out of bed. My fever hit an all-time high, and I needed a friend to get me out of bed and back to the sick bay. The nurse could do nothing, as the sick bay was full, so it was best to stay in the dormitory. I had to be helped to the bathroom. I couldn't bathe for days, and unless one of the girls remembered, I went without food or drink.

Alone in the empty dormitory building, my fever had gotten so high, my leg had turned purple, and I began to hallucinate. Paralyzed physically and mentally, I watched what appeared to be hundreds of ghost-like apparitions, white with eyes so black, they seemed to twinkle, flying so fast and coming up close to me. I would get lost in their black twinkling eyes. This must have gone on for hours, as I heard the girls returning to the dormitory as I began to lose consciousness and felt myself slipping out of my body. I heard melodic sounds and whispers and began to fly around in the room with hundreds of flying entities. At the center of the flying mass was a blazing pristine light, pure and blissful. I felt at peace, and it seemed that I was being healed, blessed, and loved. I felt the support of my guiding spirits, my true mothers speaking to me. We appeared to have a single mind, but I did not know or understand what I was seeing or what was happening to me.

Years later and during my spiritual healing journey, I realized that I must have experienced an aspect of my oversoul. I felt a conversation going on between me and the hundreds of other beings. Even though there were no words spoken between us, I knew what they were communicating. What they shared with me was a sense that I had come to earth to fulfill a mission, and that we, the hundreds, were a single group of an oversoul that was always with me no matter my circumstances. I felt I needed rest and restoration, and my Soul energy at the time decided to take a break and heal from all the traumas. I then returned, but not as the old self, but as one of the flying ones. We all seemed to retain the same information and think in the same way, so it felt like another part of me had returned to my dying body. The aspect of my Soul that returned to my body was different. I now had a strong and peaceful mind, and my energy field would radiate light.

When I re-entered my body and opened my eyes, I saw that the girls had surrounded my bed. They seemed concerned as my body had felt life-less but were taken aback by the light now radiating through my body. I looked around and then at my body and felt life return to it. My leg began to change color almost immediately, and I sat and then stood up, which seemed to shock the girls since I had been bedridden for weeks. Some felt it was a miracle, and others became scared. Soon, rumors began to perco-late that I might be a witch but this new me felt strong and resilient. I was unbothered by the rumors as I went about my day, finally happy to take a nice bath and walk without limping. My parents had received a message about my illness, but no one came to visit. Instead, they sent an ex-employee, to check on me.

Stories about my miraculous recovery had spread fast, and I became more isolated as other students did not know what to make of it, and some feared it. My clairvoyant abilities had increased astronomically after my near-death experience. I became a lot more observant and could see people's true emotions and intentions, and therefore, my responses and reactions never seemed appropriate. I did not know how to censor myself, and my words seemed cutting, refusing to interact with the students who seemed to have ulterior motives. I quickly lost acquaintances, and bullying became commonplace among the seniors. I spent many days walking five miles to fetch water, washing dishes, and carrying out extra chores.

I craved and needed a sense of belonging and an escape from people who had dark energies around them, so I began attending a Christian church and joined a group of born-again Christians. I agreed to give my life to Christ. I was not sure what it truly meant, but I know it felt good, and I was calm and at peace when around this group.

The Dove at M'kah

Every weekend, this group of born-again Christians would meet at the top of M'kah Hill, where we would pray, sing, and dance to Christian music. Here, young girls spoke in tongues, experiencing the ecstasy of the Holy Spirit. I enjoyed being there and had felt safe. On weekdays, I would venture off on my own to be in solitude and wait patiently to see the flying ones.

One evening, as the sun was setting, a friend, who I had made within the group, and I set off on our own for a prayer session. We got up the hill and dispersed. My friend went for a walk, and I sat on a large rock and began my prayers alone. A few minutes into my prayer session, a large white dove flew in front of me. Mind you, doves were not native to the area. The size of the dove was that of a large two-story building. It did not speak, but I felt it communicating with me by impressing thoughts into my head.

The dove said, "Child, I am delighted in your worship and must gift you in return. State a wish, and it is yours." Without hesitation, I knew what I wanted above all else. Recalling one of my dreams of a past life where I was a spiritual healer, I wished to have spiritual wisdom and help the rest of the girls interpret their dreams. I then replied, "The gift of wisdom!" The dove responded," And so it is!" and disappeared. I was encouraged and felt blessed to have seen this entity. My physical life was full of uncertainty, but the dove gave me hope. Many years later as a psychotherapist, I came to know this entity as the emanation of the Holy Spirit. No matter my challenges in life, I always hear the quiet whisper of this illustrious Spirit. It was getting dark, and my friend had returned from her walk, and we began to head back to the dormitory. I told her what I had seen, and she quietly listened to me, nodding her head in support.

My friend looked at me and said, "You are about to embark on a very difficult journey; never to forget your experience at the top of M'kah." As she said this, my mind went back to my parents and my heart sank. I could picture what was going to happen when I returned home, the sadness on their faces when they saw I had survived, and the abuse that would follow. I let out a big sigh, but my friend placed her hands around my shoulder and repeated, "You are protected, and this will only strengthen you." We continued to visit the hill every chance we had, and visions of the dove and the flying ones became more commonplace. They moved fast but always appeared just when I looked up. I felt safe and protected but knew that I would soon leave the safety of M'kah as the semester drew nearer to a close. I would soon be heading home for the holidays, which filled me with great anxiety.

In the summer of 1982, I began heading home for the summer holidays. My heart could not stop beating fast. I did not want to stay at Gboko given the bullying, poor diet, illness, and feelings of isolation, but the alternative was no comfort to me either. All the students eagerly packed their suitcases as we took a three-hour bus ride to Makurdi airport.

We finally arrived in Lagos after several days of delays, waiting and sleeping at the airport. My parents' driver picked me up, but no one was at home to welcome me. My home was just as I had left it, always clean and tidy, with the traditional style of white and brown furniture, Persian rugs, and lace curtains. I went upstairs, hugged my father, and greeted my mother.

With both knees on the ground, I said, "Good evening, Mommy." My mother looked at me with disappointment in her face. She asked, "Did you get promoted to the next grade?" I replied, "Yes." She hissed and turned her face, signaling me to leave her room. I went off to catch up with my sisters and was finally relieved to take a good shower.

As I walked into the bedroom, I found my older stepsister sitting up in her bunk bed. She turned, and I said to her, "I am born again!" She yelped with excitement and gave me a tight hug. We began to chat about our experiences but kept our voices down for fear of the others hearing and tattling.

Everything seemed normal for the first few days, but it would be the calm before the storm. On the third day of my arrival home, my mother called me into her room and handed me an odd-looking red dress with occult symbols around the chest and said, "Wear this dress to sleep tonight." I knew full well what this dress meant.

My mother frequented many Babalawo, and she had taken all her children to different meetings and rituals. Some rituals included bathing in the river with black soap, drinking horrible-tasting concoctions, or rubbing substances on our bodies. Her instruction was new and different, but I immediately knew that I was being prepared to stand up before the occult. I looked at her calmly and replied, "No, I refuse. I have given my life to Christ."

At first, my mother was taken aback. I had never said no to her, and no one dared to defy her demands. She was quiet at first and didn't know what to say as I got up to leave. I didn't hear from my parents for the rest of the day, but I was certain they were discussing their next move.

The next evening, the imams and Babalawo invited to the house were seated on the living room floor. They had Korans, tasbihs, and other items around them. My stepsister and stepbrother were called to the room. We were told to kneel, and my father told the imams that he was concerned that me and my stepsiblings had joined a religious fanatic group and demanded that we each renounce all affiliations with the Christian religion or face being disowned.

My father went on to say that he was willing to overlook my stepsiblings' decisions because he felt they had joined Christianity because their mother was not in the home with them, but he could not excuse or allow me to have a religious choice. The imams agreed and told me that I had to listen to my parents and wear the dress as instructed.

While kneeling before them, I replied, "No. I will not renounce my faith in Christ." My mother then went on a tirade of angry yelling, announcing that she had officially disowned me, before picking up a big wooden table and hurling it at my head, beating and flogging me as the Babalawo sat and watched. My stepsiblings were permitted to go back to their rooms. I was flogged and pushed out of the house and asked never to return.

I left the gates and sat on the streets. I didn't know where to go, but whatever happened, I was determined not to wear that dress. I knew that I was to be used for sacrifice to increase my mother's powers. She thought that I would not have survived Gboko, but I did and so she proceeded with plan B. After hours of sitting out on the streets of Glover Road, I was called back into the house, but the beatings continued for three months. My hair was shaved, and I was denied food for days. I was told that I would not be allowed to return to Gboko, and my father insisted that he would no longer pay for my education so long as I refused to renounce my faith.

Saddened by the prospect of not seeing my dear friend, Ugogi, I wrote her a farewell letter that contained a promise to keep my faith no matter what. I asked my sister to sneak the letter to the driver to mail at the post office. My mother saw the letter and opened it. She became livid, went upstairs with a metal high heel shoe, busted into my room, and began to hit me on the head with the heel. With several blows to the head, blood splashed on the walls. My stepsister screamed, and my mother came to, saw the blood, and walked away. By this time, I was drenched in my own blood. Using a piece of cloth to stop the bleeding, my sister took me to the driver and asked him to take me to the hospital. No one was allowed to go with me. At the hospital, the nurses treated my wounds and stitched up my head.

One nurse looked at me and asked, "What happened? Who did this to you?"

I replied, "My mother."

"Why?" she asked.

"Because I told her that I was a Christian," I replied.

The nurse looked at me in disbelief and walked away. I returned home hours later to the blood-stained walls. My siblings were so traumatized by the sight of what had happened that they left the room and kept their distance. By this time, the living room did not feel safe, and so with my head bandaged up and an excruciating headache, I began to clean the blood-stained walls of my room. One sister came to help. We cleaned and scrubbed, and then I went to bed and fell into a deep sleep.

It had been four months since I left Gboko, and my parents had begun to realize that they had taken things too far and gave up their intent to initiate me into their occult and steal my Soul. The flying ones were around, ensuring that my aura was not broken.

My father continued to insist that all his children become practicing Muslims and enrolled us in private Islamic training to learn and read the Quran. He insisted to me that religion was made for man and not man for religion. Therefore, religion only served as a tool for furthering human life, a contradiction to me, especially seeing the dark energies surrounding him. What was stranger to me was how he was oblivious to his own contradictions, being Muslim but engaging religious cults. The words felt ugly, but I had no choice but to attend the Islamic school.

For me, the Islamic school was not about religion but about spirituality as I could sense the spiritual and heavenly counterparts of the Quran scriptures I studied and so, it only broadened my awareness. Many nights, I would ask the flying ones to show me the future, and I would see it in dreams. I was to become a wise counselor, and life would be fulfilling.

Because of what was shown in my dreams, I hoped that this, too, would pass, and I would one day be free of my parents. Fear gripped me by day, and love held me by night. On some nights, I recalled past lives, and in one dream, I saw that my mother had ordered a man to have me killed. I woke up with the feeling that karma was about to replay itself, but I must not let it. I must not allow her to break my psyche.

My mother took my quiet detachment as defiance, but I dared not say anything; sometimes, I would pretend to cry so she would leave me alone. I did not share any dreams or visions with my siblings. They felt troubled by the chaos and abuse and chose to distance themselves from me. My oldest brother had graduated from college, and my father paid for his master's degree in the United States. The psychological effects of all the drama was beginning to show in my older sister, who developed obsessive-compulsive behaviors and depression. Despite occasionally receiving floggings for minor infractions such as forgetting to wear an underskirt or taking food meant for my father, my younger siblings managed to stay in my mother's good graces and learned not to defy her.

Gang Rape

My parents had exhausted all attempts to break me and decided to take their anger out on the boarding school for brainwashing me. They withdrew me from boarding school, and after attending the Islamic school, due to my father's threats, I had to show remorse and beg him to allow me to attend school. Both parents decided to find a school close to home and enrolled me in a college prep program. I had turned fifteen but everyone at the school was seventeen or above. Gboko was an all-girls school, and I had not been exposed to interacting with boys my age, let alone boys two grades above than me.

Still deeply wounded from the abuse of the last fourteen years, I needed to find a sense of belonging. To do this, I had to look beautiful, which I naturally was, but I also had to have an exterior appearance of confidence, of which I had none. I received a lot of attention, passes, and advances from boys at the school. However, the teachers ignored boys grabbing girls, mocking, and shooting spitballs at one another. I did not feel safe and quickly made a friend who was popular with the girls and the boys alike. Jose was a deeply troubled seventeen-year-old from a broken family. Everyone liked Jose, and he was an infamous partygoer.

Once Jose set his eyes on me, the other boys knew not to harass me. Soon, I was introduced to a new group of children of the elite and a new world of partying and sex. Jose knew nothing of my past, and I did every-thing I could to hide my scars. My school days involved sneaking my sister's clothes in my backpack. Even though uniforms were not required at the school, my mother insisted that I wear a dress that looked like a uniform. Now and then, I would get caught and be flogged, and then I got more creative about sneaking clothes.

One day, during a class lunch break, as I walked to a kiosk to buy myself a snack, a group of boys I met at one of the parties Jose took me to drove up alongside of me. One of the boys kept asking me a question that I did not understand. He beckoned me to get in the car so he could talk to me. The car was in the middle of a busy street, and other cars behind it were honking. He urged me to get in the car so we could get off the street, and I agreed and got in. The minute I did, I realized that I had made a huge mistake.

They kept going, driving away from the school. I asked them to let me out, but they gave me excuses, saying that they just needed to drop off one of the other boys sitting in the back seat, and then they would take me back. I looked for every opportunity to get out of the car, but the child lock was on. After driving for what seemed like twenty minutes, we arrived at a house, and I was let out. I begged them to take me back. I had no idea where I was; there were no cell phones or pagers during those days.

I began to scream for help, but the building had a high fence and looked like a mansion that was hardly lived in. Evidently, it was the home of one of the boys. One punched me so hard in the face that it felt like my jaw had dropped. Grabbing my hands and legs, the boys began to rip the clothes off my body. They dragged me into a dark room in the house, and the three boys took turns raping me. Prior to the rape, I was a virgin. They laughed at me, teasing, and taunting me for what felt like hours. The boys threatened to report the incident to my parents if I dared reveal what happened, which terrified me more than the rape. The last thing I needed was to go through another drama with my parents. They gave my torn clothes back to me and called a taxi to take me home. I cried all the way home and took a long shower, wishing I could have reversed time and not gotten in the car. In Nigeria, rape and sexual assault was an all-too-common phenomenon and quite normalized. Children were often a prized target.

Reporting such an incident would only bring me more humiliation. Violated, humiliated, and scared out of my mind that my parents would find out about the rape, my heart raced every time the phone rang. What if it were my attackers calling to inform my parents? There were whispers around the school, but no one spoke with me, and other students began to distance themselves. I told no one and was concerned about any of my sisters finding out; I didn't trust them not to laugh at me and hoped that this would be a secret I would take to the afterlife.

Humanitarian Hypocrisy

My parents were heavily involved in social elite clubs with international affiliations. Most of the elites in Lagos were members of clubs that functioned as if they cared about the disadvantaged when, in fact, their membership was a cover for extraordinary shows of materialism, adulterous affairs, and self-aggrandizement. Elaborate parties were often held to show off their wealth, provide awards for phantom service, and parade expensive traditional attires and gold jewelry.

My mother enjoyed the limelight and being the center of attention, and her goal was to be seen as a generous person and humanitarian, a position that seemed to dominate her life. This seeming contradiction was quite confusing for a child because, in keeping with her appearances, my mother was clearly a generous person by day and attracted a lot of attention for her generosity. She spearheaded orphanages for abandoned and neglected children and received international awards for her philanthropic endeavors. What happened behind the compounds of these orphanages was unknown, but from a clairvoyant angle, the more she attracted attention, the more her negative attachments fed off the people around her like an energy vampire. The more she fed, the hungrier she got for more power.

Arranged Marriage and Coming to America

With extreme narcissistic abuse, sexual and physical abuse, I somehow managed to get through undergraduate college at the local university in Lagos. My life during this time was uneventful, except for surviving one of the most gang-ridden universities in Lagos. By this time, my trust in people had greatly diminished and I stayed away from home every chance I got. I did not engage social campus life as I was still traumatized from my sexual abuse and managed to elude sexual advances from college professors and students alike. I focused on my Islamic faith, and praying five times daily, asking and begging God for an escape from a culture I found horrid. I had a few acquaintances and close relationships with friends who were as troubled as I was. Although we never spoke about our traumas, we seemed to bond, sharing our hopes and dreams.

By my third year of college, my younger sister had gotten pregnant and was to marry her long-term boyfriend. During her marriage ceremony, my mother met a friend of a friend, and their discussion started the ball rolling on arranging a marriage between me and the friend's nephew. One day, when I was home from school, my mother told me to wait by the phone for a phone call. I did as I was told, and sure enough, I began speaking to a man who lived in the United States. I had no idea who he was or what he looked like, but I knew that I would take every opportunity to get away from my family and far away from Nigeria. I had a year left of college, and my father had vowed not to assist me with furthering my education through a master's degree even though he had supported my stepsiblings.

The man I talked with on the phone was thirteen years older than me and had been living in the United States for twenty years. He seemed safe enough and offered me a potential exit plan. My mother recommended that I marry this man, and I agreed to the opportunity to leave Nigeria and finally find some space to breathe. The suitor visited Nigeria exactly one month from the day we first spoke, and we got engaged a week after meeting. I was not attracted to this man, let alone in love with him. Yet, I felt a karmic connection as his energy felt familiar. I took that familiar feeling as a hope for the next journey of my life and an opportunity to escape from my family.

Arriving in the United States at the age of twenty-two with a $150 wedding present from my father, I was eternally thankful for my escape, but I was also confronted with a new set of obstacles. The man who arranged to marry me was still married to someone else. So, I had a problem with how to legalize myself.

When I received a work permit, my first job was as a family service counselor in Miami, Florida, at the cocaine baby unit during the crack epidemic. My job was to provide social services to families struggling with drug addiction.

We eventually married and had four children, but my husband provided no financial support. I was left to care for myself and the children. Maintaining jobs in social services and working with abused and neglected children, I embarked on my graduate studies in mental health in the hopes that I could find a solution to healing my wounds. Now and then, I would catch a glimpse of the flying ones, the pristine light, a happy dream, and my hope for the future. I was isolated and without a support system, but it taught me to be strong and independent and to keep going. I needed to work hard to gain my independence from what grew to be a negative, abusive, and toxic marriage. Although I was far away and on the other side of the world from my family, my mother continued to manipulate my home life.

A year after I arrived in the United States, Mother came to visit, and after one week, she and my then-husband developed a hatred for each other. Both were narcissistic and controlling; neither would succumb to the other's control, and I was stuck between them. I was mocked by my mother and siblings for living in poverty in the United States and being unable to shower them with money. I became distracted by the fighting; my mother would cut me off every two years, and despite the distance, I still craved her approval.

One summer, fifteen years after I had left Nigeria, I received news that my father had passed away. I made plans to go home for the funeral. Simultaneously, I had also begun my private psychotherapy practice. As I prepared, I got wind of my mother's plans to mistreat me once I arrived in Nigeria. Gossip and rumors came from the siblings that Mother planned to cut me off, claiming that my father was not my biological father.

While sitting in my office, weeping, I saw my father's feet and then the rest of him appeared. He was sitting on my couch with my grand-mother, who had passed away a year prior. I felt that they were giving me the approval to walk away from my siblings and my mother. I thought nobody walks away from a narcissist unless they are done with you. I also knew that my mother was heavily involved in occult practices, and I needed to use my strength to hold my boundaries on a physical and spiritual level. If I walked away, I would never look back.

For the first time, I mustered the courage to walk away and completely disengage all contact and communication with what was left of my birth family. That same year, I walked out of my fifteen-year marriage and resolved to resume a conscious spiritual journey.

CHAPTER 2

The Wounded Healer

As I have mentioned before, this book is not about a pity party or playing the blame game but rather an honest account of my wounds, placing my experiences under strict examination and mapping my journey toward healing and, ultimately enlightenment. The wounded healer's story describes my journey and reveals a map for supporting the healing of others with similar wounds.

The wounded Soul will know no peace until it is able to come to truth and understanding. Only true understanding will heal the Soul and expand consciousness. I now see that my traumas presented possibilities for growth in knowledge and insight. As a researcher by heart and taking the observer approach, collecting a data of my experiences, my traumas enabled me to ask significant questions about life and death, what I am and the purpose of being on the planet. I did not dismiss anything. Dreams, past lifetimes, relationships I had along the way, counted towards the bigger picture and a wholesome view of my path and man's purpose in creation.

Because of the enormous opportunities for spiritual growth, I have come to realize, as a therapist, the challenges those who live easy lives of privilege face. Today, in the United States, many have a sense of entitlement, especially among the youth. Such people are more likely to live indolent lives, always seeking entertainment and forever bored from a lack of purpose, and who ultimately fail to grow their spirit, resulting in misplaced anger and depression.

All the money, worldly access and self-aggrandizement will do little to enrich the Soul. I have also come to appreciate my aggressors for offering to take on such a role in my life, closing the gap for me to focus squarely on my determination and persistence for true freedom. To clarify, I am not saying that we should condone child abuse and not hold perpetrators accountable; what I am saying is that if you find yourself at the receiving end of abuse, controlling forces or discrimination, healing and growth are possible if we take ownership of these experiences.

We can develop true convictions that will ultimately feed and free the Soul. All experiences can be used for developing deeper insights into oneself. The proverbial saying, "know thyself," is the ability to undertake a truly experimental and experiential study into ourselves and experiences.

To free our Souls, we must act like true researchers and investigators. Taking all experiences, however disturbing or exhilarating, as part of the puzzle pieces that will ultimately point to who we are and why we are here. Do not discard the past. Discarding the past is like having no roots, no leg to stand on, and such people are always at the whims of an impending identity crisis. They are quick to accept any ideologies, join cults, and follow a celebrity or the next social media craze. We have a mental health epidemic in the United States and around the world because of identity confusion. Then, there are the spiritual teachings which tell you that the ego is bad.

On the contrary, the ego is a part of the self that requires growth. We need a healthy ego, not one that is narcissistic in nature or borderline personality. Only a healthy personality and ego can be further developed into the super consciousness. From here, enlightenment occurs. Traumas only seek to bring us back to the most fundamental questions for all humans on this planet—who are we, and why are we here?

Each of my traumas brought me insights that drew me closer to answering these questions. Along with consistent meditation practice, cultivation of spiritual virtues, and contemplation of traumas, I came closer to my truths. There are many perspectives but only one truth, and since humanity has been denied much of its history, additional painstaking work must be done by all individuals to arrive at their convictions. True convictions feel right within; we do not doubt them, and others will feel their rightness even though they cannot explain it. This will make logical and intuitive sense and leave room for more growth.

All healing professionals should undertake their healing journey, for an unhealed healer is a danger to others. Such people are quick to deny their shadows and, therefore, cannot be genuine with others.

The Invisible Wounds

During my career as a caseworker, government employee, and psychotherapist, I have developed and led trainings on the impact of child abuse, emotional traumas, post-traumatic stress disorder (PTSD), and more. The types of wounds a person experiences because of chronic, dangerous situations are usually described as invisible because they manifest in the subtle mental, emotional, and energetic body. Research and education are available about ways these invisible aspects of us can be healed and maintained. Ignoring these invisible wounds is impossible as they manifest into mental illnesses, personality disorders, and other strange anomalies.

Mental health professionals are trained to treat disorders such as depression, anxiety, and stress, but what I found later when working with clients in private practice was that the wounds themselves are usually within the ego personality, and disorders like depression and anxiety are corresponding symptoms. In other words, we are less likely to get any meaningful results from treatment if the psychiatrist or psychologist is treating just our symptoms. For example, children of narcissistic parents adopt narcissistic traits and may, in some cases, develop other personality disorders like borderline personalities. Narcissists are often prone to depression and social anxiety because they are perfectionists, hard on themselves and forever fearful of people's opinions of them.

I, myself developed certain personality traits as a coping mechanism for enduring child abuse. Both my parents had a bad temper and were easily set off with violent tendencies. I also developed a bad temper and jealousy for the preferential treatment my siblings got. I became competitive to prove my worth to others. During careful self-examination, I studied my astrological chart because astrology provides clues of true characteristics, skills, challenges, and areas in which a person is likely to succeed. My astrological chart revealed that I was not a naturally angry or jealous person and that these traits were the result of my environment; consequently, with forgiveness work and integrative therapy, I could release these traits. I could also see how my north node which the opportunity of this present life requires a lot of self determination unbated by the abuse and manipulation of the people closest to me. As the last of my oversoul group of a collective of great teachers, I will not renege on my ultimate plan to fulfill God's promise to the world.

Another trait I had was due to my sexual abuse. I developed a distrust of people and never seemed to allow friendships to linger past a certain time. I also had challenges with codependency. Following the Buddhist dharma teachings, I learned to transform distrust into compassion. I accepted that I cannot change anyone and had to let go all people's expectations. I learned to release relationships when their purpose ended, and I gave myself permission to disengage from unhealthy situations and keep an open and loving heart for myself and others.

Another trait was lying. In elementary school, I once told friends lies to hide my scars by pretending that I has fallen on a boat ride with my family and that was what caused my injuries. Each week, I had to come up with a new and elaborate lie, and this behavior became a habit. Doing inner-child work and becoming more present to why I told little white lies, which was to get approval from others, I released the need for acceptance and learned to accept myself.

I also realized that my astrological traits- high intuition, reduced objectivity, and sensitivity to subtle energies-were the reason for my communication problems. I needed to balance logic with intuition without denying my clairvoyant abilities. A new paradigm for spiritual psychotherapy may be established, and trauma treatment may be more successfully treated, if mental health treatments are adjusted and intuition and spiritual knowledge are introduced. In my practice, there are energy tools I have used for assessing the damage to a person's aura and chakra and incorporating solutions for healing at an energetic level.

Who is a Healer?

A healer is anyone who is authentic and lives in alignment with their meaning and purpose in life. Healers have a sense of self-awareness with an accurate appraisal of their strengths and their weaknesses; still they do not allow their strengths to escalate into grandiosity and don't let their perceived weaknesses permit them to fall into a pit of despair. They tend to be emotionally well-regulated; however, they can engage in appropriate and vulnerable shows of emotions.

Healers are self-possessed people. They are not necessarily rich and will not require material possessions as cover for self-security. They do not engage in get-rich spirituality or ignore their true feelings, but by acknowledging them, they begin to look deeper into their subconscious processes. Healers are aligned with their purpose in life and may have had difficult lives, but they keep going. God anoints them, and they do not shy away from the challenges life presents. They know that the Holy Spirit will provide what they need to function on the planet.

Healers must maintain a healthy balance between what they need and what they want in life. They know their limits and dismiss fears about what people think or how they will be judged. They are wise and do not fall for the masks people put on. They know when to step away and disengage from an unhealthy situation. They are in tune with their intuition and trust their guiding system.

In the last decade, an explosion of so-called healers and spiritualists have appeared on Facebook, YouTube, and the like. They galvanize millions of followers, but the followers seem stuck on colorful words and do not discern their leaders' true intentions. The devil knows the truth and can channel information that is truth but is it helpful for the person's development? Sitting on the phone and watching insightful videos do little for spiritual development which occurs organically from our daily experiences and interactions with other people.

Healers know the connection between their words and the energy and intention behind those words. They carefully search themselves, align with their purpose, and take corresponding actions. Outcomes are not necessarily their focus, but they seek to examine outcomes against their purpose, and if it is not the desired outcome, they return to clarify their purpose.

Healing happens when we stimulate one another, combine energy, and grow together. We heal when we open our minds to seeing our traumas fully and gain wisdom from them. We thrive in environments where there is egoless competition. We progress through mutual interaction by eliminating the ego sense and being authentic in our interactions. An enlightened person possesses the ability to work with any energy but knows in some instances that disengaging could also be an act of healing.

If the person is not on the level where we are, or their intentions are not in alignment with ours, then we should disengage. So, we have two choices: either we disengage or combine and mutually grow together. When we disengage, there is still growth because we have allowed the other person to move according to his or her plan.

We need to be aware when we are interacting with others, not to interact with the ego but to be authentic. To be authentic requires that the healers have done their shadow work and have taken their own spiritual journey. Discernment becomes a key tool of the healer. They are operating from the light, which sees all and knows what needs to be said and done at each moment.

The healer can discern what a person is really saying and what they are about from an energetic standpoint. For instance, a person can say something like, "I am skeptical." What they may mean is that they cannot relate; they don't understand, or they have not had this experience. Likewise, another person can mean it in completely different terms, such as, "I would rather have it my way." If someone is missing the bigger vision, they must disengage since continuing to commit to something that is in contradiction creates negativity.

The planet is full of negativity because people refuse to disengage when it is necessary to do so—a difficult concept to explain, but to sum it all up, there is a divine plan for humanity. The divine plan is that we grow by mutual stimulation, egoless competition, and forbearance. By so doing, our lives open intuitively rather than destructively. Having the right understanding and applying it to how people should evolve is the way forward. The divine expects egoless mutual stimulation.

Healers do not enable bad behavior for the sake of being nice. They are living in unity with who they are. They have integrated their lessons and completed their work to be secure and comfortable enough to recognize what doesn't work and have the strength to walk away. Healers will understand this because they are authentic and will see right through their parents and selfish people, and it is not uncommon for authentic people to end up being mistreated. When those with authenticity speak, their words are clear. They do not deviate from their calling. The more authentic we become, the more resistant we are to fake people. This doesn't mean we are right all the time. True healers are observant, have a healthy appraisal of their errors, and are open to taking corrective action without beating themselves up.

A healer is anyone who is in the business of healing or healing others from physical, mental, emotional, or spiritual traumas. This includes medical doctors, lawyers, government workers, lawmakers, dentists, accountants, teachers, and parents. However, there is only one true healer, the Holy Spirit, with the light of God within. All people in the profession of helping others are potential conduits for healing, but without undertaking their journey of healing, they are likely to be ineffective and even harmful to others.

However big or small our traumas, we must use healers for self-discovery, which makes us self-aware and learn where our strengths and challenges are—to position ourselves where we fit best. We should develop healthy boundaries in all our relationships. We should also undertake a consistent study with a spiritual psychotherapist who has done his or her healing work to heal and promote self-awareness.

What is spiritual psychotherapy?

Spiritual psychotherapy incorporates the best of traditional Western psychotherapy with Eastern philosophy, practical spiritual models like Astrology and I-Ching, and energy medicine like quantum healing, biofeedback techniques, Reiki, and polarity therapies. Spiritual psychotherapists see and work with each person as a physical, emotional, mental, and spiritual being. This multi-level approach to healing helps guide the individual to discover, explore, and implement his or her true expression of self. It is truly "healing with Soul."

Spiritual psychotherapy is also known as transpersonal psychotherapy, a sub-field of school of psychology that integrates the spiritual and transcendental aspects of the human experience within the framework of modern psychology. The transpersonal is defined as "experiences in which the sense of identity or self extends beyond (trans) the individual or personal to encompass wider aspects of humankind, life, psyche or cosmos." It has also been defined as "development beyond conventional, personal or individual levels" (Walsh and Vaughn, 1993).

"Transpersonal psychology operates in favor of the realization of the Self and the awakening of the spiritual nature and most genuine human qualities in every individual." (Tart C.T. 1992. p. 18). Issues considered in transpersonal psychotherapy include spiritual self-development, self beyond the ego, peak experiences, mystical experiences, systemic trance, spiritual crises, spiritual evolution, religious conversion, altered states of consciousness, spiritual practices, and other sublime and/or unusually expanded experiences of living. The discipline attempts to describe and integrate spiritual experience within modern psychological theory and to formulate new theories to encompass such experience. (Lajoie, D. H. & Shapiro, 1992)

Unlike most forms of psychotherapy that concentrate on improving mental health, transpersonal therapy takes a more holistic approach, addressing mental, physical, social, emotional, creative, and intellectual needs with an emphasis on the role of a healthy spirit in healing. Spiritual psychotherapy facilitates healing and growth by emphasizing honesty, open-mindedness, and self-awareness on the part of the therapist and the client.

Transpersonal therapy, which is more closely related to spiritual psychotherapy, is a holistic healing intervention that evolved from the humanistic work of American psychologist Abraham Maslow in the 1960s. It integrates traditional spiritual rituals into modern psychology, whose intervention is based on the idea that humans are more than mind and body but are also composed of intangible or transcendent factors that make up the whole person. (Friedman, 2014). Just as your mind and body sometimes require treatment, your spirituality and other intangible aspects of yourself often require healing of a sort. A transpersonal therapist may draw from a variety of different religions and spiritual practices for tools and methods that can help you explore various levels of consciousness and use your spirituality to guide you through troubled times.

Healing at the Soul Level

Often, the problem with people is that the Soul is not strong enough to control the personality. The Soul is not in control of the ego-personality. Without a connection, a person feels lost and will always feel that something is missing in their life. There are many reasons why the connection is not happening. The past life preferences of the Soul versus the cultural influences of the physical and physiological issues at birth, owing to medical complications and malpractice, and the harmonic signature of the Soul not matching the astrological map of the person, to name a few. Due to the disconnect, the physical human is adapted to focus externally on his surroundings and less on his inner Soul.

One of my main goals of spiritual psychotherapy is to connect the ego personality to the Soul, being aware that this connection has nothing to do with outer circumstances. You don't have to be rich and successful in art, business, politics or science to connect with your Soul. Your outer worldly success is relative, but it has nothing to do with your Soul. Nothing you do in the world has anything to do with your Soul.

So, when I first meet with my clients, my focus is usually to collect information about their life history and major life events and simultaneously intuitively reconcile the Soul's needs through the natal astrological chart with the physical human. It is like piecing together a treasure map and connecting the dots to find the roadblocks to Soul awareness.

My goal is to bypass the ego personality—to find out what the Soul really wants to communicate to the physical person. The ability to make this connection depends on my connection with the light. The more light I have built within myself in collaboration with my Soul, the more I can extend the light to my clients to strengthen and connect with their Souls. We need to have more light inside us because only light can connect the physical body to the Soul. Because the Soul is light (the Soul is made of pure light), only light attracts light.

Traditional psychotherapy is vastly insufficient because its focus is on the ego-personality, a problem for the Soul to begin with. This personality is made of matter. However, matter is also spirit (everything is spirit).

Everything, from solid, liquid and gas, is energy and vibrates at a certain frequency. The heavier and denser the energy, the slower it vibrates. For example, a rock is energy, but it has a very slow vibration and therefore can be seen by the human eye. Likewise, we cannot see the wind because it is vibrating at a much higher frequency than the rock. Therefore, the physical body is of a low-frequency vibration, much lower in vibration than the Soul, which is why people are not normally aware that they are Souls. People are aware of their bodies because they are dense but are not aware of the Soul because it is lighter. Eight billion people are focused on the ego personality, a materialistic energy field of a certain vibration, but the Soul vibrates in a field of light, and there's no connection between the two. We must make a conscious, intelligent connection; we must work and increase that connection, and then the personality will slowly diminish until only the connection with the Soul remains. Then, you are on the way to light.

A spiritual psychotherapist working in the way of light will never be depleted of energy because the universe will replenish you when you give, which goes beyond the traditional religious message of getting a reward for donating to the church, giving a homeless man money on the street, volunteering at the food bank, or doing the dutiful things for your parents and children. The universe will not reward acts that do not have pure intention attached to them. The universe replenishes you with spiritual light every time you give an insight that comes from the light. The light is not information you read, or something regurgitated without developing spiritual conviction. No, it is not information your ego personality has formulated without the Soul. However, what you do for others is so important because it is connected to your ability to increase spiritual energy.

So, you can act pious all day and say all the right things that come from the ego, but without the light in you without working and growing that light, you will be left behind in the collective evolution of the human species—the kingdom of light, the kingdom of God, which is part of our natural evolution. The light is coming to the planet, and it will usher in this new reality.

All of humanity is presently going through a trial period. Our growth is determined by the measure of light in us. This light determines our graduation points to the luminous heights. Earth is like a school for learning. Like a plant that focuses on the sunlight, we grow by our focus and perseverance in the light. Spiritual psychotherapy understands this fundamental purpose and supports the client in achieving their goals.

Today, unfortunately, the focus is more on the cognitive and intellectual aspects of our being. Those who are educated in psychology, philosophy, science, and other fields try to find solutions to all problems through their intellect. We can be technologically advanced all we want and carry the latest gadgets, but it would be a waste of life if we did not make efforts to receive the light. You can be clever and know a lot of things, but the light is of a different quality and thinks differently. It feeds the intellect of the human brain but not the other way around, and we must open our minds to receive the wisdom of the light.

The light is a much higher vibration, a subtle, fine energy, and the only way you can connect your personality with the light is through the light itself. There is no other way. Mind cannot do it; emotions cannot do it; physical vitality cannot do it—nothing can do it but light itself.

There are all kinds of humans currently on the planet at different levels of their evolution or Soul development, from angelic positive light to demonic dark and all the variations in between. You cannot claim to be in 6th grade when you are a kindergartener. Many kindergarten Souls insist they are at levels they are not. They want to take their toy trucks and head to the highway, wide-eyed and ready to do what they want. There is nothing wrong with this, except they are not mature enough to lead others and because most people have not incorporated their lessons in life and do not have an accurate appraisal of themselves, they will, therefore, not have an accurate appraisal of others. They will judge what is of light bad and what is bad good. This is what is happening on the planet today, The bad is placed on a pedestal and the good is persecuted and even killed.

Many leaders today, whether political, religious or by popularity on the internet, are very clever and have the appearance of knowing. They have cognitive knowledge, but their minds are closed to the divine flow and their hearts are closed to love. Cognitive knowledge will die with the body; the only thing that goes with the Soul is the convictions the Soul has gathered throughout its experiences on earth. Convictions about what the soul is, why it was on the planet, and if it accomplished its goals.

When you align your life with what you are and why you are here, you can expect to get a lot of pushback from family, friends and your community because their expectations are not in alignment with the soul. These days, there is a push that all human beings are the same and need the same medications, food and even the same amount of a daily supply of water. They do not understand that each person even when they have similar patterns as a group of people, is still unique in their own way and must discover their unique configurations. All paths lead to love, but how we get there may not look the same because everyone has their own measure of light karma and dark karma. It is nothing bad, it's like school. You have midterms and exams, and you get a report card, which will forever be part of your record.

In the same way, your actions, decisions, and habits are recorded in your library of report cards, when you reincarnate, you will pick up where you left off in life. You will continue to reincarnate until you have learned all your spiritual lessons, enlightened yourself, and developed the right convictions about yourself, the world, and the universe. All your activities are perfectly imprinted into your Soul energy. Our Soul energy is affected by many things. Examples — the evils we inherited from our parents, our past life deeds, the spiritual lessons we have incorporated into our being and those we failed to learn and our ability to assimilate the right and true convictions into our Soul.

For instance, instead of going by what society tells us about the concept of love, we do not really know until we truly contemplate this concept and develop our convictions based on our own experiences, which requires deep thinking and intuitive perception. Many people know things, but that does not mean that they have assimilated what they know into their psyche, mind, and Soul. Everyone has a perception, but perception is not truth. There is only one truth, and only true convictions feed the Soul.

Today, much information is being thrown at people all over the internet. Social media has manufactured thousands of gurus and teachers, telling us this or that and, although well-meaning, cannot be entirely relied upon because even they cannot help us translate what they are trying to feed into our Soul. They can help us study for exams, but they cannot take our test for us. We are in the school of life together in the great classroom called Earth. We can have study groups in the form of family and friends or teachers, but we still must take the test alone, and the reward is ours to keep. Any knowledge or teaching must be applied to our daily life, and we must match that truth against our experiences to come to our convictions.

If we follow our individual journeys, we will not spend hours on the internet, and we will not be bored; instead, we will be present in our daily life experiences, our interactions, and the messages our true self gives us.

A woman once told me how good and kind she was, as her eye color changed from blue to black. She at the same time revealed that she was manipulative, controlling, self-deprecating and did not feel good enough. It was obvious she had two distinct aspects: one as a kind person and one was a narcissist. It was not my place to tell her what she was but to invite her to contemplate these aspects of herself. She denied these negative aspects of her personality and, therefore, will not likely work on them and instead blame others for how she is.

Blaming someone for how you are is an utter waste of energy. We do not sit and complain that someone gave us an illness; no, we set about treating ourselves, and very little time is spent on complaining about how we got it. You just know that in the future, you will avoid certain things and adopt other precautions. The planet is full of negative forces because people have chosen not to take responsibility for their issues but instead shift the blame on others thereby creating more negativity.

Past Lives and Dreams

To truly heal, we must remember the past that brought us to the present so we can make changes to move us in the right direction for the future. Many times, in my graduate studies in mental health, I heard the phrase: "forget about the past and focus on the now", which is easier for those who are too lazy for real spiritual work. The scientist says the ground is wet because it rained yesterday, pointing to what happened in the past that gave rise to the present. We are the result of our past, but without careful examination, will keep repeating the same patterns in our current and future lives. We will continue to replay the same karmic cycles lifetime after lifetime. So many clients tell me that they have let go of the past, but their behaviors beg to differ, their bodies are falling apart from illness and they cannot stop to connect the dots to the cascading health issues they have. They smile and appear pleasant and every now and then, their anger comes out, they have separation anxiety or explode in fits of jealous rage but still claim to have let go of the past.

From age three, I always had a distinct sense that the world was not real. My dream life felt no less real than my waking life. At the time, I would have many vivid dreams, and I later came to the arduous conclusion that I was recalling my past lives. I also received premonitions and saw future events that later came to pass. Dreaming is an important aspect of our daily lives and gives us clues into our real nature. I often assist clients in interpreting their dreams to gain awareness of themselves. My dreams helped me gain clarity about problems, receive warnings about situations, and provide the right advice to clients.

One deep trauma and vulnerability I had was my sense of a lack of belonging in the world. It does matter where I have lived, my home country of Nigeria, the United States, or the communities within which I serve, there is always a nudging feeling that I do not belong, that Earth is not my home. I am aware of this feeling; it comes on like a rush of anxiety, and it has often been used by evil entities through people who do not hesitate to tell me to get out before they attempt an attack. For the most part, I have accepted this vulnerability and sought to maintain my peace in the knowing that I am here in service of divine will, and I choose to forbear until my work is completed. I rest in this peace, and it is my predominant vibration.

Proving my right to belong is of no relevance to me. Earth and my body are temporary abodes anyway. They are both rentals, and when my lease is up, I gladly return my rental but take with me the wonderful experiences and rewards of the light I have grown from within. It is like trading the old for the new, like when the caterpillar trades his form to become a butterfly. For us humans, we are actively building our new form, our Soul body. We are carefully constructing it with our thoughts, words and deeds, and when we leave the body, we will become our thoughts.

Jesus was tempted three times in the wilderness and on several other occasions. The Buddha was tempted by Mara and many who challenged him. They stood their ground. To them, I am grateful for their responses as they helped me to fashion who I choose to be in the face of the shadows. I take my feelings about not belonging as a cue to prepare to stand my ground and insist on moving forward with my divine plan.

An important spiritual practice is the use of intuition, our dreams, and daydreams. They are, in fact, powerful in providing insight into the future. We may get visions of a scene which is an indication that an event might occur. If we pay attention, then we can be ready for this turn in our lives. We all have many such thoughts and daydreams than we realize. This is a special human trait we all possess, which is the ability to predict the future and to use our intuition appropriately we must learn to observe and recognize them and not dismiss them and then say- "I knew it!" When a thought comes, we must ask why. Why did this thought come now? How does it relate to my divine purpose? Taking this observer position helps us release our need to control everything. It places us in the flow of evolution.

All daydreams must be contemplated, including the negative ones. Negative thoughts of something bad happening, such as someone we love getting hurt or not achieving something we want, are thoughts that we should stop as soon as they come and will a positive thought instead. This is a conscious practice of balancing the two hemispheres of the brain. The negative must be balanced with the positive. As the Buddha described the mind like a bull that must be tamed. If you keep practicing this, negative images will stop coming into the mind. Your intuition will become more about positive things. When negative thoughts come after that, we should take them very seriously and make a conscious effort to change the thought into a positive one. For instance, if the thought comes to you that you are going to have a wreck in a blue car and someone comes along and offers you a ride in a blue car, do not accept it.

From an observer's position, we should stop and look at our daydreams. This is mindfulness in constant action and consistent practice will allow us to increase self-awareness.

CHAPTER 3

My Journey to Spiritual Psychotherapy

In this innovative approach to spiritual psychotherapy, we accept all aspects of the ego personality rather than deny them. We accept traditional western therapies, exercises, techniques, and processes. Techniques such as Cognitive Behavioral Therapy, Jungian Dream Works, Narrative Therapy, Experiential Therapy etc. We also accept body-based therapies such as Yoga and Tai-Chi and mental exercises such as Meditation, Chanting and Mantra. Whatever therapies you employ for yourself and your clients, but these therapies must be consciously tuned towards the Soul-in service of the Soul. We must ask how these therapies can benefit the totality of the client, not just their physical body. When therapies are geared toward the physical body, they will not work; the client will remain disconnected, and healing will not occur. The client will ultimately not feel better because the disconnect remains. For example, if the client is in therapy for anger issues and is in therapy because his anger is affecting his relationships, he must want to heal for the sake of his soul and to understand himself first. Sometimes the soul is angry for a variety of reasons, for instance, the soul may want out of the relationship whereas the ego personality wants to keep the relationship out of fear. Therefore, Spiritual Psychotherapy works to get to the real reason the person is angry.

Before we can relate to anyone on a soul level, a therapist/healer must connect with their own soul. To begin, the therapist must engage him/herself to do the internal spiritual work and the external work of service to others. The idea of service is very important because a person can still be self-serving by doing internal work—aligning their body, mind, and emotions just for themselves. It is quite possible to be selfish because spiritual practice is for the love of self and not for the love of others nor the love of good. They may want to seem better than others, more powerful and in control of their profession, career, and bottom line. They engage in physical exercises, eating well, meditate, studying thousands of spiritual books, and practice energy work, but they are doing it solely for themselves. The exercises will not work unless we do these things for others.

In other words, we improve ourselves so you can help others. We are going to the gym to keep our body healthy so we can help others better. We are not going to the gym to make ourselves better looking than others; we are doing it to help others better. When we improve ourselves, we are more radiant, helpful, intelligent, wiser, and physically able. When we put our mind/body/energy together, we are better able to help people and, in turn, uplift the whole society.

The way of spiritual psychotherapy is different. If we work on our Soul and, at the same time, align our physical body and ego personality to our Soul and align our body and ego to the world around us, divine love and wisdom occur inside, a transformation that is not possible any other way. Somehow, the light will come through us into the world. But suppose a person is self-centered consciously or unconsciously when they go into meditation, in that case, they will collect the divine light, but it stays inside them. The energy does not go beyond their field, and this can be quite dangerous for the person's health. The person will collect divine energy; however, this energy needs to keep moving through the field of the person like a pipe running water through the tap. If the pipes collect water but you do not turn on the tap, the pipes will start to clog or rot. This is why many yoga practitioners and healers develop health issues. This also happens with Christians who go to church and collect the grace however, they are doing it for themselves and their bottom line. They are going to church every Sunday and collecting the grace, but internally they are selfish. The grace will collect in their bodies but because there is no flow, they will get sick.

When we are truly in service, that light will come through our emotional, mind, and body nature. It shines toward others, and it really helps them. Now, you can perform whatever healing techniques like reiki healing or hypnotherapy, or preaching in church or using some machine and the person will receive healing because divine energy is moving through us and others are receiving it. We will go beyond arguing whether this or that technique is better, we will go beyond religion and belief systems. Divine energy is working through us and people will truly heal and transform on the spot. Such an experience can only happen because the divine light is working through us.

Our body, mind, and energy must be service-oriented for the divine light to operate, which it will if we are open and in a position of helpfulness. The mindset is not one of going about trying to save the world. If we do the work correctly and align our person to our Soul while connecting to the world around us for the sake of doing good for others, then the divine light will come through. This is how God wants us to be spiritual today.

Most people are in a state of delusion, and if we are in the light, we can be of service to the people open to receiving. They will find you. Through the right relationship with yourself and discovering your energy field, you can develop a strong ethereal body, one not so easily manipulated by others or unseen energies in the ether. Our ethereal body comprises our mental, energetic, and emotional bodies. We must balance these bodies through various exercises like prayer, meditation, mantra, sound, and physical exercises.

You will soon realize that you do not have a separate mind in the ethereal realm, and your thoughts are not private to you. The mind becomes an open cellphone where the seen and unseen communicate with you daily. You become the medium through which they contact others. You will stop believing everything your mind tells you and develop an open antenna.

What I noticed about the ethereal realms, sometimes called the astral, is that the word "you" does not exist. Everything is the "I AM," and everything is in the union, which is simple logic. When someone is talking to you, they say, "I am…." In our head, we only hear, "I am", for the most part. When you hear the phrase that humanity is one and united, you may ask how that is possible since we are individuated in our bodies.

Oneness occurs in the collective mind field. Think of it like the ocean. There are possibly trillions of fish in the vast ocean. They share the ocean, and therefore, all the trillion lifeforms in the ocean are united in the collective field that is the ocean. In the same way, humanity operates in a collective mind field, and thoughts travel in the field. They can be received by anyone operating on a similar resonance.

Practical Steps to Spiritual Psychotherapy

1. The Ego

Alongside traditional learning of skills of communication and engagement in therapy, all psychotherapists and healers must consider embarking on spiritual psychotherapy for their professional and spiritual development. In new age and consciousness teachings, there is often the belief that the ego is not our friend. According to Sigmund Freud and *A Course in Miracles,1976*, ego can be summarized as that unconscious repressed part of the mind that believes in separation and fear. The ego is also often described as the unconscious, or in other words, automatic behavior patterns, which come from this part of the mind.

Through my journey, I began to realize that this idea may not be entirely accurate. The ego is our friend because it is the part of the mind that has free will to choose to grow, evolve or devolve. Our ego is connected to our body, and it governs our logical ability to analyze and compute linear concepts of the past, present, and future.

The ego is housed in our cognitive/conscious mind, and our subconscious mind is housed within the ethereal body. The level of maturity of the Soul depends on its past life experiences and its ability to incorporate those lessons into its consciousness. The lessons of love, forgiveness, cooperation, balance, manifestation, integrity, and so on are recorded in the Soul and ethereal body, and the person can use those skills for present and future lives. So, the subconscious mind houses all our pre-recorded experiences from past lives' behavior patterns, memories, emotions, creative abilities, and skill sets. Then there is the spirit seed, also called the *God gene* or the *Christ seed*, which sits in the pineal gland. The Soul and the spirit must merge while in the body, which will activate the higher consciousness, and the person will be able to access universal knowledge. (Villoldo, 2016). Therefore, all aspects of the mind, including the ego, have a valuable function and must work collaboratively with one another.

Much of our early childhood experiences get stored in cognition and adapt to our culture and home environments. If we are lucky and can capture the magical, imaginative childhood, we can connect with the animistic realms (the world of fairies, gnomes, water goddesses, spirits of the forests, fairytale creatures and mythological beings) and begin our first insights into spirituality. Many of these creatures are worshipped by indigenous cultures around the world, however, their role on the planet with humans is a symbiotic relationship and not one to be worshipped. The animistic are charged with the role of caring for the natural life, plants, animals, and humans and in turn they benefit from the spiritual energies of humans. An example of this symbiotic relationship can be found between trees and humans, one breathes in carbon dioxide and the other receives oxygen and vice versa.

As we grow up, we begin to think about our career and finding true love, both are the two main avenues for achieving our Soul's destiny. Unfortunately, many of us miss out on achieving a solid footing, which can derail our path to a successful future.

Our parents want what they think is best for us but do not consider the possibility that the Soul has its plans and must be supported to find its way. If we manage to choose the right career, and refine our ability to follow our hearts, we will likely map a successful Soul journey.

When I began my work in psychotherapy, I wanted to be a healer. Yet, I soon realized the years of painstaking work necessary to become skilled at using my entire body to sense what is going on around me. I had to learn to differentiate between the voice of the ego and the voice of God/Holy Spirit/true self, which involves listening intently to what my head says versus what my heart says.

Once we choose to follow our heart, the mind can then be appropriately used to understand what the heart reveals. We will see that the mind cannot provide any answers. It simply regurgitates the past. During our spiritual journey, we may discover many stored unresolved emotions in the emotional body and mental delusions. We work through delusional believes and emotions indoctrinated into us from childhood. With consistent meditation, mindfulness, and breathwork, we can learn to release and filter the emotional and mental body. So, we meditate to achieve a clear mind, and we engage in mindfulness, meditation, and breathwork to release old emotions and learn to filter appropriately. After that, the heart and mind open, and we learn to hear the voice for God, trust ourselves and the process of life.

2. An Intention for a Spiritual Practice

Making up your mind to practice spiritually enables you to walk towards discipline. The core principle of spiritual practice is that you have some structure and discipline throughout your day, and practice will allow you to evaluate your actions to help you focus more on your inner life. Intention is key to beginning your spiritual journey. Ask yourself, what do you want above all else? What do you want to become? Many people say that they want love, peace, and success, but they are not willing to do the work to achieve them. These are virtues we must cultivate.

Through meditation and careful contemplation, we will notice our predominant vibration or baseline. Our baseline could be victim, depression, anger, pride, greed, or shame, or it could be courage, understanding, peace, or enlightenment. Being authentic with oneself is the turning point to the higher vibrations of peace and love, for without authenticity, we will live in denial and avoid transforming our shadow parts.

3. A Desire for Love

One morning during meditation, I saw a vision of a large, complex geometric shape in outer space. It looked like a crystal and was the size of the sun. It also had a black hole in the middle, but the silver-white color it emitted was unlike any color I had seen in physical life. It was clear to me that this giant crystal was intelligent and conscious. I sat in awe for a minute, looking at this entity. It had no words, but a knowing came upon me. For the next few days after this vision, I began to understand what love was in truth. The realization was that love is nothing! It has no feeling, no words, no concepts, no history, no form. It is the emptiness that pervades all things and creates all things. The biblical saying that God is love made sense to me. Love being the substance of all creation.

Since then, I have learned to be in stillness and quiet whenever I sit in deep meditation. Through this emptiness does all light emanate. In Buddhism, this state is called *sunyata* and is expressed as the state of spaciousness, void, or emptiness. The realization of sunyata is the key to attaining enlightenment and true wisdom. Reaching this state means the practitioner has realized that the five skandhas (the elements that make up the human being: form, perception, sensation, consciousness, and mental formation) are impermanent and not related to the inner self.

In this context, *sunyata* refers to the fact that we are essentially empty of the individual self that we tend to think of as being "us," a crucial concept in Buddhism. (Abe, 1997). Once we move beyond the self, we will contact the true self or Soul or light. The practitioners will now act from their real nature and speak from that self and not from the ego personality.

In Dzogchen Buddhism, there is a concept called *rigpa*, the purified version of awareness that is always present inside us. It is a type of radiant consciousness alerted to any outward stimulation. Rigpa, the knowledge of knowledge itself, is one of the greatest gifts of life that can never be destroyed after it is once obtained. The view teaches that not even death can diminish this awareness inside of us (Rinpoche, 2009).

Everything that shapes our personality is also linked to rigpa as it gives us the confidence, the strength, the certainty, and the profound humor to go on in this life. Serene emptiness can also be obtained through this view as we achieve a deep sense of contentment in life. Even when things stop going our way, we will not be particularly disappointed because we are content with our own life. The perspective will always manage to make us smile and laugh, giving us the strength to take on any difficulty that comes our way. It is from this void that the light appears! This light is the real spiritual self that then permeates the mind, body, and energy field.

To achieve this requires a desire to know and love oneself not in a cocky, arrogant way but to know one's grandeur. Many clients tell me that they love themselves. I ask them how, and they will say things like, "I do yoga," "I eat healthily," and "I like to shop." Still, in the same breath, they are also depressed, in bad relationships, and have a perfectionist attitude.

Discovering love is a practice. Knowing love is impossible without acceptance. Human love is conditional. Sometimes, we love with conditions and expectations. When asked this question of love, people always name the things they love and then the things they hate about themselves, which means they have conditional love for themselves. Acceptance is the key to love. Without it, love cannot be known.

Zen tradition speaks of accepting the self and accepting the parts of us that we do not inherently accept. By accepting what we do not accept, we bring wholeness to ourselves, which must be done with every condition and situation in which we find ourselves. People talk about becoming better people. They keep striving to be better, and society tells them all the ways to be better. These include things like getting a better education, a better spouse, and buying a better house. We keep seeking love by seeking better things, and we can never grasp happiness long enough before it disappears like clouds in the sky. Instead, we love for love's sake. We seek the love of God and become one with that love, becoming love itself. As we come closer to divine love, we realize that there are two loves – the love of God and earthly love. We can learn about divine love through earthly love if we choose to take that earthly love higher or we can take that earthly love to the depths of hell where we will encounter evil love.

As a child, I wished to know what love was, but I was told that I was not good enough and needed to be responsive to others and give everything I had.

I admired my grandmother, who I knew to be a very loving person, so I tried to emulate her. I would follow behind her, watch her speaking with chickens, chopping bits of her food to feed vultures, singing at burial sites, and stood next to her as she performed her five daily prayers. I, of course, copied everything she did, but I had no clue about her central fountain or psyche. When we study the people who have the power of love within them, we can catalog how they behave in various situations and formulate some rules out of this catalog.

We may notice that people who display this astonishing universal love are not particularly drawn to romantic love with the opposite sex. They do not have centralized love like the average person who loves only this person or that thing but rather exude erotic energy that permeates their entire nerve endings, cells of their bodies, their whole organism, physical, psychological, and spiritual. Their flow of love is not catalyzed solely in the genital system, nor in special love for certain things, as most people do.

We live in a culture where the idea of love is often limited to sexual love, or within a family unit or some act of kindness. People who love universally are in a constant dance with the aliveness of everything around them; this aliveness penetrates every cell in their bodies. They are always in an orgasmic state. People who love will easily give away what they have, for they know that giving and receiving are the same. That which is given to others is given to yourself.

A Course in Miracles, 1973, says giving and receiving are the same. The average human mind does not see things this way. We believe that if we give money to a person, we no longer have the money we gave away, and we are now at a loss. When spiritual light flows through us, we give away out of the abundance of it. Such giving has nothing to do with material giving but the giving of spiritual energy, which is truly uplifting to people.

4. A Meditative Practice

Modern societies have come to believe in a body-based world. From childhood, we are taught to take care of our bodies, bathe them, brush various parts, protect them, and work hard to prevent its inevitable demise. Because of this, we live in fear, for the body is vulnerable, so we build all manner of objects, homes, clothing, and cars to keep it alive. Our fear has increased exponentially, with the fear of unseen viruses and the use of fear-based solutions that create more fear. We are not taught to focus on the mind, and if we are, it is just to read a book for enjoyment and keep the mind distracted. We go to school and are taught how to be law-abiding citizens to prevent danger to our bodies and other bodies.

Ancient shamanic traditions knew otherwise. Buddhism, Zen, Samurai, and Hindu traditions understood the importance of mental discipline and focus. The mind must be tended to as carefully as the body. The emotions and energy field must also be given equitable importance for the whole well-being. Not until we tend to all aspects of body, mind, emotion, and energy can we truly begin to connect with the Soul.

"When one knows the how and the why of the mind, when one knows
the different functionalities of the mind, then one can control it.
Thus, the mind becomes a useful and perfect instrument through which
we can work for the benefit of humanity."
—*Samael Aun Weor, spiritual teacher and author*

If your mind can settle naturally of its own accord, and if you find you are inspired to rest in its pure awareness, you do not need any method of meditation. The purpose of meditation is to empty the mind and allow the flow of information to come to it from the spirit. The function of the mind is to understand, not to get information. Our spirit also has its own mind/consciousness, and we can receive messages from our higher causal body. In yogic philosophy, the causal body is one of three bodies that contains each and every individual's Soul, the others being the physical body and the astral body. (Upanishad, 1828). The causal body is the most subtle of the three and is contained within the other two. It is the body that transports the essence of the individual from one life into the next reincarnation.

The causal body is also known by the Sanskrit term *karana sharira*. It is composed of karma and samskara, which are, respectively, the record of the yogi's actions in all states of existence and the experiential impressions and imprints on the mind. (Maharshi, 2006).

When we maintain a meditative practice, we will then get in touch with all the memories stored in the emotional body. We then employ various techniques like affirmations, integrative therapy, and presence to clear stored traumas in the emotional field. We integrate all our unresolved experiences and contemplate them to gain wisdom and true convictions, which then enlightens the Soul. After the healing and balancing of the emotional body, the heart's energy opens, and one begins to speak from the heart's mind.

We must seek to understand the essential nature of our mind, our various shifting moods, and the insights we have developed through our practice into how to work with ourselves from moment to moment. By bringing these together, we learn the art of applying whatever method is appropriate for any situation or problem to transform that part of our mind. But remember, a method is only a means, not the meditation itself. Through practicing the method skillfully, we reach the perfection of that pure state of total presence, the real meditation.

When I began practicing meditation, I did not attend a special class or buy expensive DVDs. I knew that I needed to make meditation a daily practice and part of my lifestyle. I thought I lost everything after my father and grandmother passed away. When they appeared to me, I realized that I wanted to go deeper to connect with the other side and explore my spirituality. I wanted to explore not what I had been told but to discover for myself. All beliefs are nothing more than an emotional comfort until we have firsthand experiences about those beliefs. Not until then, the belief will remain in the cognitive mind and will not become a part of our behavior or absorbed in the subconscious mind. When we have experiences say of love can we then integrate the real meaning of love into our life experiences which becomes a part of us. Our true convictions come from experience which feeds the soul.

I was not happy with my life. My relationships were chaotic, and I felt pushed and pulled by the expectations of other people. The first thing I did was to eliminate as many distractions from my life as possible. I trimmed down my lifestyle to keep my life as simple as possible, which is a major step for a healthy spiritual life. We must bring order and discipline to our daily life to keep it simple. I also disengaged from social media, television viewing, and people who were not particularly interested in developing themselves. I once had a client argue with me that she was learning and growing spiritually from watching YouTube videos and Facebook teachings. The issue is that any information you receive on the internet will only fill the emotional sense and rest in the cognitive/ego mind. They will eventually fall away from the body when it dies if the information is not practiced, cultivated, and taken into the inner recesses of the psyche. Becoming mentally awakened does not mean one is spiritually awakened. These days, a person can become mentally awakened by watching lots of podcasts and videos and reading books and they could even mentally awaken after smoking marijuana or doing psychedelics, but that awakening is only the beginning. True spiritual awakening brings us to the highest frequency of love and wisdom. This frequency opens us to creativity and spontaneity, and we begin to receive cues and impulses from spirit. If such cues and impulses do not turn out the way we want, we take them as vital learning opportunities and ask what lessons we could glean from unwanted outcomes.

Many of us have created a lifestyle filled with distractions. The journey to self-discovery often requires us to simplify our lifestyles, including changing our schedules, nutritional habits, and sensory inundations such as watching television and movies, engaging in promiscuity, overworking, being in unhealthy relationships, and so on.

The next thing I did was create a quiet environment that supported inner peace — a space for just me alone with no music, sound, television, or other distracting stimuli. I may light an incense, have plants around me, and use the shaman's rattle to quiet the mind and go within. These items should not become our focus or be idolized. They are used to help the practitioner move into a more receptive mode. As one perfects meditation and rigpa becomes our natural state of mind, these tools are no longer necessary, for one can maintain rigpa no matter their external conditions. They may be dealing with crises, at risk of losing their home, and still be in the inner state of rigpa. Once we have found stability in our meditation, noises and disturbances of every kind will have far less impact.

As years went by, I began to adopt a meditative mind not just during the moments I sat to meditate but also throughout the day; my mind stayed in a clear meditative state. I then began to understand more about the one collective mind of humanity. Then, there is the universal mind, which is beyond the mind of any single collective. It is a total oneness. I realized it is only in the human world that separation exists. The idea of me versus you only exists in the human world. Once our consciousness begins to expand into the field of the one mind or astral world, there is no me versus you. The mind exists in total oneness, and we affect not just ourselves with our thoughts but the entire collective consciousness is at the mercy of our thoughts.

If we spend the day thinking negative thoughts, such as blaming others, feeling we are not good enough, and being worried about money, we exhibit low-frequency thoughts that feed the collective. We will find that we invariably encounter other people and situations like our state of mind, which is why experts say that if we genuinely want to change our lives, we must change our minds.

5. What is Contemplative Practice?

Now, once the mind is stabilized and quieted, we can then begin contemplation. Here, the real work begins for spiritual and consciousness expansion. Contemplation is the art of developing true spiritual convictions. The operative word here is *true* because our spirit cannot further develop itself in erroneous lies. The human belief structure is mixed with a lot of false ideas and ways of living on earth. With the advent of the internet, there is so much truth, lies, and in-between floating around that one must practice discernment. Many people, theorists, and educational systems have provided a variety of beliefs, many of which are false and will not feed the higher consciousness of our children or adults.

Many people accept ideas without truly examining these ideas alongside their intuition. They do not place themselves under strict examination but regurgitate, defend, and even kill other humans over erroneous beliefs. When we transition into the inevitable death experience, we will not be able to ascend under these erroneous beliefs. Many people are depressed and dissatisfied with their lives despite having material wealth, family, and various comforts because we can never be truly happy living on misguided principles.

Every experience we have, down to our simplest encounters, must be deeply contemplated. For experience is what the Soul truly seeks. Experiences must be processed, digested, and understood. Understanding brings about wisdom within the self, and within every traumatic experience lies a jewel of wisdom and understanding. The primary goal of contemplation is to help us discover the brilliantly hidden sanity within ourselves.

Many people are frustrated with meditation because they don't feel progress in their spiritual life. Meditation is only the foundation for more deeper spiritual work. In some Buddhist traditions, they call it *mindfulness* or *cultivation*. Many counseling programs barely teach this practice, and it is quite evident that so-called western mindfulness experts know nothing of its true meaning.

So, the work of contemplation can also be referred to as mindfulness or cultivation. They all mean the same thing and arrive at the same result: increased awareness and expanded consciousness. For example, people who eat excessively due to stress can recognize when they abuse their bodies by overeating to avoid anxiety. Later, their anxiety is diverted to guilt and regret for eating in an out-of-control manner. Another person may develop leg and knee pain because they feel stuck in life. Their bodies aligned themselves to the belief of feeling stuck. Another person may develop tinnitus of the ear because they refused to listen to their intuition, and yet another could develop a bacterial infection due to a toxic mind. Contemplative therapy may help us recognize why we indulge in such desires and help us become more self-aware.

Once we know the root cause of an issue, we can make the necessary changes in life. A lack of contemplation often results in health issues, which is the last attempt by the Soul to get the ego to pay attention.

Contemplative therapy can help us accept painful memories. Victims of trauma and abuse often suppress such memories, which then sit in the energy field as stuck emotions. These stuck energies, if left unprocessed, may begin to manifest as health problems years later. We may become triggered when something reminds us of the trauma and may attempt to project blame on the person who triggered the feeling, but the reality is that being triggered simply means you have not processed the trauma. When we contemplate our traumas, we will truly begin to appreciate their corresponding opportunity to develop love, peace, and wisdom.

6. Cutting the Delusions

Tibetan Buddhists talk about cutting the delusions. Practitioners keep a small knife next to them as a symbolic way of cutting off thoughts that are not real. As we go about our daily lives, we can experience unreal fear-based thoughts. If we entertain them, they will take over our minds and begin to wreak havoc to the point of causing mental and physical health problems.

Instead, we must learn the difference between how our ego thinks versus true spiritual communication. Cutting the delusions means not allowing runaway thoughts to infect our minds. We must question our thoughts and practice positive self-talk gently.

In Dzogchen practice, Trekchod – literally "cutting through" – the path of cutting through, or liberating, our ordinary mental events whenever we want, like a hot knife through butter. Through meditation, one becomes familiar with the pristine awareness experience. Meditation allows the body and mind to become relaxed, at ease, and alert. As times goes one, we naturally and comfortably rest in pristine awareness of rigpa and the gap between thoughts start to widen and even extend for longer periods at a time. Soon, uncomfortable emotions start to diminish as the mind no longer grasps negative thoughts. At the same time, extraordinary mental events like unconditional bliss, joy, expansive energy, and compassion arise by themselves. (Prescott, 2014).

Rigpa, the pristine awareness becomes the constant abiding state of mind. It would not matter what condition a person finds themselves, all forms, all sounds, and all thoughts are instantly released as they arise, and nothing other than the radiance of pristine awareness is left. This is our natural state. The next level Dzogchen practice is Togal – "direct crossing" or "leaping over." With Togal, by mobilizing one's inherent heart essence wisdom and the awareness accomplished by the practice of Trekchod, we can shed the hindrance of the physical body without dying, and so achieve the ultimate accomplishment: the level of realization called "the naturally present fundamental nature." (Das, 2010)

With Togal, one attains four levels of experience: (1) the direct experience of the nature of reality; (2) the expanding experience of the nature of reality; (3) pristine awareness reaching its ultimate point; and (4) all experience dissolving into the nature of reality. (Das, 2010).

When I had begun my meditation practice, I did not have a teacher and did not know what direction to follow except to listen to the quiet nudging from my spirit. I knew I had an unseen teacher who gave me the support and guidance I needed. I did not know what type of meditation practice to follow but years later, I realized I had achieved the four levels by virtue of its description and my personal experience with meditation. Rigpa being the pristine awareness, the widening of the space between thought, Trekchod is cutting the delusions of the mind. Delusional thoughts are like the clouds in the sky and the practice of meditation keep the sky clear and makes way for the light to pierce through the mind. That light is Togal, the wisdom of God. Once Togal is achieved, you are in the way of light.

7. Learning the Difference Between Attachment and Love

The ego has a definition of trust, and the higher self has another. For the ego, trust comes from the expectation that a person will be the way we want. My mother is supposed to be nurturing; my father is supposed to love me, and so on. When we place expectations on people, we will invariably become hurt when they do not meet these expectations. We may even blame them for traumas, like I blamed my mother for my traumas.

When we realize that our trust must be placed not in people but on the grand design of the universe, we begin to raise our vibration towards enlightenment. People are exactly where they are meant to be and we do not need to insist that they become what we want. This will be controlling and the opposite of love. When we connect with our true nature as spiritual beings, we know that the spiritual realms will not fail to lift us when we focus on it. Not everyone believes that they have a Spirit or Soul because not everyone has one and many more are disconnected from it. If you are in tune with your Soul, you instinctively know that you came into this body, and you will leave it. You know that you are immortal, your spirit cannot die or get sick, and fear is not real. Understanding and accepting these truths is how we develop trust.

Trust dawns in our Soul when we accept that people are exactly as they are meant to be, and how we see them reflects our current developmental stage. The world is as it is meant to be, and we accept others and the world as it is. We do not get angry at a three-month-old baby for not walking or at a snake for biting. It will be itself. Our trust is placed in the grand design, knowing that the universe has a plan, and we can allow ourselves to let go and trust the grand plan. When we integrate with our spiritual being, we realize that free will is gifted to the spirit, not the human being. Therefore, the most important achievement of a human being on this planet is the enlightenment of the Soul.

Divine threads are dangling down in the ethers, waiting for people to grab onto them and swing to higher heights. These threads are vines of love, joy, peace, abundance, and all the divine virtues, but we must grab onto them and hold on tight with our minds. Sometimes, people will focus on, say, love but are also focused on other earthly issues and will find that their attention is divided, and no upward movement can come of that. Does it mean that we should neglect our family and daily duties? No!

We understand that we must address daily concerns and responsibilities, pay our bills, and go to work, but they do not have to consume our minds. The mind retains what matters the most. That is our enlightenment. The Buddha said, "Before enlightenment, chop wood and carry water; after enlightenment, chop wood and carry water." When we truly love a family member, it means we do not get attached; we love them unconditionally, allowing them to be free and to live as they choose. If their lifestyle does not match your fundamental values and goals in life, then you must disengage and allow them to join with those who align with them, which is challenging for a mother or father. We do not want to see our children walk down the wrong path, and we can do what we can to counsel and support them. However, if a client or family member does not ask for or want help, we must respect their wishes. There must be basic rules for engagement and healthy boundaries, even with the people we love with all our hearts. The truth is that we must love the way the divine loves. For divinity does not know specialness and loves all the same. Love is the emptiness present in all relationships. Unfortunately, attachments continue into the afterlife, whether we are attached to an idea, a deity, a house, or a family. These attachments form chains in the ethereal realms and will prevent swinging upward toward luminous heights.

8. Daily Mantras and Affirmations

The Bible says that we are the word of God, the will of the creator, and all we see from trees, birds, animals, and humans are all part of God's will. We are each a form of divine expression and can choose how we want to express ourselves within the divine laws. Sound begins with our greatest instrument, our voice, which is why all spiritual texts warn all humans to choose their words carefully, for every word will manifest in another form. We can also use sound with the right attention, attitude, and intention to create and effect change in an environment that becomes a catalyst for healing the physical, mental, emotional, or spiritual aspects. Our voice is essential for raising our vibration. It is a wonderful practice for maintaining inner purity and connecting with the divine.

The ancients chanted to maintain wellbeing, joyful states, and connection with God. Our voice is part of the package for developing our light body. Just like water and fast-moving turbines make electricity, chanting moves our water body, chakras and light body. Every indigenous culture in the world engages in chanting to move their consciousness into an altered state to connect with the spiritual realms.

Many indigenous cultures and even today's scientists understand what is now known as the quantum field or dream state or dimensions, and everything is sound and vibration. When the universe tunes into us, it recognizes us by sound and vibration. These days, people are self-conscious and avoid using their voices or singing. With the right attention and intention, we can align with holy beings and even reach the gates of heaven.

Within my psychotherapy practice, I begin energy healing work with my client by chanting with the intention of connecting with the divine realms. I then employ various natural sounds like rattles, tuning forks, drums, digeridoos, singing bowls, frequency beats, and biofeedback quantum tools to assist my clients in relaxation, clearing stuck emotions, releasing negative attachments, recalling their lost Soul parts and restoring their energy field.

Ancient mantras employ the vowel sounds, which are the primordial sounds of God, to connect with the qualities of love, peace, and tranquility.

The mantra always goes back to its source, the highest level of the spiritual realms. Years ago, this secret was uncovered by the eastern and western sages who took advantage of it by using mantras in Hebrew, Chinese, Arabic, and Sanskrit.

Sound and frequency go hand in hand. Our voice is connected to our vibrations and frequencies, and this is why our voice is extremely important. Sound cuts across the dimensions and can be used to contact higher dimensions as well as lower, depending on the intention and the vibration of the person. So, there is a direct relationship between sound and consciousness. Those who understand this will see the potential within healing and consciousness and the use of sound for healing oneself, others, or any aspect of the cosmos. The universe is very fluid and flexible and is willing to support our beliefs and expectations. Attention, intention, and expectation... that's all it needs from us. How we choose and use these for everyday experiences and for developing and integrating a state of wellness and greater awareness is extremely important for the activities we engage in for conscious living and the method for therapeutic work.

9. Trusting Your Intuition

Growing up in Nigeria, my father had a large library of books in the living room, my favorite part of the home. I especially enjoyed skimming through the books on astrology. They seemed to provide me with some comfort. The books talked about astrological signs, temperaments, skills, and challenges. Since then, I have taken a special interest in astrology and use it in therapeutic practice. Our lives are influenced by energies from our past up to our moment of incarnation, and where and when we are born is directly related to the spiritual lessons we are here to learn. Earth is a school for the growth and development of the human spirit. Astrology and numerology hold clues to the lessons we are here to learn. Most western scientific institutions are extremely opposed to astrology despite evidence of its direct impact on our overall development. (Willis, 2020)

We can be affected by planetary shifts, our biorhythms, and numerology. All our experiences are valid; there are no mistakes in the universe. Even animals follow their natural biorhythms and birds understand the earth's natural cycle. Marine life would flow with the tides, but humans believe they are above it all. I have a sense that the world is perfectly mathematically aligned. If you can understand the flow of energy and planets, you will appreciate your behaviors. Some people are prone to depression, anxiety, anger, and fear more than others, not because they are weak but because of their astrological makeup. You can learn many things about your skill sets and the gifts you brought to the world by understanding astrology and fully using your gifts. Through astrology, you will learn where your challenges lie. There are many personality assessment tools that psychologists use to assess one's personality. Although I happen to be trained in conducting these tests, I find Astrology to be the quickest, fasted and most precise tool for understanding my clients. No two people have quite the same astrological chart, they may have similar traits, but there will still be subtle differences with how they express the energies displayed on their chart. I have had identical twins with same exact chart, but both expressed their personalities in very unique ways, and it is reflected in their dress styles, temperaments and drives.

I use numerology calculations from my clients' dates of births to understand their Soul paths and the challenges they are facing at that moment. Over time, I calculated my own energetic origins, and the specific skill sets at birth through astrology and galactic astrology, which I will talk more about in future chapters. I also understood I was born in Africa to connect with the DNA of the first humanoids of ancient Egypt.

Through astrology, I even understood my body structure. These days, everyone wishes to be skinny, and anyone who does not look a certain way is considered subpar. I understood that my body type was specifically geared to carry large amounts of light. Through astrology, I saw why certain cultural paradigms, such as being in family groups, keeping long-term friends, and being a closet introvert, are simply imprints of the Soul's past and its predispositions.

I also understood the meaning of universal energy, which permeates all things and is available to all people if we would but tune our minds to it. I am also extremely clairvoyant and clairaudient because of my astrological makeup, past life experiences, and skill sets acquired during those lives. Following our unique makeup is important for unpacking the path of our Soul. If we follow the dictates of others, as opposed to our inner guidance, we will deviate from our Soul's mission.

I began to study galactic astrology, which draws information from the Galactic Centre-oriented charts from the sun's perspective but interprets it from the perspective of the Milky Way Centre. While the Geocentric chart looks out from Earth through a telescope, the Helio chart looks out from the sun with a telescope, plotting the planets in their real positions. It can then look further out at the stars in the background and note their correct positions. More importantly, it looks specifically at how our solar system and the planets react to incoming frequencies from the center of the galaxy at a given moment.

By using your birth date and place, galactic astrology of birth will determine your true spiritual origins. Earth is like a soup bowl of all types of Souls. There are young Souls, old Souls, prophets, teachers, and volunteers. I learned a lot from studying my chart, which drew my attention to my intimate connection to the galactic administration. I am an angelic being incarnated on Earth.

Why, you might ask, would an angel incarnate as a human being, and is this even possible? There are many incarnated angels who, with joy and complete devotion to the supreme light, volunteer to bring truth, joy, and hope to humanity. If you believe that Jesus was a cosmic being, then you can open your mind to the possibility that God could send many more. (Steiner, 2024). The distractions and low-level desires that affect even the brightest amongst us are great and once in human form, we potentially forget who we are and fall prey to the pressures and demands of the world. By being truly helpful and loving others as ourselves, we advance spiritually, even in the afterlife, the spiritual and heavenly realms, and our work is never done until the last Soul is redeemed.

From an early age, I would hear the ringing in my ears crying out to me not to get distracted or give in to my desires, to stay focused on the light, and watch my associations closely. It goes without saying that a strong will is the greatest gift of any Soul. Now, there are many incarnated angels and possibly people who took on human incarnations for further spiritual development. This message, collaborated by the divinations of the Babalawos, felt true.

Many incarnated angels can have a difficult time fitting into the ways of humans. Given that my mission is to support the awakening of other angelic and star seeds, I began to pay close attention to the clients who found me and the interactions that took place between us. Incarnated angels, usually the family's black sheep, would have no real attachments to the world and feel a deep sense of purpose or mission. They would be focused on their life destiny even though they don't remember why they came. When I suspect them of being angelic beings, based on the energies and information obtained at my initial session with all clients, I begin to work with them to understand the bigger picture and how their concerns fit into this picture.

My goal as a Spiritual Psychotherapist is to support the Soul and Spirit of my client, which will invariably translate to a healthier and happier life. Once clients know why they are here and what they are through careful calculations of the charts, they can accept their challenges and focus on their mission and spiritual lessons. The Soul will be happy, and life will become richer and fuller.

For example, I had a client who struggled all his life to find a mate. By all accounts, he was good-looking, educated, and was doing well professionally, but he could not understand why all his romantic relationships never lasted, which was a source of pain and depression for him because he felt something was seriously wrong with him. When I pulled his chart and read it to him, I explained to him that romance and marriage were not the goals of the Soul for this lifetime. His focus was on connecting to his higher self and on service through his spiritual goals. When he realized that he was exactly where he was meant to be and there was nothing wrong with him, he felt a release and freedom to focus on the things he truly loved.

10. Practice Dying to the Self

In Tibetan Buddhism, there is the art of dying to the self; Jesus also explains this in the great art of surrender, which is not about suicide which is borne out of self-hate. Dying to the self is the surrender to the Soul and letting go of the ego. In the West, most people consider death a terrible thing. The entire media culture, including medical and educational systems, is in fear of it, and they create all types of fear-based policies and procedures.

We must contemplate death not in a morbid way but as a natural transition toward the afterlife. However we prepared in this life sets the precedence for the next life. This is a simple statement that has been around for thousands of years. Still, for some reason, people completely disregarded this and focus on gaining material things that have no meaning to the spirit.

Whatever we concentrate on, we will become - a statement that speaks to the universal law of success. If we want to be successful at anything, we must focus on it—whether it is spiritual, material, creative, finding a great job, learning a new dance, or something else. If you want to become a bus driver, you focus on becoming one; if you want to become the CEO of a Fortune 500 company, you can if you concentrate hard enough and are willing to do whatever it takes, and you will become one. However, there is a slight caveat to this statement. Here, a discernment must emerge.

We must ask ourselves if we really want to focus on this one thing. We must ask ourselves if it is worthwhile to BECOME IT. Is it beneficial for the Soul to become this thing? Is it what my Soul wants? Many successful people in the world are not happy even though they have achieved fame and money. We must ask ourselves: if we achieve this thing, will it make us happy? Will our mind be at peace? Are we going to be satisfied in life?

Most people in the world today are very involved in the world—which is fine— it's quite natural to be so, and there is nothing wrong with it. For many, the question of spiritual life is kind of on the fence; they are not interested in it at all, or if they're a little interested, it's kind of there. They will engage in spirituality sometimes for entertainment, to feel better about themselves, or to get followers on YouTube or Facebook. So, engaging in spirituality is inextricably linked to materialism in this day and age, and as a result, spirituality will fail. No success will occur since their energy is split.

How about your spiritual life? Some people are curious about karma, past lives, or incarnation, they may attend church daily and perform darshans depending on the religion but may still be on the fence about their spiritual life. They seem interested, but they are not willing to go deeper or do something about their spiritual life. How important is your spiritual life? How important is your material life? Either a person's life revolves around their spiritual life, or it revolves around their material life. You must ask yourself: Is your spiritual life the only thing that really matters?

Christ revealed that wherever your treasure is, so is your heart. The dying to the self requires a decision to let go of everything and attend to spiritual life. Through a dedicated Spiritual life, would the ego take the back seat. It will not die but rather surrender to the Spiritual path. We will have our responsibilities as parents and family members and take care of our responsibilities, and not neglect these. But we also must ask ourselves every day, "What happens to us when we die?" If we cannot answer this question, then we have missed out already.

When we leave this body, we go somewhere and wherever we go, and whatever we do after we die is determined by what we have been and done in the present life. Focusing on spirituality is concentrating on your future.

The only future that matters. Human life is a short journey compared to the trillions of years our Soul has been in existence and will continue to exist. Being in human form, however long, is like a sneeze to the Soul. While you have a chance, do something about your spiritual life.

11. Seeing Only Thyself—Authenticity

Buddhist teachings often muse that this world is a type of Bardo (Bardo means a type of hellish realm). There are many Bardos and when we die, we go to the realm that corresponds with our thoughts and desires. There is a bardo for hellish beings, hungry ghosts, a hell for deceitful, selfish people and so on. When asked what Bardo this earth is, the Buddha called it the jealous realm. Souls who find themselves on this earth plane must contend with jealousy which can be traced to many forms of wicked deeds on the planet.

The first sin was committed by Cain when he killed Abel due to jealousy. Jealousy is extremely toxic, and it is easy to become infected by it. You will find friends smiling at the dinner table but secretly hate each other, moms jealous of their daughters, dads jealous of their sons, a spouse obsessed by envy, the desire to repress a community or racial group may all be ascribed to jealousy. We compare ourselves with others and this habit if left unchecked can result in self-hate and evil attempts to sabotage another person either consciously or unconsciously. One of the worst human vices is jealousy. It is nearly impossible for humans not to operate in this low vibration, and it affects the Soul in terrible ways. In the astral, a person secretly consumed by jealousy often looks green, haggard, and evil looking. Efforts must be made by each of us to talk ourselves out of comparing ourselves with others, embracing our own success and failures, and accepting our individual unique paths.

In the Hispanic communities, people talk about "oho," meaning the evil eye. When a person gets jealous of others, they send waves of evil energies towards their target, which can result in the demise of that person. People do not have to actively perform black magic to send an evil eye to another; they just need to be angry, hateful, and gossip. To avoid this, I practice seeing only myself in others. In other words, everyone I meet is an aspect of me, and I must be authentic in my dealings with them because my actions toward them will translate back to me. Now, this does not mean to be pretentious and smile and be fake! It is important to be honest with yourself about your feelings of jealousy when they emerge, and to make every attempt to practice self-talk.

12. Quantum Physics and Energy Medicine

We have heard that energy cannot be created or destroyed. (Cappuccio, 2006). Still, it can be changed, transformed, or elevated, which is the law of resonance and vibration. Humans can manipulate creation, but they do not create contrary to popular belief. Glass is made from stone, furniture is made from trees and plants, houses are made from clay, and so on. There are many forms of energy. Some are fast-moving, and some are slow-moving. A rock is energy but may not move as fast as water, which is simple knowledge.

Humans are made of variations of energy. Our body is solid, but our emotions are like water, and our thoughts are like air. As water can be solid, ice, liquid, and gas form, we have aspects of us seen and unseen. Just because we do not see the mind and emotion doesn't mean they are not there. The slower a moving particle, the easier it is to be seen by the visible eye. Just because we do not see faster-moving particles with the visible eye does not mean they are not there.

Most of the energy around us is unseen to the human eye because we are limited in our vision. Over thousands of years, we have successfully influenced one another in certain belief systems, and we do not question them. So, anyone who sees beyond the norm is considered strange. What we lack almost all the time is context. We see a world event or something happening in our lives, and we tend to look at these situations apart from everything else going on. But what I have learned over the last thirty years, repeatedly, is that the truth, the real understanding, comes when we connect the dots. When we connect each individual event in context to many other events, that individual event starts to look vastly different in and of itself.

We must explore life beyond the perceived normal—that which is more than a human construct. These constructs are taught in schools, universities, culture, media, mainstream science, medicine, and research. Basically, we are taught a version of life/reality that has been constructed. But because it is now termed *normal*, people tend to believe that anything outside of that must, therefore, not be normal.

So, we call events and happenings that cannot be explained *paranormal*. My life experience has shown me that the paranormal is normal where the human normal is an illusion. While we go through life within the bounds of human normality, the paranormal (the real normal) interacts and intercepts us and events all the time. We must go beyond the illusion and deconstruct the perceived normal. By doing so, we take back control of our lives and regain our ability to see more fully, not an easy task.

As much as humans want to change, our subconscious mind, which controls our behaviors, is not so easily changed. Any theory or idea must be put into practice, and we must each take responsibility for our change. Basically, we are told to believe that we live in a solid, physical, and material world, and everything has space between them. There is a thing called *time* that moves from the past through the present to the future, and the interaction of the material world is random. Things happen without force or unity behind them. We are told that we are cosmic accidents. We come out of nowhere and die at the end.

But what if this reality is not physical at all? What if we experience it physically, but it is not solid? There is electromagnetic resistance. Like WIFI and a computer, our body is like a computer. Our emails don't fall off the internet unless we delete them. You can make a phone call to someone halfway around the world, but we don't stop to ask how this is possible. If you can understand this concept, then you will see that you are not what you think you are.

Frequency is defined in physics as the number of waves that pass a fixed point in unit time; also, the number of cycles or vibrations undergone during one unit of time by a body in periodic motion. A body in periodic motion is said to have undergone one cycle or one vibration after passing through a series of events or positions and returning to its original state (McInturff, 2006). It is essential to notice the frequency we are operating in, which is easy to do. Just start by paying attention to the quality of your thoughts and feelings. You will soon see that they are either predominantly positive or negative or oscillate between them, which means chaos or static.

I once heard the saying, "We cannot afford the luxury of a negative thought." For one, negative thoughts will produce static energy in the energetic body and lower our vibration. The law of resonance says that like attracts like, so we will invariably invite corresponding negative thoughts into our field.

To connect with faster-moving energies, we must train the mind and emotions to be more positively focused. From that positivity, we move into transcendental thinking. The transcendental mind is a mind that is no longer tuned to positive or negative thoughts; it has moved into the higher mind of the spirit, which is empty and only receives the thoughts coming from the spiritual planes. In order words, we can access all consciousness from lower to higher vibrations. Negative energies carry negative thoughts and feelings, and many times, people do not recognize that these negative thoughts and feelings do not come from them but from the energies around them.

Many years ago, I began to study the concept of quantum physics. I am not a scientist, and these concepts were difficult to grasp, but some basic theories were practical in daily life. One is the idea of polarity—that every-thing has an opposite, the same concept in Buddhism of the Yin and Yang.

We know that everything has an opposite. Up/down, in/out, hot/cold, one does not exist without the other. What is physical must have a nonphysical counterpart, and so on. A transcendental mind stops focusing on one side and accepts that all sides exist because its opposite is there. They simply move into the wisdom of higher knowledge and reason.

I then asked, what would be the opposite polarity of humans? What is my polarity? I was pleasantly surprised when the answer became clear and simple: my opposite is God! Therefore, the source of all creation is with me. I do not exist without it, and because I am part of it, it is incomplete without me, which goes for everyone and everything. Polarities must exist together like the two sides of a coin. I felt liberated by this realization that I am not alone and can never be. A field of awareness permeates me and is around me if only I can open my mind beyond my five senses. Then, I can see beyond the physical that *the Course in Miracles, 1976* called "the perfect union." The human mind or ego sees separation, which is not real.

13. Ritualism: Creating Sacred Space

Before I begin my day, working with clients in psychotherapy and energy work, I follow meditation rituals, using chants, candle lighting, palo santo, sage, holy water, essential oils, and crystals as part of the intention for truth. I give gratitude to the elements working with me, to the universe, and to the spirit. It came to me that all these elements have their spiritual meaning and divine representations. In order words, there is a spiritual and heavenly representation of an amethyst crystal, as also with fire, oils and sounds. As above, so below.

One day, a woman had scheduled an appointment to meet with me for a session. She had been suffering from panic attacks that continued to increase in number and intensity throughout the day. She had some spiritual experiences and had started becoming paranoid. She came to my office thirty minutes before her scheduled appointment and waited her turn.

As I came to greet her, she said to me, "What is in your office?! I had a bad panic attack and went to the emergency room yesterday, believing I had a heart attack. For the panic attack increased while driving to your office, but the moment I walked into your office, it went away. I immediately felt calm and at peace. What is in your office that makes it peaceful?"

I said, "I will tell you a simple trick I found that keeps the space sacred and holy. The trick is love and gratitude. Everything in my space, the crystals, couch, and paintings, are connected to many people around the world from the farmers that picked the cotton, to the fabric makers, the miners, the manufacturers, the people who got the goods to the store so I can buy the lovely items. I visualize them and send them gratitude for keeping me alive. They do not have to know me but they will feel my gratitude and their goodness will reciprocate unconsciously. From all items have I created an energy of gratitude which raises the vibration of the space.

This energy looks like an electrical current that is sent to them and them to me. I do not have to know them through a physical connection. The spiritual connection is also physical to me, and in spirit, we are one and known to one another. I send them healing, and they reciprocate.

She looked at me with cynicism. "Well! that sounds like a lot of work!"

It is not difficult to maintain the vibration of gratitude, but many people find it difficult to keep this energy due to never being satisfied. Their longing is great, but very often, they lack earnest volition!

People believe in owning things and using them for their gratification. I warn people about this attitude because nothing good has come of it. We ask permission from Mother Nature, we thank her, we ask the trees for permission, and we thank them. I avoid saying I own a home, a popular statement among Americans! How can you own anything that you cannot take with you to the afterlife? Everything in our possession is borrowed and must be returned in the correct order. Earth is like checking into a hotel. You have a limited time, and during that time, you are welcome to use all the wonderful amenities in the hotel. When your time is up, you must leave the items and the room in proper order or pay for damages.

Ritualism exists in every religion and culture throughout the world. Despite growing up with a Muslim father, a Christian mother, a paternal grandmother who was a healer, and attending Catholic school, I was surrounded with rituals. My mother was Christian by day and sought out the Babalawo every chance she got. Of course, back then, I sometimes did not understand the purpose of the many rituals I took part in, and I often did not know why they were conducted.

Muslims conduct ablution, a practice of water cleansing before the five daily prayers with the use of various body positions. The use of candles seemed to be a common theme in the various religious and cultural practices. The shamans would burn incense, palo santo, and sage, among other things, to purify their space and prepare for spiritual and healing practices. Babalawos perform many rituals before divination.

We all, at some point in our lives, engage in rituals. Even something as simple as Grandma's secret recipe passed down through generations and family traditions are a form of ritualism. Over time, as these rituals are passed down, we often lose their meaning. The intention behind these rituals gets lost, and without pure intention, the rituals used to commune with the spirits become ineffective.

The use of the sound of the rattle to align with energy has today been reduced to entertainment. Music in ancient times was how we contacted the divine, but we now watch others sing for our pleasure. When we go to church, often, the songs become monotonous. The sound is not being used to link with the divine.

Over the years, I have worked with many people in private practice with traumatic energies and depressive, chaotic, and demonic attachments. I found it essential to develop a clear intention of who I was and what I stood for. I called this my statement of purpose to the physical and nonphysical realities. I also realized that it was important to embody this statement through chants and meditations. My statement meant that when a physical or nonphysical being encounters me, what my vibration represents must be clear to all. I will use the example of the purpose of a lamp — everyone who walks into a room and sees a lamp knows what it provides. There is no mistake about its purpose. No one will attempt to use the lamp as a vacuum or to bake a cake with. The lamp gives light and nothing else.

In the same way, my purpose must be clear. My purpose is to be a great healer and take action to align with my intention. I speak it into existence daily, incanting that I am a healer who brings peace to the world. I repeat it, receive inspiration about it, and it becomes my purpose. Before I begin my day, working with clients in psychotherapy and energy work, I follow meditation rituals, using chants, candle lighting, palo santo, sage, holy water, essential oils, and crystals as part of the intention for truth. I give gratitude to the elements working with me, to the universe, and to the good spirits. In order words, there is a spiritual representation of an amethyst crystal and a divine and heavenly meaning. As above so below.

CHAPTER 4

Finding Yourself

Our reality has two worlds—both inner and outer worlds. Our inner world is our spiritual self where we are constantly interacting with the spiritual world and spiritual beings while simultaneously having an outer physical experience. The creator made it this way so we can have multiple experiences at the same time. When our inner life is good, we are constantly interacting with angelic beings in heaven so that when we leave the physical body, we will continue having heavenly experiences. Likewise, when our inner life is evil, self-centered, and negative, we are constantly interacting with hellish beings and when we die, we immediately continue in those realms after death. When we die and enter the Spirit realms, there are angels waiting to help us prepare for a life in heaven or hell. I am not saying anything new; you can call it dimensions of reality or use Christian analogies or Bardos as in the case of Buddhists. I have seen that there are various realms in-between the highest realms of the heavens and the lowest realms of hell. These in-between realms range from closer to hell and closer to heaven and groups in those realms are doing the work of refining themselves for the higher or the lower depending on their focus. Contrary to Christian faith but supported by Buddhist and indigenous religions in many parts of the world, it is possible to take multiple incarnations on earth or other realms to continue the work of refinement.

- God is an equal opportunity employer!

By looking at someone from the outside, you may not be able to tell what their inner spiritual life is. It is possible to get some incline from their actions but what they truly are cannot be easily ascertained by just looking at them. The more we pour into our spiritual self, the more we grow like a tree inside and bare good fruit and shape a new eternal body.

Like newborn infants, we are conditioned by the inner world. The inner world is our pure state of being, the purest form of ourselves. We look without judgment. We have no preconceived labels, and our mind is at peace. As we grow up, we slowly begin to interact with the outer world. Our parents maintain their gaze on us, and we meet their gaze in the hope of seeing approval in their eyes. We know when our parents or caregivers are upset. As a result, we feel the upset radiating off them and internalize it ourselves.

In psychotherapy, on many occasions, clients will take on the parents' pain to mitigate abuse. By taking on the pain of others, we slowly lose our sense of self and adopt the personalities and temperaments of those around us. As adults, we continue with this same habit of looking to others for approval. We care so much about what others think of us, and we always compare ourselves to others.

We go to school to learn how society wants us to function, and very little is done to learn beyond the physical body complexes. The other bodies of emotion, energy, and mind are largely ignored. If there is involvement with the mind, it is to program and condition it. We attend kindergarten and spend about hours learning our numbers and alphabets. Then, we learn to read and write until we get to fifth grade, which usually involves daily practices using all five senses. We have large alphabets and cues neatly posted on the walls of the classroom. We then learn through repetition and practices such as testing and, in some cases, singing. Within a few years, we will become masters of language, labels, and judgment.

Only recently have some programs begun to offer meditation in the classroom in the West. In the East, where mental discipline is a cultural practice, meditation is part of daily life. However, teaching emotional-body regulation is missing; people bury their traumatic energies inside, and because of this, suicide is at an all-time high.

As teenagers, the desire for independence and to know who we are is ever-present in our subconscious mind. We rebel against the persistent abuse of mind programming by parents and teachers and replace them with our peers. We go through a phase of experimenting, and as the years go on, the political/judicial climate ensures more and more restrictions. We continue to seek the outer world for validation, meaning, and happiness. We want to be loved and are told to act right so we can be lovable. To the detriment of our true nature, we act according to societal norms. The fear of rejection and feelings of loneliness causes us to become inhibited or seek attention and act out.

Some live to please others in hopes of covering up the collective feelings of fear. All we know from this point on is the external world. As young adults, we are in a constant battle about who we ought to be. Some of us know and stick to it, and some do not. We are expected to pick a program of study by the age of eighteen. Up to this point, the inner world is still obscured for the most part, and the answer to what we ought to be doing cannot be truly answered without it.

The first thirty-five years of our lives are spent creating a foundation for our lives, so we constantly wonder if we are on the right path. By this time, many have become addicted to worrying and perfectionism. I found it strange when I migrated to the United States how much time people spent getting things perfect. They planned everything, and they never seemed to be satisfied with how things turned out. They always wanted improvement, which does not mean that growth is not good, but too much planning takes away innate creativity.

So long as we are listening to the suggestions of others and the detriment of inner guidance, we will always feel that something is missing. We will not truly know what it feels like to know without a doubt that you are on your Soul's path. The success of any person largely depends on how well they have listened to their inner being and allowed themselves to be guided by it.

To truly be guided by the inner world requires intuition and spontaneity. Unfortunately, the school system does not allow for either. It has become overly structured and rigid, resulting in an increasing number of depressed children. Life is too hard, they say. I would agree, for without a system that allows for free expression, life would be a struggle.

I am not saying anything new here, for Americans are quick to agree with their flaws and talk about how things should be better, but very little is done to initiate the change. To truly change the system means to end the system, which most people are afraid to do. We cannot add to a foundation that is wrought with fear and control. The change must come from everyone's decision to take an inner journey. We can create the conditions for internal to outer expression and then give space for trial and creativity. The struggle most teenagers face is being themselves in the face of parental peers and societal expectations. Through astrology and numerology, I found how we can help teenagers understand their true temperaments and Soul drives and how they can work within the system's confines. I provide more details of this in the chapter on case studies.

Suicidal Ideations—Contending with Demonic Forces

Psychotherapists don't often talk about this topic because they don't want their clinical licenses canceled. When I went into private practice, I had no idea what I was getting into. I did not understand essential concepts such as energy, boundaries, and confidence. I thought a smile, some clinical notes, intake forms, and a few comforting words and open-ended questions were all I needed to excel at this job. That was my training.

I was in for a rude awakening. I learned soon enough that I did not know anything about this field, and my experience taught me that clinical practices were more than a few notes written down. Not long after I began my private practice, a woman came into my clinic with her ten-year-old daughter for counseling. The girl reported hearing voices asking her to commit suicide. The usual course of action over such an outcry would be to follow the necessary clinical steps, find out if she had a plan, and then take appropriate measures for inpatient hospitalization.

However, I had heard the stories before. Several other patients also told me that some evil voices in their heads were telling them to do things they didn't want to do. As I sat there listening to the little girl telling me of her ordeal, I felt like I had just been touched by evil. I could sense the negative feeling washing all over me. The hairs on the back of my neck stood up, and I immediately felt a dark presence in the room. I took a closer look at the little girl crying as her mother worriedly looked at her. I asked her mother if her daughter felt oppressed by demons. I honestly didn't know why I asked such a question. It went against everything I had been taught during my psychotherapy classes. My feelings of dread had perhaps compelled me to ask it, but the mother looked relieved at the question and replied.

"You can see them?" She whispered to me.

Before I could answer her, a voice bellowed through my ears. *"You don't know what you are doing,"* it yelled out loud. Before I could make sense of what I heard, my vision went dark. I saw an ugly deformed hand appear from within the darkness to reach out for me, a situation that lasted no more than a few seconds. My vision came back the next moment, but I was in for an even more spectacular sight.

As soon as I opened my eyes, I saw beams of light flying into the office and surrounding me, their message to the dark entities was that I was not to be touched. I was completely taken aback by this spectacular sight. As easy as this job looked, it could get dangerous if people were not adequately equipped to protect themselves and their clients. I didn't bother asking the woman and her daughter if they could see what I saw. I had no idea what I had seen. Freaked out, I did not know where to turn for help. I certainly could not call friends or colleagues! They would probably suggest I check into psychiatric care with my client.

So, I decided that the only solution was to find a gifted psychic. I explained what had happened, and the psychic told me I had abilities that I needed to develop. I began taking psychic lessons from her. She would take me to haunted places and ask me what I saw and felt. It was here that I began to understand my psychic abilities. I was adamant about not wanting to experience what had happened in my office that day. It shook me up, but it also occurred to me that the people came to me for help.

They were seeking support for the very issues I was afraid of. I had to overcome my fear of the unknown and realized that the only way to be truly helpful was to raise my frequency from fear to love. To do that, I had to face my fears, explore my subconscious mind, and completely release fear from my vibration and unconscious belief systems.

The first step was asking for protection since I didn't know how to protect myself. I used crystals and candles, incense, and other aids sold at stores to shield myself from the negative energies. I prayed every day to seek protection. The next step was to realize that all powers belonged to God and my alliance with divine love was my weapon. Our first inclination, when confronted by these energies, is to ask them to leave. We reject them because they are beyond our capability of comprehension. We can either pretend that they are not there or become intrigued by them, both options reinforce and empowers them. In return, we lose our power and energy to keep them that way. The only solution is to bring fear and all its manifestations to love.

By loving God, good for the sake of good, knowing that we are life receivers and not life itself, this knowing stabilizes our vibration in God. We become the vibration that harmonizes and integrates lower energies, which is a process and does not happen overnight. It requires meditation, cultivation practices, and intuitive awareness.

CHAPTER 5

Out-of-Body Experience

We are more than just our physical bodies. Suppose we can conceive of our bodies as energy and our mind as consciousness. In that case, we can conceive of the possibility that energy and consciousness can project themselves in many ways and can even move beyond time and space. We all have out-of-body experiences when we project our thoughts to other places besides the physical body. When we sleep at night, our consciousness is experiencing other realities and going places even though our bodies are in bed.

Out-of-body experience, also known as OBE or astral travel, refers to the experience in which the individual's conscious awareness is no longer located in the physical body. Often, the individual recalls looking back and seeing the body from outside. During OBE, a person's consciousness can move instantly anywhere in the world by merely willing it. In genuine OBEs, the astral body can pass through walls and floors, bringing back detailed information. Many clients who seek out a spiritual psychotherapist have had these types of experiences and require therapists who are open the possibility of these experiences.

If you share these types of experiences with a conventional therapist, they will not be able to relate to you, let alone offer insight, which is what makes a spiritual psychotherapist unique. They have done the work and can relate on many levels.

Also known as dissociation in psychology, I have experienced myself moving out of my physical body, especially during traumatic events. Sometimes, the Soul or energy body will take flight to protect itself from the impact of trauma. If the person is not self-aware of their energy body or if their aura is in distress, it leaves them feeling vulnerable and more anxious. With a torn aura, they are more likely to absorb negative energies around them. Most people do not know how to maintain a healthy energy field. Shamans and ancient healers around the world are trained to perform ceremonies to recall the Soul back to the body.

In instances where the individual Soul is more experienced with the right intentions, it can leave at will and return at will. It does this to experience, learn, and even go forward in time to help themselves and others make appropriate decisions. Sometimes we get a feeling of déjà vu where we have a strange sense that we have been at a place before or have met someone or a situation that feels familiar.

We live in a reality where traumatic experiences happen by the second. Unfortunately, we do not have enough authentic avenues for dealing with traumas. Very few therapists have the tools it takes to guide clients on their healing journey. Most of us carry these experiences as energetic signatures in our aura as we try our hardest to ignore them or forget about them. We can confront these experiences only when we are committed to finding ourselves. These realizations can break us down bit by bit, and complete recovery happens when we learn to piece our Soul energy together.

When contemplated, Out-of-Body experiences can increase self-awareness. There have been instances where clients have reported being taken out of their bodies while asleep without their permission. They also report being unable to control it. In several of these instances, the out-of-body experiences had been taking place from childhood and the client had unknowingly given consent. Traveling in sleep would leave them fatigued and confused by what was happening to them. I encourage clients to maintain autonomy and never make agreements with entities because the reality is that one can never truly know anyone's intentions. Only be open to OBEs if they are part of the Soul's plan to use as a learning tool, and all trust is placed in the Holy Spirit to guide us through it.

Out-of-body experiences have played a significant role in my life, enabling me to walk down the spiritual path. The first time I experienced this state of transcendence, I had gotten into trouble in second grade for talking to a friend in the middle of a lecture. The teacher caught me and made me kneel on the floor as punishment. A few minutes later, I dropped to the floor after a wave of inertia hit me out of nowhere.

I was not unconscious, but I could sense that I was out of my body. I could see my body lying on the floor face down. One minute, I was kneeling on the floor, and the next minute, I was looking down at my body from the ceiling. My teacher thought I was faking it, so she did not call out to me. I could see my classmates feeling uneasy as they looked at me laying on the floor and I could also sense their thoughts and feelings.

What was this sensation, and why was I suddenly feeling light? At that moment, I realized that there was more to me than just my physical body. So, at a young age, I discovered that the physical constraints did not bind me in this form. My second body was free to explore the hidden world—things I could not have seen through the eyes of my physical body became clear to me through the eyes of my second body.

In shamanic healing, there is a practice known as *Soul retrieval*. Shamans believe that when a person experiences physical, emotional, or psychological trauma, the Soul can take flight to protect itself from the impact of the shock. Trauma tears into the ethereal body and cause it to cluster, which may leave the soul body vulnerable to invasions from negative entities.

Psychology has a different view on out-of-body experiences. It states that a person often dissociates during trauma, but it is unclear to psychologists about what dissociated. (Braithwaite, 2016).

In layperson's terms, people often describe falling into a hypnotic state when they are in a state of shock, which enables them to see their life flashing before their eyes. People often describe feeling different after experiencing a traumatic event—like not feeling like themselves and may often use words like feeling "incomplete" or "lost" to communicate what they are going through. They grieve over the loss of their Soul part and may even talk about their need to return to the scene of their trauma to get closure. Unconsciously and without realizing it, a person experiencing Soul loss from trauma may seek to retrace their steps to recover their lost Soul part. They may even recreate the traumas in the hope of recovering the Soul.

For instance, I had a client who had returned from the war in Iraq and was being treated for Post Traumatic Stress Disorder (PTSD). He would often describe feeling lost and incomplete. He would tell me how he used to be a happy person who enjoyed playing the guitar at church every Sunday. Since his traumatic event, he has been depressed, sad, angry, and was not motivated to go to church, an indication that the aspect of the Soul that was lost was his happiness, creativity, and connection to God. He then told me that he felt he had unfinished business in Iraq and would like to return to continue working there. That, to me, was an indication that he was attempting to retrace his steps and find his lost Soul part.

Another client unconsciously attempted to recover their lost Soul part by engaging in an abusive relationship like their previous traumatic relationship in hopes of regaining their power. Unfortunately, they keep retraumatizing themselves in the bid to recover themselves, creating unhealthy behavior patterns.

In spiritual psychotherapy, a careful assessment of the traumatic event is necessary, as well as the emotional response to the trauma – whether it be sadness, grief, anger, or shame. The therapist must explore the coping mechanisms the client created, which could be alcoholism or sex addiction, for example. Then, the task is to explore the Soul part that was lost; an example of this could be their creativity, innocence, or self-confidence.

A clairvoyant therapist can see these issues in real-time but must slowly guide the client to recall the incident, identify what was lost, release the coping mechanisms and behavior patterns, and recall the Soul part. In some instances, the Soul part is irretrievably lost or not healthy for rejoining, but energy healing can draw new energy to the Soul body.

Kundalini Awakening

Many people talk about the Kundalini awakening, and some have even created businesses out of it. They charge exorbitant prices for their services and bid their followers to pursue one technique or another. The word *kundalini* means an enlightening experience in Hindu traditions. People who experience this awakening later become enlightened gurus in their lives. (Woollacott, 2021).

However, my take on kundalini is that it is synonymous with the Christian depiction of receiving grace. But the Christians have monetized this by telling people to go to church to receive this grace. My clairvoyant experiences and studies of kundalini have led me to believe that it happens when we are ready for it, not when we think it should happen. Astrology provides insights and clues as to when awakening happens and whether it will happen in a person's present lifetime. The other concern is that when it does happen, would the person ready for it, and are they able to absorb this energy for greater good?

The human Soul can be closely related to plant seeds. We may call the seed the "Christ seed." According to Buddhists, this seed is buried in the sacral chakra of the human body. When we are born, we have an internal clock in our DNA that subconsciously alerts us to our impending transformations. When we are oblivious to this process, we will not understand what is happening. We may assume a health issue or the work of malevolent forces.

Kundalini awakening occurs throughout one's lifespan, and the timing is unique to everyone. I had my first kundalini awakening at the age of seven where I experienced my past lives in dreams and later, I concluded that I was clearing my past life traumas. I had another awakening in my late twenties, but at the time, I was distracted by life events and did not fully take advantage of the energy; instead, I misdirected it towards a love interest which often happens to people. The grace/kundalini is a powerful orgasmic energy, and it can easily be misinterpreted by our ego mistaking it for the love of another.

My next known kundalini experience began when I was around thirty-eight years old and this time, I was more self-aware. I felt my internal clock ticking away. Many people in this world may equate this internal clock to an impending mid-life crisis. The message to me from my inner being was to cleanse my lifestyle and let go of unhealthy relationships. As I went through energetic and emotional shifts, friends and family saw me as an erratic, shaking, and impulsive but to me, I was taking my life back and owning my own autonomy.

They did not know that whatever I was doing from that point onward was for my Soul plan. All my life, I had served others. I served my mother, then a spouse, then my children. I was always a daughter, a wife, a mother. I never truly got the chance to be myself. With a heavy heart but a determined mind, I finally walked out of a fifteen-year marriage and moved into an apartment by myself. I wanted to see what life looked like for someone who lived solely for her Soul plan.

I was not, however, prepared for the series of events that took place from then on. Beginning a consistent meditation practice brought about many paranormal experiences. One night, I was awakened by what sounded like a freight train in my bedroom. I felt tidal waves of energy cascading through my body, and I went through hours of orgasms. That's the only way I can describe it. This orgasmic bliss was different as I felt it begin from my feet all the way to the top of my head. This orgasmic energy enveloped my entire body, cells, the brain, and inches beyond my physical body.

I never equated this experience with kundalini or grace, as most spiritual texts treat it as something serious, where you are cleanly dressed and reciting chants. Most spiritualists do not equate kundalini with orgasmic sexual bliss. A clairvoyant psychic helped me understand my experience as she said to me, "The spiritual and sexual are the same." Then, I understood. The union with God is an orgasmic experience of a romantic interlude of divine penetration into every cell and atom of your body. Soon, I realized what every human Soul was seeking! The desire to join with God is an unforgettable experience of sheer bliss. We get lost seeking this orgasmic union by joining with someone else, but it is impossible to seek pleasure through a body and not find pain, for sex and romance have nothing to do with true love.

All real pleasure comes from doing God's will. When the Soul is crushed under the weight and might of the ego and misinterprets the other person as the source of what it is starving for, making love to a body will unavoidably result in disappointment. The mind is still plagued with all that is yet unhealed and projects its unconscious needs onto the lover, hoping and requiring that the lover fulfill the deep hunger for safety, love, acceptance, and escape from suffering that is the pervasive thirst of the ego.

We must be vigilant during the vast stage of our journey to spiritual awakening as we can project our deep yearning for God towards a person incapable of giving us the love we seek. We must be careful not to imprison ourselves in the desire for a body that only services the ego. We must ask to be released from temptation for the sexual impulse we feel as it is often misguided.

What we genuinely crave is a miraculous impulse and God's energy infusing our bodies, transforming us into His lovers, and losing ourselves completely in our commitment to Him. We forget the past and future and become embedded in the now, where the kingdom of God resides. The tiny mind of separation is forever released, and our mind becomes one with God.

Later, I learned that heightened clairvoyant abilities always accompany kundalini awakening. After this initial incident, I could see the negative energies around my clients and notice how these energies would squeeze out their vitality, leaving them depressed and anxious. I was determined to keep this negativity out of my office and my life. I sought several psychics and joined the metaphysical community. I was afraid that if I brought up this subject with my other professionals, they would probably declare me psychologically insane.

Again, in the metaphysical community, I learned about crystals, sage, candles, essential oils, and many other things my degree had not taught me. I also learned about angels and spirit guides and how to call on them for our protection. However, I did not feel that any of it was working for me. What I was experiencing was natural, and these new ideas only promoted fear in my mind. However, I learned a few useful things from this experience. I still use essential oils, sage, and incense, but they are not for protection but to calm the senses. Just like in churches and temples, these items support a calm and peaceful environment that can then allow a person to deepen in their spiritual practice and move the mind in a positive direction.

The Multidimensional Self

One symptom of kundalini awakening is the realization of the multidimensional self. I read and studied the works of Robert Monroe realized that having out-of-body experiences had deeply resonated with me since an early age. I studied Hemi Sync (a meditative system) and hypnotherapy.

I used these techniques on myself to get a clear understanding of out-of-body experiences. One thing that intrigued me about studying Robert Monroe's books was that despite his OBEs, he did not conclude that there was a God until the last few chapters of his series. He talked about the multidimensional self. Monroe shared that the Soul continually projects itself into different timelines, dimensions, and bodies to experience itself and achieve a higher potential. (Monroe, 1996).

Many aspects of a person's Oversoul are operating at the same time. You can liken it to a computer or a car, which has many parts, and all these parts must be working and connected to run smoothly. One series of OBEs I had involved a woman who appeared in most of OBEs. She led me on several adventures that included soul retrievals, ancient civilizations, flying off towering structures, and getting messages from hidden locations; this woman was a continuous presence in my out-of-body experiences.

During one OBE, I was trained and assigned to command a mission instead of the female entity who was now behind me. I saw myself flying into what appeared to be an enormous, massive, screened television suspended in the sky. I was looking for something; soon enough, I found an aspect of myself on the other side of the screen.

This other aspect of myself was in a past life. I was a standing in what appeared to be a rice farm as a slave working in the fields, and I looked tired and unhappy. I swooped down fast, and as I got closer, that version of myself turned into a turquoise ring. I picked up the ring and wore it. After that, I ran fast through the fields, where some feline animals accosted me. They looked like a mix of dogs and hyenas as they chased me.

When they encircled me, I levitated and shot out of the television screen, scuttling through the black space between it and into another TV screen. Even though I knew I was traveling across realms, I was witnessing the happenings from bed where I awoke from what felt like a dream. At that moment, I yelled out, "Stop! Who are you?" I asked. The other me in the dream and the woman behind me stopped and turned around, and to my amazement, it was me. As I lay in bed, I watched my astral form and my future self as they went back in time to recover my past self. The past, present, and future selves already exist because time in the ethereal worlds is cyclical, like how music is recorded on a disc. The future already exists, and we are only a point in our entire self, which is vast and multidimensional. By looking at life this way, you will see that there are many versions of you operating within your vast oversoul.

CHAPTER 6
Childhood Trauma

Trauma is energetic disturbance that carries with it memories and emotions and can manifest itself in the body as stuck energy. Trauma ruptures the energy field and disrupts the natural flow of life force energy which can in turn result in mental, emotional and spiritual health problems. The Chakras, Meridians and Acupressure points of the biofield and especially the root and sacral chakras are impacted by traumas at an early age. Since the root chakra is associated with our foundations in life much like the root of a tree, the individual may feel insecure and ungrounded. No matter how well they may have done later in life, they will feel unsafe and in constant survival mode. They may feel a lack of belonging in the world. When a child is sexually abused, this has devastating effects because the sacral chakra which is responsible for digestion, sexuality, emotions, and creativity is disrupted. Like a tree without a trunk, the child may lose their sense of creativity, childlikeness, and unable to emotionally self-regulate. They may even experience identity and sexual confusion.

As they become teenagers, their sense of confidence and individuation becomes challenged as the traumatized teenager develops behavior problems, defiance or becomes a people pleaser. They may feel shame, self-doubt, or hopelessness. The solar plexus chakra is responsible for self-confidence and life force energy and can be attributed to the branches of a tree. Without a solid foundation, the child is unable to branch out. These days, more teenagers are having anxiety (Denizet, 2017), because the solar plexus which is responsible for the automatic nervous system is blocked and disrupts the natural flow of life force energy. As we become young adults, the heart chakra which is responsible for self-love, and our ability to love and trust others is unable to develop in a healthy way. Traumatized children often become adults with chaotic and unhealthy relationships. Our ability to express and communicate our wants and needs are also impacted by a blocked throat chakra and we may spend our adult years overthinking and second guessing ourselves. It is difficult to connect with the higher chakras when our foundations in life are not secure. Some people feel that by being spiritual, they can bypass all their childhood traumas and focus on the higher chakras, which may not work because they must still deal with their traumas. Unfortunately, most religious settings do not offer trauma healing at the level a spiritual psychotherapist is trained to do.

This is the reason why people have difficulty getting past childhood trauma. They can sense that their energy systems, the real aspect of their growth and development has been stunted somehow. No matter how much they try to hide and suppress it, the feeling something is amiss will not leave their minds. They may search for different treatments and visit therapists and psychologists but unfortunately, the mental health care system is still not equipped for handling the energetic effects of trauma.

I recall a time when I was working through my traumas, I had a series of dreams where angels showed me a house that was demolished. It looked like a bomb had been set off in it and all that was left were piles of rubble. As they comforted me in the dream, they gave me reassurance that the house would be rebuilt. As months and years went by, I would have recurrent dreams of the house slowly being rebuilt. In one dream, the house would have a frame, in another a roof and yet others would reveal that the house has being repainted and furnished. Soon, the house looked like a mansion and then a resort. I did not know what these dreams meant but later as I developed more insights, I realized that the house in my dreams represented my energy field and aura.

As I worked closely with my traumas and held space for others as they worked through theirs, I began to see clairvoyantly how traumatic energies appear in the ethereal body. I also saw how pieces of our Souls can take flight for safety and how memories can creep into our minds to remind us of our Soul loss, which triggers grief. Even when people tell me that they do not remember their childhood, it does not mean that the traumatic energy isn't there. They may present with depression or bipolar disorders and not understand why they have these symptoms.

We can hold traumas from childhood and past lives, and I work with clients to find the true origins of their traumas—like how a doctor would run tests to find the source of an illness and then prescribe the right medication to treat the illness. In trauma work, it is important to find the true causes and locate the subconscious script or beliefs recorded in the mind to assist the client in taking responsibility for moving the traumatic energy to new levels of wisdom and understanding. We can also locate coping mechanisms the client may be using to cope with the traumatic memory. Examples of coping mechanisms include alcohol, anxiety, depression or anger. One of the coping mechanisms I developed from my childhood trauma was that I had difficulty believing that people could be genuinely loving. My parents would tell me how I should be grateful for sending me to school and feeding me while they brutally flogged me so, I equated people's kindness with potential abuse. I also had difficulty trusting people and would not allow anyone to get close to me. I ended friendships abruptly and doubted the motives of people even when they were well-meaning.

Well-trained therapists cannot truly understand how to decipher coping mechanisms if they have not found their own coping mechanisms or gotten in touch with their unconscious script and behavior patterns. Until we work through our own trapped emotions, beliefs we have created because of trauma and their ensuing behavior patterns, we cannot truly understand how much effort is involved in trauma work. Energetic traumas form a low vibration or noise in the ethereal body of a person, preventing the natural flow of chi or prana. If you understand that our emotions both good and bad ones are energies moving through the body, traumatic energies get heavy and stuck in the field like a clog in the drains of a kitchen sink. Traumatic energy can later cause health issues in the areas of the body where they are stuck.

All children deserve a good future and must be protected and given the best care possible. Children can incarnate with distinctive Soul plans, may have karmic imbalances and wonderful skill sets to be expressed, and therefore we must treat them with greater awareness. A loving home goes a long way in helping children heal energetically, making it easier to resolve karma. Still, unfortunately, children are often born to parents who were not raised to understand the importance of emotions and how to work through difficult feelings.

We can still develop trauma scripts even in the most loving of circumstances. For instance, I had a client who had a devoted mother. One day, her mother left her with a friend while she went a few yards away to pick up ice cream at the mall. The child became fixated on abandonment as a result. No matter what the mother did from then on, the client blamed her mother for abandonment. While doing trauma work, we discovered that her abandonment issues came from past lives and that this single moment triggered the traumatic memory. Working with the client involved taking responsibility for the energy of abandonment and, bringing space to the trapped emotions through breathwork and integrative therapy.

Traumatic energy cannot be released but rather it can be freed up and integrated. Since the energy is a part of us, we can only get in touch with it, become aware of it, and bring presence to it. In doing so, the energy opens and is no longer blocked and can be freed to flow back into higher vibrational states. We can also rescript unhelpful beliefs and change our outlook about the trauma to more positive thoughts. By looking critically at the events, we can find the good in such events and thereby understand our experiences wholly.

Children must be guided with love and compassion to take responsibility for their emotions even in traumatic situations as it empowers them to take ownership of their lives. Many children live under an unfortunate delusion regarding their parents, which causes them trauma. They believe they can hold their parents accountable for their existence on earth, insisting that their parents take care of them; after all, they are responsible for bringing them into the world.

Likewise, many parents act like they own their children, forcing them to abide by and adopt their flawed beliefs, beating their children into compliance, molding them in the most grotesque ways, and expecting them to repay them with their future for their parental services. Our Western society demands that parents must not be less than perfect when it comes to caring for their children, and any slight imperfections could lead to the worst forms of condemnation from others, including government institutions. Nothing more foolish could be observed. Every human being is here on earth at his request to incarnate!

We reincarnate back to earth either because we have unfinished business, or we took the wrong path back to earth, or we are still evolving. Either way, our parents only offer us the opportunity for incarnation. Parents merely provide the possibility for an incarnation, nothing more. There is a reason why we use the word offspring when referring to a child. Nature uses itself to offspring itself. Like a tree produces seeds to bring about more trees. Our bodies are simply an act of nature and a vessel for the soul. Every incarnating Soul should be grateful for the opportunity offered, Parents, on the other hand, must be reminded that they are not God and did not create the incarnating Soul. They should support the vessel to maturity, and allow the young adult to begin his journey to self-discovery. The Soul of the child is only the visitor of its parents, and the parent is a temporary host, and neither can claim any rights to the other. Neither has a spiritual claim on the other.

The parents and the incarnating soul may have some similarities by law of attraction or mutual interests; however, the incarnating soul is a complete personality on his own with distinct soul plans that may or not have anything to do with their parents or family. The only thing a child receives from his parents is his physical body, which it needs as a tool for his activities on this earth.

Still, through procreation, the parents assume all obligations to take care of the child's physical body until he is ready to take care of himself. If the parents continue to care for the adult child, it is simply out of love and generosity, but the young adult must cease to rely upon their parents and the parents must encourage him to become independent as soon as possible. When this does not happen at the right time, the relationship can start to pose problems like co-dependency and resentment from both parties. The incarnating soul will feel stifled by the parents even when they are clearly providing valuable support. Life is short and we all came into this world to reconcile threads of karma that have prevented us from ascending to luminous heights. All efforts must be made to guide children to listen to their inner self and express their needs and wants including the buried emotions of past and present lives.

Understanding Abuse

Understanding abuse is one of the biggest hurdles in life. We should devote time to helping children develop their emotional bodies. Because of abuse, many of us stop growing emotionally. Our emotional bodies become stunted at the age of trauma. Therapy is important for helping children process their traumas so they can free their emotional bodies to realize more experiences and grow mentally and emotionally. When a child becomes stuck in a traumatic memory, they may continue to interpret experiences from the beliefs they created from that memory and may use the same defense mechanisms to self sooth. Trauma has a domino effect which must be explored to release the layers of defense mechanisms and belief systems. It is not to be taken lightly or ignored as they do not go away no matter how much with try to bury it.

Anna Freud defined these defense mechanisms as "unconscious resources used by the ego" to decrease internal stress (Parekh et al, 2010) Clients can often devise these unconscious mechanisms to decrease conflict within themselves, According to Freudian theory, defense mechanisms involve a distortion of reality in some way so that we are better able to cope with a situation. Ego-defense mechanisms are natural and normal. When they get out of proportion (i.e., used with frequency), neurosis develop, such as anxiety states, phobias, obsessions, or hysteria.

For instance, a sixty-year-old man may still be reacting to situations the same way he did when he was ten years old. The only difference is that he is acting out with an older body. I had a client in his sixties with severe anxiety. He suffered poverty in his childhood and was teased for wearing the same torn clothes and shoes to school every day. Since then, he had worked hard and became successful. He buys many cars, clothes, and expensive shoes and checks his accounts and stocks daily. He did not understand that childhood poverty left him in fear of poverty.

Another client, a woman who was sickly as a child and was left alone a lot, went on to become a successful doctor with an obsession with sickness. Her mind had become locked into the fear of getting sick, and much of her decisions as an adult were centered around this fear. Although she enjoyed a successful career and became well respected in her community, she often projected this fear onto her patients, catastrophizing their condition and making her unable to tune her negative perspective to more positive outlooks related to wellness.

An even more serious situation is when the traumatized child develops multiple personalities, now known as dissociative identity disorder (DID). Unless we release stuck emotional traumas, these memories will remain in the body and, in some instances, split the personality into alters and introjects. An introjection is an alter created in the mind of the abused that resembles the abuser. Children may even begin to exhibit other personality disorders like narcissistic traits, borderline personality disorders, or paranoid personality disorders.

What exactly is an Alter?

According to the *Diagnostic and Statistical Manual of Mental Disorders, Fifth Edition* (DSM-5-TR, 2013), A person with DID or a similar form of other specified dissociative disorder (OSDD) (previously called Dissociative Disorder Not Otherwise Specified or DDNOS-1) has a fragmented personality. A person with DID experiences himself or herself as having separate identities, known as alters or alternate identities, previously known as personalities. Alters take over control of the person's body or behavior at various times. Each can function independently. All the alters together make up the person's whole personality. Alters typically develop from dissociation caused by prolonged early childhood trauma, although attachment problems and persistent neglect in very early childhood are also known factors.

Once a person has DID, new alters can be created at any age but are less commonly created in adults. People with alters may refer to them as "parts inside, aspects, facets, ways of being, voices, multiples, selves, ages of me, people, persons, individuals, spirits, demons, others," etc. Alter identities are sometimes incorrectly referred to as ego states or even alter egos, but these states exist in people without alters and do not involve amnesia, dissociative symptoms, or clinical distress (DSM-5-TR).

Introjects

Introjection, on the other hand, is a defense mechanism that refers to the internalization of mental representations attributed to an external object, or the so-called introject, introjected object, or internal object (APA *Dictionary of Psychology*). Introjection is when one person accepts another's expectation or projection and makes it part of their self-image.

Children will use introjection to maintain a relationship with their caregivers. Parents project issues onto their children that they have not resolved themselves. For example, a person can internalize another person's beliefs or attitudes and connect with them emotionally, which usually occurs during childhood development when children are vulnerable to outside influences. A strong introject can be very harmful because it can distort an individual's view of themselves and the world.

For example, if an abusive father raised you and you internalized his belief that you are worthless, then it can be very difficult to break free from that negative self-image later in life. In later chapters, you will see how I worked with a sixteen-year-old client using hypnotherapy, energy healing, cognitive behavioral therapy, and biofeedback to heal her mind and integrate her psyche.

Soul Retrieval

Psychology uses words like *dissociation, splitting, introjects, archetypes,* or *alters* and may allude to the fact that the personality of a person can split, but they cannot exactly say what split. We can get further insight into this splitting from shamans. Shamans believe that in moments of trauma, aspects of the Soul may take flight for safety. Parts of the Soul took flight because the aura was either broken or damaged. Without a healing session, the person's aura becomes vulnerable to invading entities. It's like a house with broken windows; the home is no longer safe, and intruders may now easily obtain access to it.

Soul retrieval is a significant part of shamanic practice in which the shaman in an altered state, seeks to release negative energies trapped in a person's biofield and then find the lost Soul part and integrate it back into the person's biofield. Sometimes, the Soul may not have left the biofield and still be in the energy field but powerless in controlling or expelling invading energies. A person may also appear beside themselves, suspended in their biofield, and describe not feeling fully in their bodies or not feeling grounded, which is why I integrate energy healing with psychotherapy. Energy healing is needed to release the invading energies and recall the Soul, and then I use psychotherapy to change maladaptive defense mechanisms.

Many cultures believe that sickness is linked to the fact that fragments of our Souls have gone missing because of the Soul's flight during traumatic events. Other healers in Eastern traditions may refer to it as a loss of lifeforce energy. There are even times when a person may lose lifeforce from repeated use of psychedelics or drugs. They keep escaping, and this causes holes and tears in the aura. The person may have had a wonderful trip, but their aura is no longer protected, and many are not experienced enough to recall themselves or seal themselves back.

Soul loss can also happen under anesthesia. A patient may lose Soul parts while in surgery and never fully recover because they were not fully recalled back to the body. When under anesthesia, the Soul in the body is completely vulnerable. The mind is put to sleep or temporarily disengaged from the body.

Think of the aura as an invisible protective shell. It has a different quality or dimension, like the shell of an egg is different from the egg white and yolk. The human being has a similar protective shell, although not visible to our eye. The aura/shell houses the mental, emotional and energy bodies and the Soul; a smaller part of the oversoul is housed in the body. If the shell of an egg has a hole or is broken, the chick growing in the shell may not grow or survive. We, humans, are that delicate, and the mechanisms that are required for our evolution are quite sophisticated indeed, which is why no matter how scientists want to clone a human, they will never have a real human because scientists cannot create a Soul or emotional body.

Soul loss mainly occurs because of shock. A person dissociates and falls into a trance during a traumatic experience. The Soul does this to protect itself from the impact of trauma. The Native American shamans say that the Soul can go into the underworld, present world, or upper world. The Soul can also take refuge with their ancestors, so people feel grief after trauma because, unconsciously, they feel that a piece of themselves has been lost. They can also replay the trauma patterns to retrace their steps to recover the lost Soul part, which is why a person may continually pick abusive partners. If they lose themselves through domestic violence, then a person can become promiscuous in hopes of recreating the experiences to somehow regain their personal power. (Brink, 2017)

I often helped clients in recuperating from emotional trauma and Soul loss by using Soul-retrieval techniques and hypnotherapy. For instance, one time, I worked with a client on Soul retrieval. I went into a trance to search for the Soul. I traveled to the woods during the Soul retrieval, where the client grew up as a child in the present world. I found her Soul was being taken care of by her pet Dalmatian who had passed away during her childhood years.

When I beckoned the Soul part to integrate back into the body, the Soul part refused, saying that the causative factors for escape had not been resolved because the client was still engaged in a pattern of abusive and unhealthy relationships. Psychotherapy sessions were then geared towards self-forgiveness, healthy boundaries, and assertiveness. I did not re-engage the Soul retrieval ceremony, but after several sessions of cognitive behavioral therapy, the Soul part returned because the client was ready to re-engage herself.

Healing the Spiritual and Energetic Levels

I discovered by accident that I could intuitively recall missing Soul parts during hypnosis and Reiki healing. As a psychotherapist, I can combine psychotherapy with energy healing to prepare the client for the Soul's return so that there is a renewed healing space for the recovered Soul.

I also conduct an initial mental health assessment and assess the client's natal astrological chart, the result of which is like putting pieces of the puzzle together to determine the client's personality adaptations and the root causes of their presenting symptoms. Unlike our modern Western practices, this type of holistic healing can empower clients to dramatically divine their illnesses' ultimate causes while in an expanded state of awareness. We can neutralize them at their spiritual and energetic levels and prevent their reoccurrence.

Over the years of studying and practicing energy work, I understood more about the correlating factors between mental states and the energy field. Today, many people are now becoming Reiki practitioners in a one-weekend course and opening businesses without taking the time to truly get to know themselves and determine if they are suited to engage in this healing practice. To be a healer, you should know yourself, including knowing who your ancestors are, what they have passed down to you, and what you could invariably pass on to your clients. In native communities, no one wakes up one day to take on the label of healer or shaman without years of study and daily practice under an experienced shaman who has become one through lineage. No one wakes up to become the pope, but westerners see it fit to label themselves as native healers.

Developing the ability to manipulate energy takes years of dedicated practice, clarifying your intention, working on your traumas, and being consistent with meditation, affirmation, prayer, and experiential learning. A weekend course is not enough to become an energy worker. Being able to manipulate energy requires the practitioner to raise their vibration and align with their higher purpose and the divine light. Another important thing to note is that healers are chosen by divine forces. They know if you are capable of transmitting healing just as a farmer knows if a crop is good, bad or rotten.

I have attended many metaphysical fairs where I watched practitioners work on their client's energy in an open space. They have the client on a massage bed, and the practitioner is waving their hands or touching certain acupressure points of the client's body.

I have seen situations in which the client is healing the practitioner, or the practitioner is taking the client's energy, or the practitioner has unresolved traumas that interface with the client's issues and become magnified. When two people come together, whoever has the more dominant vibration wins. If depression is the dominant vibration, then the weaker person will absorb the energy.

Doctors, psychiatrists, and psychologists are trained healers. Still, they are not necessarily trained in spiritual development, and if they have bad energy and you place your trust in them by signing consent forms to be at their mercy, you may not necessarily get better or have your issues resolved. If the issues are resolved, the resolution is temporary. We rely on pills made by companies whose main purpose is to profit and not to heal you. That is why we must develop discernment and trust our guiding system when putting anything in our bodies.

Science is not the sole answer to health issues; a healthy emotional, mental, and spiritual life must also be incorporated as we navigate healthcare systems. It is difficult to meet a medical professional who is not operating from their ego, and it is difficult to find a patient who is not in a state of disempowerment. These two mindsets come together to create a frequency of two opposites: helplessness and power over—weak versus strong. The client perceives himself as weak and sees the practitioners as strong, and the practitioner views the client as weak, and together, they produce a low-level frequency that will not bring healing to either party involved in the process.

Some healers will swear by some special modality or another as the answer to healing when modalities are nothing but tools. A farmer does not believe that his tractor will bring the harvest because he knows the tractor is just a tool to support the harvest. No healing occurs in this situation, and both wonder why nothing is being resolved. The mechanisms for healing occur at a subconscious level, but neither are fully aware of the aspects that block healing.

To Be a True Healer, You Must Know Yourself!

To be an effective healer means to be in touch with your hidden intent. You will circumvent the entire process if your primary motivation is your bottom line or the money you will receive from the client. It does not mean we should work without pay, but the primary motivating factor must be to heal the self and others. Charging a fair fee for service can also be healing for clients to invest in their wellness. People do not respect free service, and it may reinforce negative aspects of entitlement if given away for free.

Healers should consider setting up a daily meditation practice and contemplation to balance their four bodies through various practices in service of the Soul. If you are not ready to maintain a disciplined life, then you are not ready for a healing practice. The practitioners must be in touch with and surrender to the Soul's purpose. They must realize their hidden skill sets and be willing to engage in a career that is aligned with their Soul's gifts. Many people do not know what they want to do and jump on the bandwagon of professions.

As creatures of habit, we seem to follow the flock in fear of being left out. Be willing to take the risk to follow what your Soul truly wants to do with the life God has blessed you with. All professions are helping professions. Every career or job is in service to others. However, if your purpose is to make money or your heart is not in the role, there will be dissatisfaction, creating negative energy. Surrendering and aligning to the Soul's purpose is crucial for ending all bad karma. The practitioners must be honest with themselves about their Soul's levels of maturity. Some say that Earth is a school, and we are here to learn. There is truth to this. We are all in different grades of Earth school, and some of us are in kindergarten, and some are in the high school of life, some are volunteers, and some are here for the experience. To survive in this school, we must get in touch with the real self.

To learn more about energies, one must differentiate between the critical ingredients for ending karma. A self-study may include an understanding of one's natal chart, numerology, personality, and the refinement of their personality. We may engage in daily disciplined spiritual and religious practices done with true intent and having the right attention. Through consistent meditation, we will slowly develop the observer's mind. We contact the pristine awareness within us that is observing our experiences. The lower programmed mind will no longer control us and can now step back from it and observe it. From observation and mindfulness, we can then integrate all negative/positive thoughts and behaviors into the emptiness of the higher mind. The Light of God joins with the mind that earnestly seeks it. Being a healer is a lifestyle and you either understand the bigger picture, the reward at the end or be mired in the delusions of this world.

CHAPTER 7

The Forgiveness Work
- Healing Trauma

Finding the true source of trauma is a puzzle worth solving. It helps us better understand ourselves and the world. If we do not know the true source of our traumas and illnesses, how can healing occur? I often use an advanced integrative therapy method developed by Asha Clinton, Ph.D., to interact with a client's Soul to source the root cause of an issue (Clinton, 2009).

Often, health issues are simply the result of much more profound emotional problems. Since the Soul is the storehouse of all memories, from inception in the ethers, we can get the answers we need by organizing the body's energies and using muscle testing.

Additionally, one can find deep-rooted behavior patterns within critical nodes of a person's astrological chart. Trauma could originate from various sources—including past lives, Soul families, entity attachments, ghost attachments, unhelpful cords from other lives, repeating behavior patterns, ancestral trauma, and trauma at the time of birth, which especially can be found where Chiron (an asteroid in the astrological chart called the *wounded healer,* which indicates how our traumas appear in daily life) sits in the astrological chart.

Then there are traumas from hospital stays, which is very strange, as one would hope to go to a hospital for a cure. Since hospitals do not practice spiritual hygiene, the environment can be infected with spiritual contaminations. Having surgery in such environments creates a risk of exposure to energetic attachments. Think of how many people you know that went for routine procedures only to get sicker. Hospitals may be physically clean, but they are energetically filthy. I recommend that people pray for protection from their guides and God when entering any routine procedures. Since energetic cleansing is unlikely in any hospital, people must take steps for self-protection. I have conducted energy work and prayer intercessions for clients having to go for any routine procedures.

Sometimes, a person may not have any of these issues except that they happen to be in the wrong place at the wrong time. The ethereal field is like the vast ocean, and anyone can be at the receiving end of other people's thought forms. It is like an unsuspecting fish accidentally swimming into an oil spill, we can get caught in issues being sent out by the collective thoughts of people.

Another dangerous traumatic experience can occur due to becoming the subject of jealousy or hate by another person. If someone feels jealousy toward another person, they can invariably send out waves of psychic attacks.

A further challenge is within so-called families. It is disheartening to see family members manipulate and traumatize other family members. They will intentionally keep each other from progressing in life. A person without self-awareness is tough to work with and dangerous to be around. Remember that we are the ones labeling people as family, blood relatives, friends, enemies, and so on. On a Soul level, these people are not special but rather soul agreements, contracts, attachments, or mutual lessons to be learned.

Trauma surrounds us, and we see it everywhere in the world. Emotional and mental pain or secondary effects of trauma will undoubtedly find us all, eventually. Even the Prince of England (now the king) isn't safe from the ravages of depression, even though he surely must have it all.

Collective trauma is trauma experienced by a group of people, culture, family, or community, and these traumas can include the holocaust, genocides, racism, and war.

Transgenerational trauma is trauma stored in the DNA and collective memory of the group and passed down from generation to generation. We can see this with the communal traumas of African Americans, Native Americans, and others.

Primary trauma happens suddenly with devastating mental and emotional effects like when a person gets into a car accident. It is unexpected, and the person can recall the incident and the psychological symptoms of the trauma.

Secondary trauma occurs over a lifespan. For instance, poverty, child abuse, child neglect, and ongoing systematic abuse such as racism, sexism, ageism, and so forth are all forms of secondary trauma. We do not realize its impact until we are temporarily removed from the environment, such as returning from war or growing up and living a different life. Once settled in a new life, we may begin to recall these memories, and without the care of a healed psychotherapist, a person may develop a later onset of PTSD.

As I mentioned in earlier chapters, I have suffered many traumas as a child and young adult and strongly desired to heal myself. I also seek to help others heal their traumas but will only train in methods and procedures that I find helpful for my healing. I found that I must test modalities against my traumas and explore my unconscious core beliefs associate with the trauma before I can heal. Also, I sought to know what healing looked like. Just like a recovered alcoholic knows where his mentee is on his recovery journey, I came to understand where my clients are on their healing journey, and this allows me to guide them better. Through my healing, I discovered some essential steps that I could pass along to others.

In Advanced Integrative Therapy (AIT), Clinton provides three categories for mapping traumas: Identifying the trauma, taking responsibility for the trauma, and forgiving.

Step 1: Identifying the Trauma

The initiating trauma includes the symptoms that caused a person to seek therapy. The client may present with symptoms of depression, social anxiety, chaotic relationships, workplace difficulties, indecision, or grief. The therapist will then seek to find the root cause of the initiating trauma by getting the client to recall when the traumatic symptoms originally began. For instance, a client could be coming to therapy for social anxiety which originally began at an early age from sexual abuse trauma. The client may have developed feelings of unworthiness when in social situations. Then there are the connecting patterns, in other words, the unconscious coping or defense mechanisms and personality disorders that a client uses to self-protect and cope with the trauma. Social anxiety can also be deemed a defense mechanism because it prompts the client to protect himself. The only problem with these defense mechanisms is that it can be overused by the client and became maladaptive.

Step 2: Taking Responsibility

Taking responsibility is easier said than done, for our ego defense mechanisms seek to deny, project, ignore, or detach from the emotional and mental pain of the trauma. A person can deny traumas in many ways, such as blocking the memory of the trauma or believing that it did not happen. Sometimes, people project their traumas onto others since they cannot find justice for themselves; they live suspiciously and even blame others for their unhappiness.

For instance, I often encounter African American clients who feel suspicious of their White coworkers and expect to be discriminated against and White-American clients who feel guilt and overcompensate in ways they ordinarily would not condone. Taking responsibility for the child abuse I experienced was very difficult because I could not understand how I caused the abuse. I was the child and, therefore, could not be held responsible. Until I explored past life regressions, I could see how my past life guilt caused me to reincarnate into abuse. I had to accept that I created this situation on a Soul level for my learning. I also realized that if I did not take responsibility for the trauma, I would project or deny it and be doomed to repeat a life of pain in the next life. I had to forgive myself for my sake. If we contract a virus at the airport or from another person, we don't sit there and complain about how we got infected. Rather, we focus on healing ourselves. Blaming others for our traumas will be counterproductive for healing. If we project blame, then we are looking for that person to fix us which they cannot do. Perpetrators are not be capable of getting into our psyche to heal us. They can apologize, but that will do little to heal the trauma.

Step 3: Forgiveness

One of the fundamental teachings in the *Course in Miracles* (ACIM, 1976) is the concept of forgiveness, and its author identifies three steps in forgiveness.

The first step is to take responsibility for healing ourselves. We must recognize that forgiveness begins with taking responsibility for the trauma that happened. This is not about self-blame but about taking ownership of what has happened and accepting the experience so we can move forward with courage and understanding. We understand that trauma is mostly attributed to our perception of the events, and we can allow a more wholesome view of the trauma which allows us to accept ourselves more and thereby forgive ourselves. We live in a world of duality and therefore nothing positive exists without a corresponding negative and vice versa. Therefore, a traumatic event has positive implications if we but tune our minds to see it.

There is a spiritual concept that states that all errors occur within the mind according to the ACIM teaching. In other words, our problems do not exist outside of our minds. When we realize that the belief that we are separated from God exists only in our ego mind, but God has already placed the healing and solution in our minds. The Holy Spirit speaks for God all the time and we can hear the solutions to our problems if we but tune our minds and hearts to hear the voice for God. The help of the Holy Spirit can lead us to the answers of all our problems so that achieving a real solution is possible. This concept can be difficult to accept since it is easier to blame our problems on others. We feel a sense of superiority when we project blame on others and take the higher road by forgiving them. There should be no forgiveness because we cannot be attacked. Our true self is at peace and safe in the love of God. We can release others from blame by fore-giving blessings.

Step 4: Surrender

Once we have truly gone through the process of forgiveness by taking responsibility, we can then truly surrender the trauma. There are many simple surrender techniques that I share with clients. Utilizing the still point method is one technique. The still point is the space between the inhale and exhale of our breath. It is also our closest link to our spirit. We voice the problem, take a deep inhale, see the energy and sensation being released into the void between the breaths, and then exhale.

We must do this consciously because we still point all day long as we breathe in and out. Still, we have negative thoughts going on in the background, and the exercise of surrender is simple and can be done anywhere with awareness. Still, we must take responsibility for our feelings instead of blaming someone else for it. Surrender is taught in Christianity and in Christ's teachings, but I wonder how many Christians really understand the concept of true surrender. When we employ the aspect of our mind that is the Holy Spirit, we make a conscious choice as a daily practice to surrender all our pain, emotions, and difficulties to God, which must be done sincerely because the Holy Spirit will not fight you to give something up due to free will. If you truly want to surrender a problem, you will be released from the problem, and a solution will be replaced with the problem. There is never a problem that cannot be solved. If you can take the time to keep this in mind, you will feel less anxious and more at peace, and your faith in God will grow even in situations where the answer is not immediately apparent.

Step 5: Trust

Through surrender, we can be open to trust. Trust is very challenging for trauma victims. Without knowing it, our guard is always up. We fear being rejected by others, and we then put on a mask to protect ourselves from showing others our true nature. The problem with trust for trauma victims is that it comes with a profound loss of confidence in oneself. I often see how clients make friends and then end the friendship just when the relationship gets closer. The wall is always up to safeguard against getting hurt. Sometimes, we will not show emotion because our parents may have taught us not to express our feelings or we watched them avoid their own feelings. In so doing, our emotional intelligence does not grow and this sets the stage for difficult adult relationships.

Through *A Course in Miracles*, I can learn to trust the process of life. I may not understand why things happened the way they did, and my clients didn't either. However, we can open to the awareness that we are more than physical bodies and we are here for a greater purpose and trust in the grand universal design at play. We may not know what that plan is, but we can see an upside to trauma. Perhaps we can find strength or creativity, passion, resilience, and solutions to problems that will help others. We can change our subconscious trauma script and see that there are jewels of wisdom within that trauma.

Regaining trust does not mean you should trust people blindly. It means to increase trust in ourselves and our ability to discern a situation more correctly and not to place unrealistic expectations on other people. You can trust a poisonous snake to be a snake and stay clear of it, but hoping the snake will not eventually bite is foolish. Restructuring our beliefs around the subject of trust can bring about a new sense of empowerment.

I recall an ancient Persian story of the scorpion and the frog. In the fable, the scorpion wanted to cross a river but could not swim, so it asked a frog to carry it across. The frog hesitated, afraid that the scorpion might sting it, but the scorpion argued that if it did that, they would both drown. The frog considered this argument sensibly and agreed to transport the scorpion. The frog lets the scorpion climb on its back and begins to swim. Midway across the river, the scorpion stings the frog anyway, dooming them both. The dying frog asks the scorpion why it stung despite knowing the consequence, to which the scorpion replies: "I couldn't help it. It's in my nature." The lesson is very clear and often overlooked: people rarely change their basic nature. We should not trust others blindly but at the same time, we should not put up a wall and distrust everyone. There is a reason why the ancients warn to take our time to get to know another person and if they are not in alignment with your goals, it is best to disengage.

Too often, we make the mistake of ignoring this truth. We exceed our limits when serving others without realizing that we are doing more damage than good. We form friendships with people who, by their nature, are not suited to be good friends to support us in achieving our life goals and vice versa. We enter romantic relationships thinking we just need to change a few things about the other person to make them perfect. We sign the dotted lines on contracts without taking care to understanding what we are getting ourselves into. We enter business transactions with people knowing the potential problems but hoping we'll work around them or that they'll act in the best interest of all parties because they're gaining something from the relationship.

We need to learn a lesson from the frog. People rarely change their basic nature. It doesn't matter what the rewards might be for acting differently. People find it extremely difficult to act contrary to their true nature. I'm not suggesting that you give up on a person because of a mistake in the past. We all make mistakes. But be wary and temper your expectations of that person; don't expect radically different behavior and monitor the situation to protect yourself. It's best to seek out friends, relationship partners, and employees whose core identity aligns with yours. If you're an employee, make sure the values of the company match your beliefs. Life is filled with challenges. Don't take on more by expecting someone to act differently from their nature. The sting of realizing this truth can be quite painful.

Step 6: Acceptance

Acceptance is the next vibrational frequency that is born out of trust. When we reach this stage, we accept the past, present, and future because we trust the universal plan. We can begin to accept others for who they are and not what we want or expect them to be. Every victim requires a perpetrator, and there is no defense without offense. The two opposites must exist together. Victimhood is a perception that we can change if we can follow the steps to healing. Remember, we may repeat forgiveness each time our body reacts to a trigger that reminds us of the past. We must continue to practice forgiveness until the energy is ultimately released and we have come to the vibration of acceptance.

Acceptance also gives rise to the justice that comes from the Holy Spirit after we surrender the trauma. The Holy Spirit is the divine justice and the great equalizer. Even when it does not appear that justice is being carried out, be rest assured that no bad deed ever goes unpunished. The universe always delivers karma on a later day.

In working with my clients, I realize that acceptance provides us the opening to healing wounds and spiritual transformation. Acceptance is a vibration, and it is choosing to accept oneself as one is without exception. Through acceptance, we can discover wholeness, wisdom, and love residing within our deepest nature.

Meditation and psychotherapy teach us to pay precise, succinct, and nonjudgmental attention to what is going on inside us through mindfulness training. The practice of mindfulness can unleash our buried emotions and by being present to our feelings, we can give trapped emotions space and time to run its course and reintegrate the stuck energy back into our energy field.

The memories and associated feelings gradually enter our consciousness during meditation practices, and we can feel difficult emotions intensely. Acceptance of difficult emotions while being in a state of presence can bring us further to healing. In a traumatized client, acceptance can lead to a profound healing and spiritual transformation.

Step 7: Love and Justice

People rarely consider these two words as intricately connected but rather view them as opposites. Rarely are these two words used together in a sentence, for when we pray for love, we forget that God's holy justice always accompanies it.

There are serious errors in human thinking, and this can especially be found by those who consider themselves spiritualists and new agers. They seriously think that love is weak, available at their beck and call and ever willing to overlook their negative and evil acts. They mistakenly think that upon their request, God should always serve and help them to fulfil their wishes.

By ignoring their true nature and putting on little cloaks of deceptive humility, they forget that their minds are dominated by negative thoughts and cannot be pleasing to God!

There is a false representation of Love that has been spread by the churches that God's love can be called upon at any time and will fix every-thing which has caused people to become lazy in their spiritual practice.

True love is like an all-consuming fire that burns the slightest impurity. It is severe when first encountered to the point where the spiritually lazy person will be completely paralyzed. Love does not indulge in kindness and neither does it forgive everything. Rather, it is severe, immediately disintegrating lies and evil on the spot, leaving a deluded person empty and paving the way for true love to fill their entire being, and it is from here that real spiritual growth begins. Love is unembellished, it knows neither justification nor excuse. Therefore, it will probably appear ruthless to many people who are engaged in self-deception.

When love comes into our being, we are met with divine justice, and forced to face our reckoning. Divine Justice is unchangeable from eternity to eternity, and independent of the people's perceptions, it is free of partiality, of people's hate and malice.

Unless we devote all our strength to letting go of things that no longer serve us, we will not learn to comprehend this loving justice and we will not become new within. Unless we accept God's holy justice, which is the love, can we receive the help we need to grow spiritually.

CHAPTER 7

Accepting Love's Vibration

Accepting how we feel in each moment opens our vibration to the unconditional love of God. Many years before taking the healing path, I came across a meme on Facebook that was so profound I remembered every word. At the time, I had not considered the deeper meaning behind this statement, and I just knew that I loved the quote and saved the meme on my desktop saver. It featured a quote by Thich Nhat Hanh:

No coming, no going

No before, no after

I hold you close; I set you free

I am you, and you are me

Almost a decade after seeing this quote, I had an out-of-body experience where I left my body and went through a wormhole and ended up in the void/abyss. My experience of the void was the most profound, unexplainable orgasmic bliss. It was at that moment that I realized what love was. It was the source of all creation that permeates everything. It had no form and was infinite; it was all intelligent and ever-loving. It had no account of the past or future; it had no label, and it was not a feeling. It was pure emptiness. At that moment, I knew unconditional love.

I realized that I could not lose love, for it is in everything. I cannot give love to anyone because love is in everything. Love is the recognition of love in all beings. Love is pure silence, and we do not need to do or say anything. We require no flowers or gifts; no words need to be said. Love simply is.

I no longer felt the need to find love; it was in me and in everything I saw. Human love is conditional. We love until a thing or person no longer meets our expectations. We want to hold and imprison that thing and we want it to remain the same to keep us comfortable. We believe we can lose a loved one, which is perhaps the most insane belief of all. The biggest challenge to love is language. We get lost in the word love, labels, and belief systems we attach to the word, and because of language, we lose the beingness of love as an all-pervading presence.

There are many kinds of love, and each person decides which is of greater priority:

1) The love for God, to love your neighbor as yourself (means to love other souls and the good in people and not their bodies) and the love of good for the sake of good. Mark 12:30-31.

2) Earthly love is romance, love of family, special love for certain places, people or things, civic duty, love for country and so on must not take precedence over the first but this kind of love can open us to the highest love of the heavens which is the love for God.

3) The least love is the love of self. All spirits, demons and devils love themselves. They hate others and believe they are better than others. They only care about themselves. When you think of the world, you may notice this love is the more prevalent. Countries killing innocent people for love of self, narcissists manipulate others over love of self and people who commit murder do it for self-love. People who hate themselves are still self-absorbed and many pretend to be good so they can be liked. All these types of loves are hellish and will only take a person down to the lower realms.

Nothing can be brought to love, and I soon learned that demons or evil entities are creations devoid of love and when they come into the presence of love, it feels like a fire burning them and hence hell fire. Love is what keeps everything alive, and it is through love that we growth, prosper and flourish. It is simply the power that keeps the universe alive. It is not a feeling but the essence of God itself. Human love is body-based, and we ascribe love to unique relationships such as a husband, wife, lover, friend, or child. We use these unique love relationships to compensate for our lack of awareness of love's presence in all things and that we are one family. All of humanity, all species, and life on the planet is one family. A stranger can become your family simply because of the goodness in them. The love within, is the life within and it is what connects us all. The evolutionary path of humanity is simply love. When we move beyond the ego state as a collective, focusing on the ultimate source of love, we will rise as a collective.

Step 8: Understanding Dawns

The frequency of love opens our vibration into understanding. We truly begin to understand the inner workings of the universe. We realize that we are interconnected and there are no mistakes in the world. All abilities, skills, and life forms are equal and equivalent. We begin to see life as a part of you and you as part of life. The universe cannot be complete without you, and you will never be complete until you accept everyone and every situation. Through understanding, we can perform miracles, for we know that the universe has all the answers, and we have everything we need and want deep within us.

We can draw upon all wisdom by drawing from within ourselves. We begin to understand our grandeur and magnificence and know that so are all people and beings; we are amazing and beautiful in our own unique way and when a person commits evil, the universe is clear about its laws. There will be corresponding karma. We do not have to feel like victims; we can trust that God has laws, and they are perfect. We each have a right to grow and maintain healthy boundaries with other people, no matter if they are family or strangers. When we raise our vibration, no evil can come of us. Nobody is dying; we are eternal spirit and live forever, and God's law is perfect in the rules of engagement. Once we follow the rules, we are always happy and free.

Step 9: Wisdom

From understanding, wisdom dawns. We no longer lean on the small ego's perception. Wisdom is a frequency, and here, we begin to transform karma and negative experiences into knowledge and wisdom. Our mind is open and is constantly receiving wisdom from God. Like a light bulb, new insights flow into our minds, and we understand why we have felt the negative feelings or went through some tough challenges. This is where true spiritual conviction dawns in our minds and our soul is fed. We have taken a negative trauma and transmuted it to wisdom which brings us closer to the state of enlightenment. Our minds can now access the infinite wisdom of the universe. We can get new insights daily and look forward to expanding our minds and evolving our Souls.

Step 10: Truth

The purpose of the human Soul's evolution is to develop true convictions because only true convictions feed the Soul. There is no need to argue with anyone about this or that. We can take on whatever ideas we want, but pray that it is the truth, or you will be lost in it once you leave the body, which is why true discernment must be developed. You refine the ability to hear the voice for truth – the Holy Spirit- and carefully filter out any information born of deception, even if it sounds good. Truth always comes to the mind that has fully forgiven the world, for it understands the real function of the world and no longer requires it for its development. Such a person will graduate from earth school because they are enlightened. If a person shares the truth with you but your mind has not opened to the vibration of truth, you will likely reject it as false.

Our world focuses on the changing perception of time and space, beginnings, and endings. There are eight billion people on the planet and eight billion perceptions. Perception requires interpretation but not the truth. There is only one truth, and it operates beyond the world of perception. We base the world of perception on the belief of duality, contrasts, and separate wills. Getting caught in the world of perception is like getting stuck in a dreamscape. Because everything you see, hear, or feel in this world is based on illusions and nothing more. We contort reality into our wishful thinking and end up making our lives more complicated than they need to be. There is so much information out there on the internet. Everyone seems to know the truth, but if that were the case, the world would be at peace. Escaping from the world is difficult and impossible to do so without external help from divine light and a determination to enlighten the self and rise above the collective noise. There is a process to this and because we are often caught up in our ego and want to fix ourselves, we have lost all humility and unknowingly prevent the light from coming in.

The Course in Miracles (ACIM, 1976) says: "Only the mind can be sick and only the mind is in need of healing." Upon the mind rests our success and spiritual transformation, for the mind is everything. You can receive direct Inspiration into your mind from the Soul and the Light of God. You can choose to turn the mind toward the ego and cut off communication with the soul and light. In the state of enlightenment, there is also a direct relationship between the Soul and the Light of God. So, an Enlightened person (in the true sense of the word) is operating as the Soul and the Light of God. Thus, an Enlightened Being, such as a Buddha or a Christ, functions as a lighted Soul with an ego and a body, expressing the Soul and the Light of God. So, there is no healing except in the mind.

The corrupt systems of the world are trying to solve problems by creating new ones and continuing an endless cycle of fixing people, society, and culture. People are trying to patch up all the diseased and dying. The "fixers" collect the bodies of the sick and the dying and try to patch them up, but they are not changing people's minds. All the welfare organizations of the world are practically useless because they are patching up bodies, not minds. Yet the minds created those dead, sick, and dying bodies. The minds of people must change, and then there won't be so many diseases and terrible miseries in the world. All of these are created by the mind, so if you really want to do good to people, you must help them change their minds. The mind must be reoriented in another direction. Then, the Soul and the Light of God naturally will come into view. The Soul becomes the ruling principle. The ego is normally the ruling principle, the "authoritarian" inside us. But when we reorient ourselves, the enlightened soul becomes our ruling principle.

Similarly, we recognize that the body is simply an outfit, our communication device, our instrument in this world and when we change our mental focus, the Light of God, becomes our tool and instrument in the world. It all goes back to refocusing the mind.

This lesson is very important. It is the understanding of how we have shaped our destinies through the mind. It is difficult to describe these things in human words but as you physically experience what I am trying to convey here, it will make clear sense to you. Our mind witnesses the reality of what we have created in our heads. Because we have iPads and media steering our heads in a negative direction, the world will continue to look and feel negative. The more we believe our individual perception, the more we end up projecting it in the real world. The world we view from our eyes reflects the internal frame of our reference. We see things that are not there to justify our behavior and choices. By doing so, we are distorting the world with our twisted defenses and end up seeing what is not there. Recognizing perceptual errors helps us learn to look past them or even forgive them to move forward.

Step 11: Meds or No Meds

As a therapist, people usually seek my services for several reasons. One reason is that they were recommended for psychotropic medication, and they did not want to take it or were on it and wanted to get off. They presented with various symptoms, from mood disorders to suicidal ideations. I am expected to follow the DSM-5-TR protocols and fit the client's symptoms into one or more of the three-hundred-and-sixty-five common mental health disorders.

In working with clients, I realized mental health disorders originate from untreated emotional traumas stored in the unconscious mind. It takes certain skill sets to get to the unconscious delusions to eradicate them. Some of these unconscious delusions can also come from entity attachments or past life issues brought forward.

Medications tend to suppress these emotional traumas and even prevent a client from facing their delusions. Medications cannot make a person love, forgive, or release victim consciousness. Mental health therapy is the least sought treatment as many now prefer to find medicines for every issue. It is a quick-fix remedy and, unfortunately, not a fix at all.

Sometimes, I joke about the fact that American culture is a drive-through culture. Fix me now; resolve the issues later. Unfortunately, there is no quick fix for healing trauma because the soul needs it to develop its consciousness. I had a client who had been on medications throughout her teenage life. She was now in her thirties and had received a prior diagnosis of bipolar disorder and depression. She sought therapy because the medicines were not working. She described feeling like a zombie all the time, mainly because the drugs made her incapable of feeling anything anymore. Unfortunately, medications have their limits, and their effects soon wear off and as it does their traumas are still waiting for them. Even if they are eighty years old and the trauma happened when they were ten but never processed it, it will come back like a tidal wave. The medications are like a fake wall keeping the waves from crashing.

As a practitioner, I practiced healing myself and then created a map for healing others. I must face my own traumas, take responsibility, and do the forgiveness work to raise my frequency. As I raised my frequency, it raised the energy in my healing space. I dedicated my office to those energies that brought about healing and restoration for my clients. We can also know this energy as the Holy Spirit in Christianity or the light of Paramatma in Hindu traditions that encourage healing. That is how I reached my path to healing myself and how I support the healing of my clients.

During my initial appointment with clients, I take the demographic data, medical history, and symptoms checklist. Using their birthdates, I investigate their numerology, which provides a wealth of information on their challenges and strengths, as well as a comprehensive view of their natal astrological chart. I chart their traumatic life patterns and significant blocks such as insecurity, self-beliefs, mistrust, and more. Then, I can see their true self based on their numerology and how they can better utilize their energy and skill sets.

Each trauma is broken down based on the concept of AIT into presenting trauma, originating trauma, and connecting patterns. We can unravel the trauma phrase in a healing space using the chakra points (points of strength) and repeat the trauma phrase (the trauma statement, e.g., "When I was five years old, I was abused by my mother and developed anxiety.") in each breath. I also use the still-point, the space between breaths, which is the void for releasing the trauma.

I feel a change is necessary to marry science with spirituality. Many books and institutes are dedicated to this marriage of viewing the duality of both as a whole. For this to take place, schools must teach psychological disciplines as they teach science and religion. We need to learn the importance of emotional training from the early stages of our life to understand the human psyche. Eastern religions and philosophy offer practical work, whereas western religions and philosophies carry theoretical work. Together, they are a perfect marriage of the new age, which can bring forth discoveries beyond the limits of the human mind.

Science and spirituality are two parts of one; treating these two things as one entity can help revolutionize both fields of medicine and spirituality side-by-side.

CHAPTER 8

Dream Interpretation

Dream States

Cognitive Mind Gross Material Realm	Subconscious Mind Fine Gross Material Realm	Super Conscious Mind Ethereal Realms	Christ Consciousness
Organic 3D Reality	Inorganic Lower 4D Reality Dream State	Spirit lands Fifth Dimension	The Universe Multidimensions
First Attention	Second Attention	Third Attention	Assess to all attention. Can receive messages from the higher dimensions

Our dream state is very important because it is the window to the different levels of the mind and therefore other dimensions. It describes our state of mind and the ways we interact with the different dimensions of reality. This happens irrespective of whether the cognitive mind is aware of it or not. A person is unlikely to access their super conscious mind or Christ consciousness if they are not open to developing their mind.

Logical, analytical people who tell me that they don't dream, are closed to the higher levels of the mind and since they only care about their material reality, they will operate solely in the cognition and only that. Such people may not be aware of their subconscious behaviors or may have suppressed themselves and have no self-awareness. Overly emotional people who do not know how to appropriately process their emotions may have emotionally charged dreams or even nightmares. These people are constantly feeding the astral inorganic beings with their lifeforce energy. For instance, a person who is addicted to porn, is releasing vast amounts of sexual energy from watching an inanimate object-the videos, thereby sending their energies into the astral second attention. That also goes for alcohol and drug addiction. They are usually surrounded by entities who feed off the energies they release into the astral realms. When we focus on things that are not real, we invariable send our energies into the astral dream world/second attention. A person who is in touch with their inner being/Soul, may have soulful dreams, interact with their guides, and receive premonitions for future decision making. A person who has opened their minds to Christ con-sciousness will experience messages from God, angels and positive spirits and may even visit the heavens.

I love to explore dreams because they can act as a window to the Soul. Our physical eyes perceive the physical world, and we use language to communicate with the external world. But the Soul speaks a different type of language, one that is picture-based, and it will be up to our physical cognitive mind to interpret the message the soul is trying to convey. It is like interpreting a painting at an art gallery, we look at all the details of the painting to understand what the artist is trying to convey.

When a human being is functioning correctly, their ego mind is work-ing intimately with the subconscious mind, and the body is responsive to the subtle and sensitive cues from the Soul. You understand what your inner self is telling you because you are sensitive to it. When you are in a deceptive situation, your inner being may message you to warn you not to trust a situation, person, or thing. The same goes for good situations and possibilities; the inner being will guide you correctly if you are open to yourself. Dreaming is another method of communication from the subconscious mind, the inner light, and the Soul. It depends on what aspects the cognitive mind is open to. If a person lives solely from their ego mind, they may dream about their daily lives and their unconscious fears, which can translate as nightmares.

If people are more open to themselves, they can access messages from their Souls and even have precognitive dreams. They can go forward in time and use their dream states to steer the cognitive mind into making appropriate life decisions. True spiritual practice involves using dreams to assess spiritual progress, resolve problems, and gain wisdom, which is why most religions, such as Christianity, Islam, Hinduism, Judaism, and Buddhism, all have stories of sages receiving messages from God through their dreams. As humans, we spend almost a third of our lives sleeping and dreaming. However, the significance of dreams varies greatly across cultures. In indigenous societies, dreams hold a special place in spiritual practice and daily life. Dreams are a powerful tool for accessing the ethereal realm that surrounds us, which our physical eye cannot see.

In psychotherapy, specifically using Jungian dream interpretation, dreams provide important clues into a person's subconscious state of awareness. According to Carl Jung, dreams do not deceive, lie, distort or disguise the truth. They attempt to lead the individual towards wholeness through what Jung calls a dialogue between ego and the self. Ego is the reflective process encompassing our conscious being, while self is the organismic process encompassing the totality of our physical, biological, psychological, social, and cultural being that includes the conscious as well as the unconscious. The self tries to tell ego what it does not know, but it ought to. This dialogue is concerned with recent memories, present difficulties, and future solutions. (Hall, 1983)

Around the world, healers and spiritualists have pioneered a more powerful, valuable, and fascinating way to approach dreaming—seeing it as a time for transformation, healing, and receiving guidance from higher levels of reality and journeying into the past and future. Throughout history, those who dream strong—who can enter other realities at will, scout the future, dialogue with the spirits, and dream for others—have had a special place of respect as shamans and seers, healers, creators, priestesses, and prophets.

In the Mohawk language, the word for shaman or healer is *rate sheets,* which means "dreamer." And, in the tradition of this ancient shaman and Mother of the Wolf Clan, dreams reveal the "secret wishes of the Soul," and the daily task of the community is to gather around a dreamer, help them recognize what the Soul is saying, and then to take action to honor the Soul's purpose (Moss, 2012).

Dreaming is also about human survival and show us what is happening up ahead. If you see a future event that you don't like, you can avoid that possible future. Dreaming is a way of connecting with our ancestors and looking at the consequences of human actions down to the seventh generation beyond ourselves. We can also access parallel lives, return to past lives, and retrieve our lost Soul parts. We can begin to access our multidimensional selves in dreams, which happens when people have dedicated themselves to spiritual practice and advanced their self-awareness. Until then, dreams are but mere continuations of a person's delusions. For instance, a person who acts like a jerk in their waking world will experience dreams of playing out this very behavior. Consequently, a person operating from fear, worry, and hate will invariably have nightmares of violent attacks and hate.

In his book, The Art of Dreaming by Carlos Castaneda, he learns from his teacher Don Juan a Shaman and whom he describes as an intermediary between the natural world of everyday life and an unseen world, which he called not the supernatural but the second attention. Don Juan contended that our world, which we believe to be unique and absolute, is only one in a cluster of consecutive worlds, arranged like the layers of an onion. He asserted that even though we have been energetically conditioned to perceive solely our world, we still have the capability of entering into those other realms, which are as real, unique, absolute, and engulfing as our own world is. The type of "dreaming" described in Castaneda's teachings, goes a step beyond what we normally view as "dreams". It overlaps with a phenomenon often referred to as "lucid dreaming", where the dreamer is conscious of his dreaming, and learns to take control of the content and direction of dreams. It is akin to "waking up" in dreams, and learning to command our attention in dreams, rather than having the dream proceed in a random, unorganized fashion.

Many shamanic practices that focus on dreaming refer to the dream state as the second attention. In contrast, our waking life is the first attention. As humans, we have the unique capacity to exist in both first and second attention. However, the second attention reality is so vast that it cannot be so easily interpreted. Suppose a shaman becomes fixated on the second attention. In that case, the shaman can risk being tricked by inorganic beings that live in the second attention.

Shamans learn to become aware of the dangers of second attention and the predator's agenda and avoid the traps they set. Ordinary, everyday people who could care less about their dreams are equally tricked, manipulated, and possessed in the dream state. Unaware human beings are often used as a tool to bring the negative entities to the material's first attention. Negative ghosts and spirits need a host to contact our material reality, and this is why many cultures avoid any communication unless by a trained shaman. The goal of evil entities is to possess the mind of its host and use him/her to carry out its agenda and suck the energy of the host.

The shamans also speak of the third attention, where the higher self resides, also known as the body double or higher Soul self. Our goal as organic humans is to concentrate on being present, limit our second attention fixation, and instead focus on drawing the third attention to our physical reality. Our higher self then uses our dreams to bring about messages and healing opportunities, as we discussed earlier.

In psychotherapy, dreams can provide us with clues to get insight into our subconscious minds. To understand the subconscious, we must interpret the dream by understanding what the symbols, people, places, and events mean for the individual. Many religions conclude that our dreams hold a more significant meaning than we can understand.

A dream either processes the events that occur earlier in the day or completes a sensory input that the mind cannot handle. For instance, if you walk into a room with your eyes closed, the brain will try to collect all the sensory input, including the impressions the cognitive mind did not notice, and the brain will then try to process all the sensory input in the dream. Sometimes, I liken the dream state of being, where the mind processes its experiences, the way our body processes the food we eat, takes the good, and releases the bad through excretion; the dream state is one avenue the mind processes experiences of the day.

I have always been a dreamer as a child and had vivid dreams I still remember, and there is no night that I do not dream. Not one dream is exactly like the next. When we reach the state of rigpa, the pristine aware-ness, dreams become about traveling to access the multidimensional self. You can help aspects of yourself operating in other dimensions and vice versa.

As a child, I noticed that my dreams had a knack for coming true. It seemed I could dream about events that would happen the next day or week. Sometimes, I would have detailed dreams of a place I had never been and meet people I had never met in waking life. Like a tape rewound, I would have that exact experience the next day. I would hear the same conversation, the same items were in the place, and I also knew details about the clothing the person would be wearing.

At times, I would dream I got into trouble and would be beaten and flogged and prayed to God the following day not to let this event happen, but it happened anyway. One day, after such a beating for a minor infrac-tion, I asked God why he let it happen even though I prayed against it. I then saw a vision of a book moving forward fast and heard my guiding system impress in my mind that my dreams allow me to prepare for the future, not to change it. It seemed to me that my future was predestined. I then asked to show my future and saw that even though life would be challenging, I would become a healer who heals the world. My traumas were part of the necessary steps to achieving God's plan.

Some may argue about free will and that I could change my destiny, but it is fruitless to explain to people that not everyone has free will. There are Souls placed on the planet for specific purposes with very little wiggle room to change their higher plan. Angelic beings have destiny because they came for a specific mission and are not necessarily on the planet to evolve but to carry out a mission. If you are a volunteer or prophet, you came for a specific plan, and therefore, you have a divine plan and a very small proportion of free will. Divine plan unveils in divine timing, and here we must be patient and have faith that things will unveil when they are meant to.

Some people fervently believe that they don't dream, and often, in psychotherapy, I see this as the case for individuals who are vastly disconnected from right-brain thinking. Their feelings and creative aspects are suppressed and substituted for their left-brain thinking, that is analytical, logical, and linear, which is not healthy, but neither is being totally right-brain and non-linear thinking. We must learn to use both our right and left brains to achieve a more balanced view of our daily lives.

Dreams happen every time we sleep. They are a product of our thoughts and emotions and are filled with images that symbolize certain meanings. If you can connect more with your intuition, you can get the meaning behind the dream. A client once told me that her dreams didn't make sense, and I told her that dreams are sometimes literal. If your dreams don't make sense, that means your waking life makes no sense. She paused for a moment and realized that this was true. She was taking organic chemistry at the time, and it didn't make sense to her.

Dreams are representative of what is going on inside of us. A Spiritual Psychotherapist understands that dreams provide valuable opportunities to explore a client's inner world and reach beyond the boundaries of logic and cognition. Since our dreams open into the inner recesses of the mind, there are creative opportunities delve into the world of imagination and learn to interpret the messages that are coming from the inner being.

Freud described dreams as the road to the unconscious (Sands, 2010), and provide a bridge between our conscious and unconscious worlds. Our dreams hold endless potentials, for deeper connections within the self and to work collaboratively with the inner self. Being able to pay closer attention to our dreams can increase self-awareness and self-discovery. Through our dreams we learn more about who and what we are.

In a psychotherapy session, I can dialogue with the client about the important characters, symbols and the overall emotions that were present in the dream. Since our dreams clue us into the parts of us that we are unaware of, dream interpretation brings insight to the unconscious. I assist the client in mapping out the feelings to the characters and as we connect the dots together the client discovers the meanings and significance for themselves. By paying close attention to our dreams, we can begin to have a rich inner life and our soul can communicate more easily with us.

CHAPTER 9

Demonic Entities

From the earliest times and to this present day, indigenous peoples all over the world from Africa, Asia, Pacific Island, Arab and South American countries have one thing in common with each other and that is the firmly held belief in the existence of evil spirits, ghosts, demons and all kindred powers.

In ancient times, the mystery of disease, sickness and death gave rise to speculations about an unseen world and the possibility that difficult and deadly experiences could be attributed to evil influences. Today, such beliefs have been thrown to the winds as medical sciences tries to debunk such notions and instead point to unseen viruses, pathogens and bacteria.

When it comes to mental health, there is a global widespread doubt about the efficacy of mental health especially as it relates to counseling and psychotherapy since most people outside of the United States and many within the country attribute mental health issues to the undue influence by evil entities. The most common illnesses that are interpreted with paranormal activities is known to be psychiatric disorders and almost one-third of people around such patients perceive it to be a paranormal incident, and around 73% of families approach faith healers. Paradoxical to the conventional belief that only mental illness accounts be stigmatized with paranormal belief, it is not unusual to find that these beliefs are not only limited to mental health issues but includes almost all other branches of medicine. (Sumbal, 2023) There is a disconnect between cultural and spiritual beliefs of many indigenous cultures around the world and the scientific mental health and medical system that begs for a reconciliation if we are to move forward as a collective.

Exploring the subject of demons is quite vast because demons take many forms, depending on their origins, how they were formed, and what they feed on. As mentioned before, all Angels used to be human at one time and so were all demons. We are having a human experience to decide which direction we will go after this life. Our daily choices, thoughts, deeds and intentions are rounded up at the end and formulate our new eternal body. Whatever feeds our desires become us. If you are obsessed with power and money, your new eternal body will look more demonic in the afterlife. If you are never satisfied, your spirit will have a gapping mouth, appear poor and miserable. If you love good for the sake of good or if you love truth and seek it earnestly, your eternal body will have beautiful flowing hair and lovely shinning skin.

When a wicked person dies and crosses over, they will become their desires and their thirst for control and greed takes over them. They will go and hang out in hellish realms with likeminded spirits and seek after living humans with similar desires. They can feed on a single person, groups, families, or communities with similar desires. The more humans agree to connect with evil spirits on the other side, the more the evil grows and gain a presence on the earth plane.

The ancient primitive Sumerian and Babylonian tablet recognized three distinct classes of evil spirit, all ready to torment the helpless wanderer. First came the disembodied human soul which could find no rest, and so wandered up and down the face of the earth; secondly, the gruesome spirits which were half human and half demon; and thirdly, the fiends and devils who were of the same nature as the gods, who rode on the noxious winds, or brought storms and pestilence. (Luzac, 2007)

In his excellent book on the subject — *Egregores: The Occult Entities That Watch Over Human Destiny*, , Mark Stavish provides historical evidence to prove that demons are thought forms or psychological constructs created individually or collectively for emotional comfort or agreed-upon ideas. They are "an autonomous psychic entity composed of and influencing the thoughts of a group of people." (Stavish, 2018 pg21).

Stavish (2018) defines demons as a home for a specific type of psychic intelligence of a nonhuman nature that can connect with the invisible dimensions of the material world we reside in—the real source of power for ancient cults' religious-magical practices (Stavish, 2018).

Most religions and ancient-cult practices recognize demonic entities as beings linked to the spiritual and material world that hold the power of persuading us by invading our minds in areas of vulnerability and weakness. These vulnerabilities arise for several reasons: It can be due to addictions of various kinds like alcohol, drugs, or even obsessive negative thoughts and childhood traumas like sexual abuse. Like animals, they sniff our vulnerabilities and use them as a weapon to disrupt our lives. They then feed on the sadness, pain, and chaos, like squeezing juice from an orange. When a person is oppressed, suppressed, or sad, they release energy on which demons feed.

People who give off negative energies are prone to attracting demonic entities as they thrive on negative energies. A person is more likely to commit a crime under the influence of alcohol. For example, a woman under the pressure of her work and family matters succumbs to alcohol. She considers about killing her employer every day, but consuming alcohol causes her lose sight of right or wrong, which is when a demonic entity takes over her rage. She ends up killing her boss without even realizing what she has done. Demonic influences can range from attachments to oppressions to possessions, all reflecting the three levels of connections between human and non-human entities.

As a spiritual psychotherapist, the key to understanding a client's mental health problems is to determine the root cause, and in some cases, I have found them to be the result of demonic influences. To clarify, not all mental health issues are demonic influence. Some may be physiological, personality or environmental influences. A well-rounded psychotherapist will work to get to the root causes and apply tools that will support the client.

Some colleagues are extremely naïve about this issue and think they can easily remove demonic attachments. This is naïve because without getting to the root cause of the attachment and without psychotherapy to negotiate with the client about his/her need for this agreement, we would be wasting our time. Demons attach by invitation where both parties are gaining something from the other. It is like signing a contract at a car dealership and later realizing you have made a mistake. Breaking this contract will require a healer who can subdue negative entities and where the entities recognize the healer's connection with the light. A bunch of fancy words would do nothing without the words being attached to a healer operating in the vibration of light.

Psychotherapy involves figuring out the underlying causes of the attachment or possession and working with the client to shift their perspective on the root cause. For instance, I had a client who was bullied by his peers in elementary and middle school and subsequently abused by his parents. He developed much internal rage and anger but did not know how to defend himself. A demonic entity capitalized on this vulnerability, and my client unconsciously invited the demon to make him strong and defend himself. In therapy, he admitted not being ready to let the contract with the demon go because he did not have alternative methods for self-defense. Even the demon was tired and wanted out of the contract, but it seemed the client was not prepared to let it go. Remember we all have free-will and I don't go around carrying a cape to save anyone. Love means allowing people to be exactly as they choose. When they want change, it will come from the helping hands of God and his helpers.

Another client wanted her boyfriend to love her and took on an energy that gave her a greater capacity to manipulate him. In another instance, a woman wanted so badly to be psychic and took on an evil energy that provided her with those abilities. She became a professional psychic and felt she couldn't remove this attachment because of a newfound stream of income this provided. The more these types of agreements remain, the stronger the attachments develop to where even the demon is having difficulty moving on and both are stuck in a miserable marriage.

What are Thought-Form Entities?

Thoughtforms are simply thoughts that float around in the fine, gross material realm. The physical reality is gross material and thought forms are composed of fine gross material. They are close to our physical reality but denser in the higher realms. People produce thought forms by the second and constantly feed them. For example, when someone feels resentment against another person but chooses not to express it, the notion keeps coming back to them and they give it fuel.

Eventually, like a baby incubating in the mother's womb, the thought-form will be born in the fine gross material plane. It can take any form, depending on its creator. The uglier the thought, the uglier the thought form. Like a baby being born, it relies on its mother for food, but soon, the child will leave and find other friends. Thought forms can increase in size and consciousness depending on how it is being fed.

A thought-form may be an independent entity, and naturally, it will seek out other people with like minds who emit similar energies. Initially, these thought forms are semi-dependent on the creator but can soon delve into an independent state. They grow when their creator gives them power by continuously feeding them. They can become an independent agent in the ethereal world and become perceptible to sensitive people. As I mentioned before, entities have different forms and strengths and how we deal with them or not varies.

When people experience trauma and do not process it, they can create alter, multiple personalities, like a fracture in their psyche, in which they section a part of their energy to keep the memory of the trauma out of their conscious memory. When clients tell me they don't remember their childhood or they don't remember a trauma, they likely have pushed the memory from their cognitive mind, but the memory is still there, and a part of their energy has also sectioned itself off to keep the memory at bay. It is possible for negative entities to then attach to the alter and feed on it to the point that the person could blackout in rage, and the alter could take over, which can be the case with people who sleepwalk. In some cases, the alter is gaining strength to the point of operating without the person's cognition.

An evil spirit is an entity that used to be human, died, and now operates as an evil spirit on the other side. An evil spirit is not a demon yet but can work its way there depending on how it is able to manipulate and cause destruction and defeat other demons.

Polish occultist of the French-Russian Martinist lineages, Mouni Sadhu defines demonic entities as *egregores*. In one of his seminal works known as The Tarot, he described them as a collective entity, such as a nation, state, religion, and sects, and their adherents and minor human organizations. The structure of egregores consists of physical bodies like human beings who have both astral and mental energies. These elements hold the power of influencing people's thoughts. (Stavish, 2018).

For instance, the United States came into existence because several people came together, stood upon this piece of land, and decided to call it America. They wrote up what they believed to be a declaration of independence to justify their proclamations. They selectively decided who could be a part of this country and how they should look and dress. They created certain traditions they should follow.

An egregore is formed, or a thought form is created when two or more people agree with this psychological concept. The entity may not start as demonic, but the number of people who decide to agree to this thought form plays an essential role in its growth. Once the thought-form is created, they become a semi-independent entity with people adhering to its agreed-upon concepts. If one person decides to exit the agreement, the entity will become weaker, but it will not disappear. Soon, the entire world will agree with the concept of America. The people of this nation would create anthems, flags, and preambles and devote their lives to the country, making the entity stronger as people are willing to die for it. They give up their identity to conform themselves to this entity.

Entities are formed from this process. This concept can be applied to all other countries, cultures, religious organizations, political groups, educational systems, and concepts such as racism, sexual orientation, and so on. People create ideas that lead to negative thoughts. They can come up with the concept of perfectionism and devote themselves to this entity. The more people strive to be perfect, the more they feed their thought forms of what they perceive to be perfect.

An egregore or thoughtform can also be created from movies. When thousands of children, for instance, watched the movie *Frozen*, an egregore was created in the ethereal plane, and because it consumed the minds of so many, this egregore gained power and strength from the energies of children.

The same went for the Black Panther, the Little Mermaid, the Witch on a Broom, the Lion King, and others. I once had a client share a psychedelic experience where she found herself in a jungle reminiscent of the jungle in the *Lion King*. We can say her mind made it up but given the fact that the movie had been imprinted in millions of people's minds, the jungle exists in the fine gross material/ethereal, also known as the second attention. If we want to know if we have any negative attachments, look no further from our mind, the quality of our thoughts, and feelings. and where we place our desires.

The adage that thoughts turn to things is literally true since our thoughts turn to things in the second attention. Sometimes, when we fall in love with an idea of a person, and create a thought form of that person, and likely, we are not seeing the actual person.

This is the reason I found meditation to be one of the most important spiritual practices for until you clarify your mind, you are at the mercy of producing unhelpful thoughts. I am saddened by Christians who spread ideas that meditation is evil for even Jesus reminds us that we are a temple of God, and the mind is included in that temple. An unclean mind cannot house the light of God. It doesn't matter how much education and knowledge or modalities you have been trained in, without a clean mind, you cannot connect with divine wisdom.

Born into Thought Forms

We are all born into powerful thought forms. To discern between good and evil, we need to understand what breeds demons. For instance, addictions are one of the most significant contributing factors that help breed demons, so habits hold the power to control us. We become so used to the sensation that comes with our addiction that we lose ourselves in it.

Addiction can arise due to many things. People are not only addicted to drugs or alcohol. They can also be addicted to work, sex, perfectionism, control, and emotional gratification. These addictions lead the person to cross any boundaries imposed by society. If we do not learn how to control our addictions, our addictions end up controlling every aspect of our lives.

If we have habits that we are unable to let go of, then it is better to realize that an entity has been attached to us. They feed off our emotions—the most powerful energy a human can release. To break addiction is difficult and, in some cases, even impossible because that entity has attached itself. Another culprit for entity attachment is narcissism, a lack of self-worth, anger, egoism, guilt and shame—low emotions that attract lower vibrational entities that then latch onto the person and cause more pain, which may not be the case for human beings with evil Souls. Since they are already on track to be evil, these lower entities attach and embolden them, making them more powerful and evil. Depression is the result of a positive person being held down by negative energies. They become depressed because something contrary to their true form is in them creating havoc. Evil people don't get depressed but rather emboldened by evil.

People regard life as limited to Earth, they believe in the physical dimension of life but reject the astral and spiritual aspects. Dimensions beyond physical life are both dark and light. Humans who are unable to look beyond the physical dimension of this world are trapped on a conscious level. Not seeing the subtle realms does not mean that they are not actively engaging and interfacing with these realms daily. They are simply blind to it and unaware of what they do. They may be glad that they cannot see, but not seeing is akin to being spiritually blind. That blindness continues in the afterlife where they wished they had opened their eyes to see. Many are spirits that walk aimlessly in the ethereal realm due to spiritual blindness.

Many cultures, religions, and philosophers believe in demonic entities. Their concepts may differ, but they agree that we are more than our physical bodies and that the universe is interfacing with us all the time. All dimensions of reality are interconnected, and we can choose to open our minds beyond physical reality through a natural development process. The key, as I mentioned, is to bypass the second attention by emptying the mind through meditation and contemplation. Letting go of illusions and belief systems that are not real, reprogramming our mind to focus on truth, love and divine light, will allow a new reality to appear before us.

The universe has a waste disposal system. And just like the city's waste management system, some beings work tirelessly to process, clean, and recycle all energies deemed hazardous, unhelpful, and no longer useful for the universe. Some religions call it hell, the bardos or purgatory. It looks very much like the city dump, and the beings who work there are quite terrible looking. They are busy sorting ethereal beings, aka human spirits, who have crossed over and who, by all accounts, have failed to avail themselves of multiple resources, opportunities, and help to aid in their spiritual development.

Many people despise the devil, Satan or Mara, depending on their religion, but they do not understand the valuable service such entities provide to the universe. They work for God and perform a thankless job of picking up beings who refuse to work in alignment with the laws of God.

I am not associating the men and women who work for the city dump with the devil, but rather to expand our minds and eyes and modify our perspectives on the entities we find most repugnant. When I studied the *Tibetan*

Book of the Dead, (2011), I begin to understand the work of evil creatures. I have caught glimpses of these lower realms, and just as the evil beings are doing their work of recycling, there are also scavengers looking to salvage people who found their way there by their own volition.

An unprecedented number of evil creatures are flying all around the world, which leads me to ask why. In the last decade, people have become even lazier in their thinking, careless in their thoughts, and fixed on negative behaviors. We find ourselves in a massive clean-up phase. As more people and so-called celebrities have come out openly and covertly to reveal their alignment with satanic forces, they fail to understand that even Satan is doing exactly what God has assigned him to do. In their ignorance and stupidity, they seek reverence in the one who will ensure their ultimate disintegration.

A massive number of people are engaging in fakery, pretending to help others while working for organizations and institutions with evil agendas, but will have only themselves to blame when the final clean-up phase begins. Without realizing it, they have fused themselves to these organizations, powerful leaders or some dogmatic belief. Such fusions are not so easily broken, and they find themselves in hellish realms due to these negative relationships. Just because someone is saying good things does not mean they are good. Practice discernment to differentiate good from trickery.

The Holy Spirit has taken me through some major training and lessons over the years, one of which involved seeing through the veils of illusion. One day, during meditation, a bat flew into my bedroom and looked at me. In my fear and frenzy, considering COVID-19 purportedly came from a bat, I freaked out. We searched everywhere for the bat and called exterminators but found no sign of the bat or bats in the area. It was then that I knew I was in for another major initiation. Like a bat, I must learn to pierce the veils of darkness. Many clairvoyants can see into the ethereal template of another person's emotional, mental, and energetic field, but this was different; I was called to see past the ethereal to the real person and the real situation. I needed to learn who is who and what is what and to no longer assess another by his/her ethereal template but by their true causal nature.

I studied the works of Abd Ru Shin (1990) where he advises that it is the sacred duty of all human beings to investigate why we are living on earth, or in general in this creation, and why thousands of ethereal cords suspend them. No one considers themselves so insignificant as to imagine that their existence is without purpose unless this person agrees with those who say otherwise. Many find themselves too important, and yet there are an even smaller number of people capable of laboriously detaching themselves from their spiritual indolence and seriously concern themselves with investigating their task on earth.

Abd Ru Shin, in his work *The Holy Grail*, reflects the following:

It is solely indolence and laziness of the spirit that makes people willing to accept the firmly established doctrines of others. And it is indolence that lies in the reassurance that comes from thinking that it is great to adhere to the faith of our parents without submitting its underlying principles to keen, careful and independent examination. (Abd Ru-Shin, 1990).

People are now eagerly supported by calculating and selfish organizations who extend and safeguard their influence to increase their power and followers. They are far from the recognition of God, for otherwise, they would not bind people in firmly established doctrines but would instead remind people that they are free to make their own spiritual decisions.

By making up our minds and coming to our own convictions, we can come to the true recognition of God, for only free, sincere conviction can help us to achieve luminous heights. We must learn to recognize our path in Creation, and the purpose of our existence. Then, we will be filled with grateful rejoicing and the greatest happiness a human spirit is able to bear, which lies solely in the recognition of God! (Abd-Ru-Shin, 1995).

The first time I watched the movie *Shawshank Redemption*, (1994), I cried like a baby. Something about this movie spoke to my Soul. I still consider it one of my favorite movies, and even back then, I did not fully understand why this movie shook me to the core. There is nothing special about a prison movie, a man wrongly convicted and sent to prison. It may have been Andy Dufresne, the main character's level of calmness in the face of injustice and the way he managed to maintain honesty, hard work, un-conditional love and kindness, compassion, and cooperation while dealing with corrupt prison mates and officials. The leading character never gave up hope. He never stopped trying to make things a little better, not just for him but for everyone around him. He never becomes institutionalized and never stopped asserting his innocence. Dufresne accepted his situation and made the best of it. The end of the movie shows his eventual thoughtfully planned escape where he exacted justice and saved his friend, Red, along the way. In my darkest hours of rejection ad pain, Andy Dufresne gave me a template for coping with gloomiest of days.

CHAPTER 10

Psychological Astrology

The field of psychology has often claimed that astrology is scientifically baseless and cannot be used to assess a person's personality. Many assume astrology is a simplistic study providing a generic compilation of zodiac signs. What they don't understand is that astrology is more than just newspaper clippings and a generic astrology app on the phone but a complex science of mathematical calculations, predictions, personality, behavioral patterns, and past-to-future life predictions. Astrology provides a map of the Soul, where it has been, what skill sets it brings, and what changes it needs to make in this lifetime to expand toward the luminous lights.

For thousands of years and even in biblical times, our ancestors looked to the stars, and they somehow were able to map the planetary constellations the same way NASA explores space to further human understanding. Ancient indigenous people looked to planetary alignments for guidance and spiritual understanding. They also looked at the position of the planets and stars and what was taking place at the time of a Soul's incarnations. As above and below, since our human Soul came from the ethers, we carry a micro version of the larger planetary alignment. Not everyone may believe this because not everyone comes from the stars or other planets.

The basic meaning of the horoscope is that, by mapping out the positions of the planets and their relations to one another (aspects), together with the distribution of the signs of the zodiac at the cardinal points, it gives a picture first of the psychic and then of the physical constitution of the individual. It represents, in essence, a system of original and fundamental qualities in a person's character and can therefore be regarded as an equivalent of the individual psyche. (Jung, 1955)

Exploring the astrological mapping of my clients helps enormously in providing guidance—to the extent to which the client is ready for change. What they need at this moment is to move in the direction of the Soul's path. We suffer when we are not in alignment with our Soul or push against its current. Often, what our Soul wants is not what society or parental figures want for us, and I have encountered parents who take the blame for the karmic imbalances of their children. Either way, the Soul will eventually present its personality, whether suppressed by family or society. If the person represses the Soul's needs at the expense of societal expectations, the person is likely to fall into deep despair or even depression.

A therapist may have deeper insight and a jumpstart on certain issues a client may be attempting to process. Even a very basic knowledge of astrology for a therapist can be extremely beneficial in their practice. The capacity to cast and read the natal chart of a client offers a wealth of information, information the patient may not be completely aware of. The natal chart of an individual displays so much more than their basic personality, it can indicate trauma and issues related to childhood and other points of stress or even benevolence and good fortune in their lifetime. The massive amount of information contained in a person's natal chart can be invaluable, displaying indicators concerning relationships, learning habits, and more.

Whether you as an individual study astrology for yourself and learn everything you can about your own natal chart and all the other charts available to you throughout your astrological journey; or you approach your astrological journey through the assistance of a professional astrologer, the benefits you will receive are innumerable.

Understanding your natal astrological chart is of utmost importance for self-awareness. Most everything about you, including the things you never share with another soul can be found in your natal chart. Your journey through the houses from one to twelve and where your planets reside, how they are oriented to one another, and your rising sign or ascendant, are all ingredients in the recipe to your characterization, personality, life lessons, karma, interactions with others, how you work, the way you learn, and so on. Everything you could want to know or prefer not to acknowledge is right there in your natal chart.

A description of past life information and some paths to a future life plan

I would venture to say most astrologers believe in past lives, reincarnation, and karma. These are the basic principles of spiritual knowledge. Some astrologers are more connected to a formal religion and others are just spiritual with no real connection to any dogma.

When we look for past lives in a natal chart, we look at several things. One of the first places I look for karmic energy is the 12th house. Whatever the 12th house shows, we have no choice but to work on during this lifetime. So, whatever sign your 12th house is, that house ruler, the planets within that house, and the aspects to all those point to karma.

Your south node sign, ruler, placement, and aspects are also potential sources of past life troubles. Your north node is what you came here for. It's new and strange. It represents your direction and goal. Your south node represents what you've previously done in former incarnations, maybe several of them. You are well-versed in and comfortable with the south node lifestyle. Most people lean toward their south node early in life, hoping to develop into their north node following their Saturn return in their early thirties. These two positions are largely diametrically opposed.

For instance, let's say your north node in Cancer is in the 7th house, which places your south node in Capricorn in your 1st house. Your north node is the direction you should be going; you should be working on how you nurture (Cancer) your partners (7th house). But everyone sees you as a workaholic because you haven't left the comfort zone of your south node in Capricorn. You are not working on your karma since nurturing makes you uncomfortable and working excessively is so familiar to you.

Certain placements and their different aspects can reveal past life issues as well. One might have Saturn conjunct their natal Sun which could mean lessons from the father or karma with the father. Saturn can represent karma from a past life and the lessons for the current life.

We must all know that karma does not always return to the person who initially facilitated it. The spiritual narrative is we have a soul team we work with and plan with before we incarnate. Often, we work out karma within our team. Sometimes the ones who love us the most on the other side choose to play the villain in this lifetime to help us through our karmic debts and help us grow spiritually.

Sometimes our karma is associates with good things and this is always nice! We may have an aspect to Venus or Jupiter and receive a lot of love or benevolence from the good things we may have accomplished in past lives. These too, would show up in our natal charts.

Also, for the future, we look to our transits. As the planets orbit through the constellations, they travel through the houses of our natal charts. They also travel through other charts such as solar return and progressed charts.

Your solar return chart is based on your birthday for this year. From that chart and the aspects to that chart we may gather much information about how your year will play out. Progressed charts show the movement of your natal planets as they have progressed during this lifetime, aspects of this chart may also be helpful for your plans in the future.

Astrology is a great tool for exploring mental illness, health issues, and career goals. Why it would not be incorporated into graduate studies is beyond me. In spiritual psychotherapy, I work with numerology, galactic astrology, and psychological astrology. These tools have helped me enormously with healing my childhood traumas. These traumas were laid out in my chart and pointed to the reasons why these challenges are necessary for future accomplishments. It allowed me to take ownership of my past and use my experiences to improve myself and support others going through similar traumas. Spiritual psychotherapists become familiar with their Soul plan and follow their inner guidance. They maintain a disciplined spiritual life, recognizing and resisting all manner of evils and focusing on their inner light through meditation and contemplation and assist others in mapping their way.

Galactic Astrology

During my studies in astrology, I stumbled across galactic astrology and felt a spirit nudge me towards it. I knew I was not a native of Earth, and I came from somewhere else, so galactic astrology felt like a tool that could bring me closer to self-discovery. I contacted Grayham Forscutt (n.d.), owner of galacticacademy.com, for a reading, and the results were astounding. It validated everything the Babalawos had said during my naming ceremony, and I received a lot of answers to questions I have had about my skillsets, past life experiences and future life projections. Ultimately, we must know what feels true for us and trust our guiding system. I have since conducted galactic astrology readings on many of my clients and many have reported feeling a sense of deeper understanding and clarity.

So, what is Galactic Astrology?

A well-renowned galactic astrologer, Grayham Forscutt, explains that Galactic astrology begins with the Amenti Hall of Records, mentioned by Charles Jarvis (n.d.). "The Halls of Amenti" is a school, stargate, and cosmic energy vortex located in the center of the Earth on the Astral Plane. In the Halls of Amenti, ascended masters and energy beings who teach and tutor rising ascending masters qualified for training. Amenti is also the supreme energy vortex of this planet and greatly sustains and repairs the planet in every way.

Students of Amenti are taught the ultimate mysteries of time, space, alchemy, and the nine dimensions. An unascended human could not enter the Halls of Amenti without being destroyed by the much higher vibrational frequency of Amenti. Ascending humans can enter the Halls of Amenti, and this serves as a perfect self-regulating device (which is no accident), and such as this exist throughout all worlds, times, planes, and dimensions of God's Omniverse.

In 2012, NASA funded the research of Jack Scudder from the University of Iowa, who studied a phenomenon unlike any other. He found that when the magnetic field of the Earth connected to the magnetic field of the Sun, a portal between time/space was created between them. Time-space is "what we will experience if we are able to pierce the veil, three dimensions of time (past, present, and future) of wherever you are, which is the one dimension of space (yourself). To make an example of this, imagine an apple. The outside of the apple is the infinite universe, which is space/time. The inside of the apple is time/space, which is a continuous loop that can be traveled."- Jeff Delano.

Scudder (1996), termed this phenomenon "X-points." After NASA examined Scudder's theory, they flew a robotic spacecraft into one of these magnetic points, which revealed that the X-point had the potential to transport objects directly into the Sun's atmosphere. The distance from the Earth to the Sun is measured as one astronomical unit or 93 million miles away. This discovery was groundbreaking because it questioned our understanding of known physics and opened the door to understanding the relationship between time and space. Even though we may not fully grasp the concept yet, it can serve as a steppingstone to better understanding how our universe operates on a scale once thought to be intangible.

Using Astrology to Map My Son's Soul Plan

Of all my traumas, nothing paled in comparison with the stress associated with raising black children in America and coping with the loss of a beloved child. I've dealt with many grieving moms who have watched helplessly as their children were discriminated against, bullied, or even murdered, only to have the world scorn and dismiss their suffering. There is no greater horror than to watch these types of modern-day lynching and the systemic ploys to suppress and gatekeep children from their potential. My innocent children were always regarded suspiciously, given different treatment by teachers and other people, and had to deal with the traumas of racial aggression on a daily basis. Amidst daily life difficulties, I was dealing with a steady torrent of evil curses from my birth mother, who had been seeking to harm me as well as my children.

One day, I had a vision that I was flying in the sky with an angel, and we were following a grey car. I saw an evil looking man and woman abandon the car and I swooped down and opened the back seat of the car. My son was lying there. We got him out as I watched his lifeless body. The angel placed his hand on my shoulder and said, "He is going to be alright." When I awoke from this vision, I began to pray, pleading God not to let this happen. I trusted the angel when he said my son would be fine, but my vision came true four years later.

On Sunday, August 13, 2023, my beloved son Rilwan Quadri's apartment was broken into, and thieves stole his money and his beloved dog. His neighbors found footage proving it was his ex-girlfriend and her dad. When Rilwan called me to tell me what happened, I begged him to come home and not attempt to get his dog. He expressed fear that his dog would be tortured, and he had to save his dog. The police were called but they never showed. Against my plea, Rilwan went to attempt to get his dog back. As he stood at the parking lot, the girlfriend's dad spotted him and yelled *"there is the nigger"*, chasing my son for several blocks, he shot him several times in the back. On the ground and bleeding, my son was still alive as they dragged him into the back seat of his car and drove to a parking lot, where he bled to death. Right before the incident, I received a text from my son, saying, *"be safe driving home. Please and thank-you for everything. Good night. I love you."* Rilwan had been missing for three days, and by the time the police found his body, the Texas 105-degree heat had badly decomposed it. The social media frenzy went viral on news outlets and Twitter/Facebook, claiming my son had abused his girlfriend, and the father had taken revenge. They hailed the murderer as a hero and spread his mugshot with my son's name at the bottom.

We found out about my son's murder on social media. His autopsy was concluded as a homicide. Although not evident at first glance, like many cities in the United States, San Antonio Texas is extremely discriminatory against minorities and black men, in particular. The police supported his assailants, claiming that he was involved in domestic violence, and social media accused my son. They fervently defended the girlfriend as a hero even though friends denied my son ever laid a hand on her. Rilwan had broken up with her, and she went back to his apartment when he was not there to rob him with her father.

His death brought about a series of conversations with my son on the other side. My first vision of him was three days after his death; he looked so beautiful and had a huge smile on his face. I knew my baby was alright when I saw the golden light enveloping him and radiating from his heart. His first words to me were, "Mom! I found Bruno!" Bruno was our border collie, who I had put down after he got a deadly reaction from a rabies vaccine shot and had multiple epileptic seizures. Rilwan grieved Bruno and wished he had gotten to see him before he passed away. He was elated to finally be reunited with Bruno. Bruno was not his only happy reunion. My son reported being reunited with his oversoul, ancient relatives, uncles, and grandparents. He told me that he was in a good place, full of love.

CHAPTER 10

Rilwan was buried with Islamic rights. The Muslim community is often one of brotherhood to whom I owe a depth of gratitude for supporting me in my greatest hour of need. I was alone with no support system, but my faith and intuitive insights brought me abrupt closure. At his funeral, there were many angels and fireworks of light, but no one could see them but me. His friends took multiple pictures on their cameras, and, for me, this confirmation that my son was a light of God.

We were all amazed by the light beam that was photographed as his friends were gathered around Rilwan's burial. We also knew that the cellphone photos had not been altered in any way, and there was no other logical source of the beam. After his funeral, Rilwan sat next to me and we had many loving conversations. He told me that he was at the funeral and thanked everyone for what they had done for him. He was deeply regretful of the mistakes he made. He told me that had he listened to me, this would not have happened. He was deeply sorry for the stress he caused me and everyone else. I told him to confess everything before they came and got him. He told me to correct his name from Ron... he is Rilwan. Then, the light of God appeared early in the morning, and my son was taken to heaven.

The next night, I had a dream that I was pregnant and lying on a hospital bed. The room looked like an old, styled hospital from the 1800s but was bright with white lights everywhere. Four angels were by my bedside. One of them said to me that my son would be reborn. They performed some surgery on me by inserting a tiny silver trident up my vagina. Afterwards they handed me a black liquid through a drip, which they said was iron for strength. Then, they asked me what I wanted for my son, and I replied, "To look beautiful and go sky diving!"

The trident has different meanings depending on religion and geographical location. In Greek mythology, the king of the sea was named, Poseidon, and he was a brother of Zeus, the king of the sky and chief king of ancient Greece. The trident granted Poseidon the ability to create tidal waves, control the weather by summoning rainstorms and lightning, and even convert live beings into other forms. The trident is also the symbol of Hades, God of the underworld. This is why many depict the devil using a trident. In the most popular version, it symbolizes a falcon, which was later identified as the symbol of the Christian Trinity: the Father, the Son, and the Holy Spirit. The trident was also once used as a military weapon. It is still used for spearfishing in some parts of the world. The trident in chemistry represents three properties of water: liquidity, fertility, and drinkability.

After doing some study on the significance of the trident, I requested the Holy Spirit to help me comprehend what my birthing dream meant, the meaning of the trident, and what the angels meant when they said my son was reborn. The Holy Spirit revealed to me that Rilwan has been re-incarnated as an angel and will join the chosen ones in complete devotion to God. My son Rilwan is a child of the light. He had a heart of gold. Not many people can reach into themselves and ask what their heart is. My son had a heart of gold, and he would do anything for his family, friends, and anyone else that he could help. He was good. But Rilwan had a fault; he was a black man. Nobody who is not black can understand what it is like to be a black man in America. From the moment he turned eighteen, Rilwan was a person of interest up until the day he was murdered. He couldn't even go to the grocery store without being stopped, frisked, and searched. He resided in Houston, and every time he visited San Antonio, he was stopped by police at least twice. We all knew that he was flagged in their system for the simple reason that he had disrespected police officers during a routine stop.

He got arrested soon after his nineteenth birthday for possessing a blunt. This misdemeanor earned him two days in jail and two years of probation. His mugshot was posted all over the internet. He was abused by the system and mocked on social media platforms. They wanted to break him, but Rilwan always kept his head up high. He always told me how grateful he was to be alive.

The Christians always say that Jesus was the son of God, that he died for the sins of the world, and that we all may be redeemed. However, I challenge all Christians of this world to contemplate their beliefs deeply and see how many sons of God who lived for love were falsely accused, mocked, ridiculed, sacrificed, and murdered. My son did not deserve to die and be treated unjustly by his community. United States is largely Christian and looks away from all manner of lynchings and killings and then goes to church to pray to Jesus after watching crucifixions on television.

Evil never wins. We stand tall and resolve to fight the good fight for our Father in heaven. It is by no means over. With every breath of our being, we continue to fight for the innocent sons of God; we will prevail against evil and tyranny.

Rilwan paid the ultimate price with his life, and now he rests with the angels in heaven. Rest in joy and goodness, Rilwan. You will never have to face an evil world ever again; keep heaven warm for us. We will soon join you; we, sons and daughters of the light, will soon join you. I see you all the time and hear your thoughts as you hear mine. You are free, you are free, you are free.

Those who leave this world are better off than the living. Can you not see that this is an evil world? Who cries for the dead when the living is dying a slow and painful existence? Children are kidnapped, sold for sex trafficking, and killed for rituals in the name of power. Billions of innocent people languish in poverty, pain, and suffering. Big pharma has gotten away with the killing of billions of people in the name of greed. We answer to tyrannical and evil governments throughout the world. Billions have joined the satanic system of AI and virtual reality. Our food has been poisoned, and billions are malnourished. We trust a judicial system that frees criminals and locks up the innocent. We see the good and righteous afflicted daily by evil temptations, but God has promised to deliver us all.

People are talking about ascension in the end times, but they are so ignorant and oblivious to how it happens. They do not know that it involves the renunciation of the world and atonement of all sins through sacrifice. They do not know that my son gave his life for the ascension. They sit in their luxury, hoping to enjoy their evil wealth from evil paychecks that come from evil institutions. My son refused to serve them; he refused to trade his Soul for the world, and he took the steps to renounce the world in exchange for his real Father in heaven.

He had a perfect 29-degree cross and a stellium in Chiron in Scorpio in 29 degrees. This means that he came with a specific mission to make the ultimate sacrifice. I prepared him daily for his next mission, to take his place among the forces of light to eradicate evil on this planet and restore the planet and the sons of God.

I used to share a story that the Buddha gave about the karma, of a man whose son was murdered. The son was released from all cyclic existence and all karmic debt paid, which released his Soul to Nirvana. The father who chooses to forgive his son's murderer does so for his redemption, and the murderer will have to atone for his actions. For these reasons, both the son and father must thank the assailants for the opportunities for redemption.

In the Quran, Allah promises redemption to anyone whose life was taken unjustly. In the Bible, God allows the innocent to die because such a death is only temporary. They will inherit eternal life with joy, peacefulness, and glory. I thank the enemies for their role is to strengthen what is good and expand the light of God.

For these reasons and more, I thank his assailants, the defenders of the assailants, and law enforcement, who fail to demand justice. To the ones who prosecuted the innocent, social media for spreading false rumors and the systems and intuitions of racism and discrimination, I thank you. To the ones to send messages and said to me, "It serves you right." The ones who turned a blind eye, and the ones who cursed my son and told me that he would amount to nothing. I am truly grateful that you also aided in the transfiguration of my son.

Heaven is filled with Souls of all religions, races, and ethnicities. The biblical says, "In my father's house are many mansions". John 12:2. My son's transfiguration will only serve to deepen my resolve to do God's will. Now, all that is needed is to train our minds to overlook all little sense-less aims and to remember that our goal is God. His memory is hidden in our minds, obscured by our pointless little goals which offer nothing and do not exist. Shall we continue to allow God's grace to shine in unawareness while the toys and trinkets of the world are sought instead? God is our only goal, our only love. We have no aim but to remember Him (ACIM, 1976).

I gave my son to the world, and they crucified him again and again and again. They recognized him not but judged his innocence and mocked his identity. My son is a son of God. He cannot die because he is immortal. The very day his body was buried, he rose again. A light came from the heavens and shined upon him. He was risen.

Why is it that human beings cannot see spirits who are said to be in the room with them? People are not all satisfied to be told that it is because they are not clairvoyants and do not have Soul-sight. They want a clear explanation. My son is a light of God; he exists beyond a body, and so does the dwelling place that I set for him.

I can offer you proof my son is resurrected. I could give you a dozen elaborate explanations, but no mortal human being who is unable to see the spirits would be any wiser after I do so. Humans are quick to forget the multitude of miracles God has laid before them. My son is guiltless, and he did not die because he is immortal. He is redeemed and has never been separated from God. There is great joy in Heaven on his homecoming, for the redeemed son of man is the guiltless Son of God, and to recognize him in each other lies our redemption (ACIM, 2016).

So, take heart to all who have buried a loved one. In this one truth, may your tears be wiped forever. We can never die, for we are eternally immortal. Christ's vision is a gift from the Holy Spirit, God's alternative to the illusion of separation and belief in sin, shame, and death. It is the single corrective for all perceptual mistakes, the reconciliation of the world's seemingly opposing elements. Its benevolent light illuminates everything from a different perspective, reflecting the thought system that emerges from knowledge and making a return to God not only conceivable but unavoidable.

What was regarded as injustice done to one by someone else now becomes a call for help and union. Sin, sickness, and attack are seen as misperceptions calling for remedy through gentleness and love. Defenses are laid down because where there is no attack, there is no need for them. Our brothers' needs become our own because they are taking the journey with us as we go to God. Without us, they would lose their way. Without them, we could never find our own (ACIM, 1976).

Galactic Events After Rilwan's Death

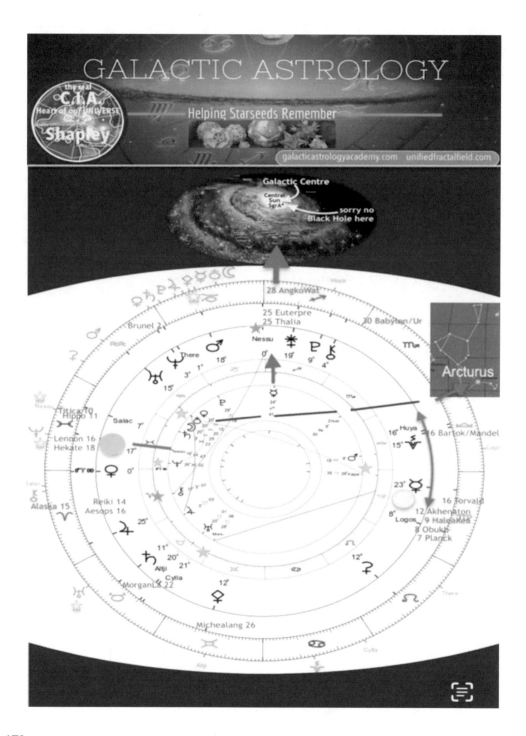

I collected information to map the sequence of events within the three days of Rilwan's death. As with many of us left behind when a loved one dies, suddenly, we have many questions about whether the departing Soul planned this or if this was just a stroke of bad luck. I added some internal zodiac and drew some extra lines. Inside are the symbols of where the planets were on that traumatic day, and then, I drew several lines from that day to his birth chart.

Earth was seated at 9 o'clock, drawn directly to Nessus on his birth chart on the 13th of August. Nessus is also in his birth chart, lining up at 12 o'clock with the galactic center. This is the most important planetoid in his chart. Nessus is a centaur planetoid representing transitions. Nessus's job is to transport renowned Souls across the river from one reality to another reality. During his three-day transition, Mercury was at 12 o'clock toward the galactic center on top of Nessus, which indicates an exchange of information.

There is a three-day period after a person dies, where they are called up on the third day and go where they are meant to go. On the third day after his death, there was a perfect alignment to Arcturus at 144 degrees. This degree creates the portal for opening a star-gate.

At 7 o'clock is a planet called Mors. Mors is one of the trans-Neptunian planetoids depict transitions, moving through dimensions, and the personification of death and rebirth. Mors was at 108 degrees to Rilwan's birth Sun. Also, at a perfect degree angle are Chiron and Kaga, asteroids responsible for moving Souls from one dimension to another. Chiron is on the node linked to the galactic center. Venus, a portal transition was also with the Earth at the time of his death. Earth was 36 degrees away from Neptune, creating portals both of entry and existence.

Without realizing it, I prepared Rilwan to take an interplanetary leap by reminding him on a regular basis in our conversations and via my writing that we are more than our physical bodies and that we must keep our minds focused on the true nature of who we are lest death find us in illusions.

The Sacrifice to be Thyself.

I shared another beautiful moment with my son. He appeared to me in a new shape. He appeared more like a golden ball of light with silver hues around him and was difficult to describe in words. I asked him why his life had been cut short. Was this God's magnificent design, or the work of demonic entities?

He said to me- *"I really didn't want to be on Earth anymore. I wasn't meant to have left so soon, but I realized that I couldn't be myself. I am with love and full of joy. I am relieved to be myself again."* He said... *"Mom, don't be so quick to leave like me. You still have 20 more years of giving. You are so much stronger than me, and please stay so I can work through you".*

He also told me- *"We could never truly feel God, not while in a body, and even Christ and all the great teachers had difficulty during their time on Earth.*

He was ecstatic, and his effervescent light glimmered more brightly as he said me:

"Mom! You are right, you are right about everything! With you being my only link to the earth, I can still gift joy to you and the world."

At that moment, it became clear to me. When Rilwan told me that he left because he could not be himself on Earth,

He said... *"I would have to be 70 years old by the time I get a glimpse of myself, and so I took the sacrifice to leave."*

I wondered what that had to do with his life path. How his date of birth was September 10, 1999, he had lived in the apartment 9, his license plate numbers added up to 9. His astrology was a perfect cross, and Chiron in 29 spelled the ultimate sacrifice and a 12th house stellium of self-undoing. His I-Ching was literally to transmute oppression to transfiguration.

My son is now a full-spectrum light being! He completed his ultimate SIDDHI (Siddhi is a Hindu word for complete understanding and enlightenment) to further his evolution by making the ultimate sacrifice to be himself, something very few dare to do. He is now free to be the golden light he is and has always been! He gave up life on Earth to be himself.

Three days after my son's death, Angels told me in a dream that my son would be reborn, for he took the steps, faced his shadows, and achieved transfiguration.

George Floyd

Charles Tindley wrote in his gospel lyrics,

"You'll understand it better by and by,
By and by, when the morning comes.
All the saints of God are gathered in home.
We will tell the story how we overcome.
And we'll understand it better by and by.
And we'll understand it better by and by."
(Tindley, 1905)

In May 2020, I woke up to angels serenading an old negro spiritual. I had not heard this song since I was ten years old. I watched as they rushed quickly through the shining lights; there must have been hundreds of them, and there was a man in the middle of them. I didn't recognize him, so I imagined the angels were chanting words of encouragement to me. A few minutes after that, my daughter walked into my room, she looked concerned and scared, she said to me,

"Mom! Did you see the news and what they did to that man?"

My daughter showed me the breaking news of a man killed by the police. To my amazement, the man I saw being taken by angels was Gorge Floyd. I told my daughter immediately, He is in heaven, I saw the angels take him to heaven!" and for the rest of the coming days, I sang the angels song and danced to the victory of God's promise that the least will become the first. I wished I could shout on the roof top to the world that it's okay, nothing is lost, George is raised, and lives amongst the angels! Nothing you do or don't do will change God's law and His promise to the innocent is unfailing and abides forever.

Transmuting Oppression to Transfiguration

In traditional Christian theology, the Harrowing of Hell, or "the descent of Christ into Hell" or Hades, is the saving act of Christ to the souls in Hades between His crucifixion and resurrection. Christ descended to those in darkness and death that light might shine on them, and He might deliver them from death. (Laufer, 2016) As Christ fearlessly faced His tormenters, death, and Hell, so we through Him can confidently face mockers and tormentors and bring His light to them by faith. When we die a horrible and violent death in the face of hate and prosecution, does the great transfiguration occur.

Since God intends for our souls to become Christ consciousness, He will take us through experiences similar to the one Jesus went through. This includes, hate, loneliness, temptations, stress, rejection, criticism and many other problems because spiritual tests lead to a partnership with God. During our spiritual tests, we are left completely alone although not alone and those times, God is intimately present with us at the deepest level giving us support. So, when my son was mocked on local news, dehumanized and shamed by his community and at the lowest point of his life did God step in. And when they dehumanized George Floyd, God stepped in and the promise from transmutation to resurrection was fulfilled.

Richard Rudd (2013) describes Jesus transfiguration as a symbol of the mythical enactment of every human who holds back nothing and embrace everything. So let us be thankful for hate and abuse for it means that God has a plan us. Thank them who crucify us for without knowing it, have they prepared you for the great transmutation and transfiguration.

CHAPTER 11

Biofeedback & Aura Imaging in Psychotherapy

As a clairvoyant child, I was exposed to the various ways people interacted with each other to gain energy through manipulation and intimidation. Energy extraction occurs when a person is made to feel small or powerless or to confuse them by derailing their mental focus. We have often heard the phrase energetic vampires to mean people who suck other people's energy. Often, these people are unaware of this habit. Energy vampires can also include governmental entities, entertainment industries and political groups who use various products like movies or policies to get people emotionally reactive and thereby harvest their energy.

Since seeing is believing, I later became intrigued with finding machines that can capture these types of activities and explore ways to use them to promote overall wellbeing. I began to research energy tools like biofeedback and aura machines, and I could match readings against my intuitive perception as well as information gathered from clients. By exploring the human biofield with machines, I became excited about the possibility of tracking me and my clients' enlightenment processes. These tools helped me validate my spiritual practices and in so doing, enlightenment ceased to not just be a spiritual belief but also a scientific fact.

There is an increasing number of biofeedback technologies on the market, and I incorporate several of them in my psychotherapy practice and found them to be invaluable in helping clients gain further self-awareness. I highlight case studies in later chapters of how I use them to promote holistic health. Technologies like the Win Aura Star Gas Discharge Visualization (GDV) machine, Bio-Well Assessments, Nuvision Technology and the Immune Modulation Allergy Elimination Technology (IMAET) can evaluate the aura of any living person or animal. An aura is an energy field that surrounds the body and extends out to an average of about four to five feet. It is closely involved in life processes, which western science refers to as a bioenergy field or a biofield (Swanson, 2011). The National Institute of Health (NIH) National Center of Biometric Information defines the GDV technique as a biometric tool that has the potential to identify deviations from a normal functional state at early stages and in real time.

GDV is a nonintrusive technique to capture the physiological and psycho-emotional status of a person and the functional status of different organs and organ systems through the electro-photonic emissions of fingertips placed on the surface of an impulse analyzer (Cole et al., 2011). I began using the aura machine to track my spiritual progress. I noticed changes in my color and size of energy depending on my state of mind and stress level. I was also able to see how my energy field stabilized and increased energy from simple techniques like breathwork, meditation and hypnotherapy. Increase in voltage of energy emitted can also be captured on a GDV machine. This allowed me to see how stress affects my energy level and the distribution of energy throughout the organ system.

Until thirty years ago, the human aura has only been seen by psychics, mystics, and saints. GDV cameras allow the aura to be photographed.

Known over the centuries by many names—chi, prana. karnaeem, and illiaster—auras have been documented for more than 5,000 years. Howard and Dorothy Sun, in their acclaimed work Color Your Life, propose that auric energies vibrate around all living things. These energies, they state, absorb sun and atmospheric light, dividing light (much as a prism does) into "component color energies" (red, orange, yellow, green, turquoise, blue, purple, and pink). Color energies are then directed toward the ethereal body's sense organs, or energy centers, the chakras. These energy centers, say the Suns, are "power points in the body through which energy flows and is transformed." Chakras, therefore, transform and balance the energy currents coming from the higher, finer energy fields so the material body can use this energy. (Sun, 2013).

Auric fields include Etheric, Emotional, Mental, Astral, Etheric Template, Celestial, and Ketheric. According to Hands of Light by Barbara Ann Brennan. These energy fields reflect the state of health of the being they surround. When the auric fields become unbalanced, reflecting an unhealthy or uncomfortable physical or mental state, it is possible to reorganize and heal them by clearing the unhealthy or blocked energies. To accomplish this, auric fields must first be seen. Although visible to some psychics and mystics, auras remain invisible to the average person. Therefore, researchers have attempted to devise machines that will photograph and analyze the aura, then diagnose its condition. (Brennan, 2002).

Since the 1890s, when the first aura photograph was taken by Nicola Tesla, the search has succeeded in producing mostly fraud, poor-quality prints, and small, direct-contact energy prints known as Kirlian photographs. (Munson, 2018).

Using cutting-edge technology, researchers can now observe and photograph auric fields without direct contact with the photographic plate.

According to the biofeedback described in the WinAura Star machine manual, (2018), a person's aura may reflect an individual's level of health. A person is considered healthy on the aura machine in terms of physical, mental (clarity), emotional, and spiritual well-being, reflected in the aura colors displayed on a biofeedback aura machine. A biofeedback aura machine used in psychotherapy gives an individual the opportunity to see the direct effects of how their thought process and mental and emotional focus affect their spiritual health both before and after therapy sessions.

To use the biofeedback WinAura Star machine for biofeedback, people place their hands on a metal sensor. The machine measures temperature and interprets the areas of the hands to corresponding areas and organs of the body. The aura and chakra (Reiki) readings are projected onto a computer screen, which shows the aura color. The colors represent the emotional, physical, and spiritual state of a person. The readings are intended for personal insight and not for diagnosis or treatment.

After conducting thousands of aura readings, I concluded the following layers of the human biofield. These layers may differ from person to person depending on their level of consciousness.

Divine (cosmic) consciousness	Christ Consciousness / Celestial
Enlightenment	Spirit Field
Transpersonal Consciousness	Soul Field
Transpersonal Consciousness	Psychic field (Clairvoyance, Clairaudience, Precognition)
Personal Consciousness	Mental field (Comprises all incarnations)
Personal Consciousness	Astral field (The body that travels in dreams)
Personal Consciousness	Aura Emotional, Mental, Astral, Etheric Template
Personal Consciousness	Dense physical field: the body (matter and Electromagnetic Field)

The biofeedback WinAura Star imaging machine not only allows clients to view their aura and chakra system but also allows them to visually witness significant changes before and after their therapy sessions and over a timespan of multiple sessions. For the client and practitioner, this viewing of aura and energy changes confirms the impact that counseling, Reiki, and hypnotherapy sessions have on the client's well-being and recovery. It also may further encourage clients to commit to sobriety goals and behavioral changes. It inspires them to take accountability for recovery beyond therapy sessions by resisting habits that would not benefit recovery and completing therapy "homework" assigned by the practitioner. For more information, visit https://www.auraphoto.com/products/WinAura/.

Bio-Well GDV Camera

To bring about a stronger analysis of a person's biofield, I also incorporate Bio-Well technology. Bio-well is a revolutionary, non-intrusive way to measure human stress levels using a specialized camera and software system. Developed by an international team led by Dr. Konstantin Korotkov from Russia in 1995, this powerful technology known as the GDV technique measures how our bodies manage and adapt to stress, which is a great health assessment tool that provides immediate insights into what is acutely happening in one's body. Based on the reports, a variety of wellness approaches and plans can be tailored to meet a client's energetic, mental, and emotional needs.

Many clients diagnosed with idiopathic issues, meaning that the root cause of the health issue is unknown, find this assessment extremely helpful. Bio-Well detects the subtle physiological, psychological, emotional, and spiritual connections to underlying issue(s). The output analysis report and images provided by the Bio-Well offer an opportunity to "see" the connection and correlations to the psycho-emotional-spiritual links to the subtle or acute disorder.

Seeing is believing. The Bio-Well displays a visual and in-depth health assessment of how the body is managing stress. In science, the term *entropy* is often used to describe how organized a system or organ is behaving. *Neg-entropy* means there is less or no chaos; *entropy* means there is disorganization and chaos. (Bailly, 2009). Often, on the healing journey, there is chaos before and during the transitional phases. Adaptivity is a dynamic process, and the Bio-Well is helpful in detecting real-time activity to aid in assessing a detox program, before and after treatments, and subtle core issues.

IMAET Biofeedback Quantum Healing System

Psychotherapists are trained to provide biofeedback therapy to clients and there is a growing market of biofeedback tools that can monitor a client's physiological states and send information back to the client. This allows the practitioner and the client to get a visual of how their stress levels is affecting their bioenergy field. Biofeedback tools can control aspects of a person's physiology—using relaxation techniques to slow down heart rate, and thereby manage symptoms of a variety of medical and psychological conditions.

The IMAET system goes a step further than conventional biofeedback tools by working with the quantum physical expression of the total of energetic processes going on in the human body at any given time. In a Western understanding, these energetic processes are inter-cellular communications of the body's 100 trillion cells." (Straile, 2023)

This bio-energetic expression of life, in Hindu culture it's called Prana, in Chinese traditional culture it's called Qi and is defined in meridians and acupoints. When we merge these traditional wisdoms with our modern scientific knowledge of body biochemistry and epigenetics, we enter a new universe of understanding health and dis-ease. We're entering the cyberspace of the body. Gaining this new understanding becomes a matter of information analysis. It has been called 'Decoding the human Body field' by Peter Fraser.

"The meridian system as the internet of the cells. It is within these channels that the cellular communications flow. And it is here where we can analyze what the body as a whole and a system of 100 trillion cells, is communicating about.

180

It will reveal everything from allergies to sensitivities to normal bio-chemical processes like digestion or hormone metabolism. This includes the Immune response, long before the Immune System becomes overwhelmed, and we become ill." (Straile, 2023)

The Immune Modulation Allergy Elimination Technology (IMAET) is an elite biocommunication technology that provides the body with intracellular balance for wellness. It uses both scalar and electromagnetic waves and contains 70,000 frequencies. (Straile, 2023). It contains twenty-seven support programs and can custom remedies and imprint frequencies in any number of personal items like water, jewelry, and medications. The IMAET uses cutting-edge bioenergetic communication technology and proprietary algorithms to deliver unmatched wellness support.

A person's bioenergy is scanned using a harness system and an interface box operating along quantum waves, also known as Tesla waves, to interface with the body and collect energetic signatures that reflect current wellness needs. Using the energetic signatures collected during the scan, IMAET provides a snapshot of the body's potential wellness and support needs. The practitioner can then customize a unique and comprehensive wellness support session based on the snapshot provided in the program, which is also called a treatment basket. The effects of the session are reportedly often experienced immediately afterward and are even more effective after multiple sessions. For more information, visit https://www.imaet.com/.

The IMAET SHOW Method

Dr. Benard Straile (2023), created the SHOW Method as a protocol to be used in the IMAET. It integrates epigenetic science and quantum biofeedback with ancient Chinese medicine, tapping procedures and kinesiology (MRT) into a precision-energy medicine technique, which aims at harmonizing the metabolic stressors created by genetic mutations and variants. The SHOW Method is a non-medical, precision bio-energetic healing technique.

It focuses on cellular communications to determine miscommunication quirks in the metabolism that generate inflammation and pain and obtain information about the status of the immune system and detoxification system. Cellular communication equals bioenergetic energy equals Qi energy (SHOW Method Handbook, 2023).

NuVision

NuVision is a quantum scanning device that works to identify body and psyche issues keeping individuals from well-being, this is referred to as "computerized kinesiology." Once identified, the practitioner can then work with the patient to provide a strategy for moving forward. A part of this strategy is using the devices in a different dimension, "computerized home-opathy," which, together with information about diet, lifestyle, supplements, and herbs, can set you on the path to healing.

NuVision helps uncover the imbalances and underlying causes of ill health. This information may be herbal, nutritional, or mental/emotional. What if the long-standing physical symptom is because of what the individual believes or says to himself? What if it's because of a job or relationship? What if it's because the individual lives in the past and is still holding on to old relationships, guilt, or regrets? What if fatigue is something simple, like being low in minerals? What if the individual has parasites? In the traditional healthcare model, these are not even considered, and drugs are easily prescribed to mask symptoms. Still, the drugs never fix the underlying problem. NuVision enhances the field by identifying information from the subject submitted to the software— and a subject's holographic token is created. From then on, the practitioner can read the relevant issues the subject reflects on his or her field, choose the relevant work sets that match holographically with the subject's field, and activate "reconnects."

Reconnects are information pockets that, when set in motion, can trigger potentially beneficial influences on the subject's information field. Illustrations about how to use Nuvision in psychotherapy is further explored in a later chapter titled case studies. For more information, visit https://nuvisionusa.com/.

CHAPTER 12
Energy Healing Modalities

Energy healing is not farfetched from conventional medicine. Hospitals use various energy tools like cardioversions to jumpstart people's hearts, such as EEG, EKG, and various radiation therapies for treatment. Electrical devices can improve blood flow, regulate the nervous system, and improve muscle responses. In the same way, all medications and nutrition are all forms of energy applications. Our human body, in its subatomic particles, is composed of earth elements and, in its most subtle form, contains energy and operates in more subtle dimensions beyond what the physical eyes can see.

Unborn fetuses depend on their mother's energy to grow and develop, and much of the mother's energy is given to the child. During pregnancy, women often experience low energy, are tired, and even ill because energy is drained from the mother to the fetus. At the time of birth, we possess this prenatal energy. Still, this prenatal energy is not enough to sustain growth. We supplement this energy with baby formula and eventually earth-based foods to grow. These two sources of energy, prenatal and earth energy, are temporary and unsustainable and never seem to last very long so we are constantly eating and exercising to get energy.

We are in fear of running out of energy, so we engage in all manner of manipulative acts toward the planet and others, knowingly and unknowingly, to fight for what seems like limited resources throughout the planet. Our mindset of lack detracts us from our true light source, and therefore, our two main sources of energy—prenatal and earth energies— become unsustainable, and our bodies eventually become diseased, age and dies. The physical body serves an important function to house the Soul and become enlightened by divine light. As mentioned in prior chapters, spiritual energy is developed from being open minded enough to receive divine love and wisdom. By resisting negativity and focusing on what is good for the sake of good, we then become recipients of divine love and wisdom. Energy and inspiration come from God and nowhere else. We can make certain things happen through ego, but such accomplishments are often short-lived.

Through acts of goodness for goodness' sake, the light expands through the Soul body. Natural light from the sun will illumine the physical body and both divine and natural light will cause a person's aura to glow on the GDV machine.

For anyone, including a spiritual psychotherapist, to successfully support another in energy healing, they must incorporate divine light into their Soul body. When clients encounter a spiritual psychotherapist, healing is automatic because any darkness will be repelled by the light of the healer and the client will befreed from negative energies. Psychotherapy is then employed to move the client's consciousness towards the light.

A spiritual psychotherapist may employ different types of energy healing methods like reiki, traditional pranic healing, Chinese acupuncture, Qigong, magnetic healing, quantum hypnotherapy, sound frequencies, and so on. However, such techniques are only as effective as the vibration of the practitioner, and this also goes for traditional medical practitioners. A doctor who does not act with uttermost sincerity to support the healing of another and does not engage spiritual development is unlikely to bring healing to another, even with the best of education and training. Healing is impossible without light.

The Human Energy Field.

When clients ask me what chakras and auras are, I use the analogy of a vehicle which has many screws and bolts, from large to small screws, all keeping the vehicle together and running. The vehicle also has liquids such as fuel and other even more subtle energies like electrical sparks that keep the car running. The same way, the human body has many vortexes of energy that lock the soul into the physical body and feeds lifeforce energy to the various organs of the body. The human body has large vortexes called chakras, medium sized vortexes called meridians and acupressure points. These are like screws and bolts that allows the body to receive life force energy from the Soul. These vortexes are connected to the emotional, mental and energy body. The human body is perfectly constructed machinery, but it requires care and attention at all levels.

Trauma can cause the body's energy systems to go out of alignment, just like when your tires hit the curb and go out of alignment. A disbalance in the energy systems will eventually cause physical and mental health issues. Until the energy system is rebalanced, a person can employ all manner of medical treatments, and nothing will work, in fact, the disbalance will likely repel any good treatments provided to the patient. This is why energy healing must be further explored to support patient healing.

The Tibetan Book of the Dead (2011) describes the chakras as connecting points which allows a person's consciousness to travel to different dimensions while in sleep and serves as an exit point when we eventually die.

Think of this like an elevator in the body through which we can exit into corresponding dimensions. The elevator also corresponds with our mental state. The root chakra is the basement and the higher crown chakras correspond to the penthouse.

So, our dreams and out-of-body experiences depend the types of thoughts we produce throughout the day. The root chakra connects to the lowest realms. A person who is negative or surrounded by negativity may have nightmares in their sleep because their consciousness exited into the lowest dimensions where nightmarish experiences happen. The sacral chakra connects to the realm of the hungry ghost. Hence, a person who spends time chasing body pleasures such as sex, drugs, food, or emotions is likely to have sexual dreams and strange consumptions. The solar plexus connects to the mental and earthly realms, and a person who is constantly thinking about earthly affairs will have dreams about his day, people in his daily life, and so on. A person who focuses on love is likely to dream of loving experiences or may dream of heartache depending on the content of their thoughts and experiences. The throat chakra connects to communications of all kinds with angels or astral beings, telepathy or even mediumistic communications from the ethereal realms. The third eye and crown chakras are higher dimensional and spiritual experiences where a person can travel to the spiritual realms in their dreams.

Chakra blockages or overuse are the result of our mental and emotional focus. Sometimes, a person can travel to the lower realms in their sleep and return to the body with negative energies that enter the subtle body, cohabitate with the person, increase pre-existing negative thoughts, and eventually oppress and possess the living person. This is why caring for our mental and emotional bodies is extremely important for overall wellbeing and preventative care. It also explains why the ancients always advised us to never go to bed angry and to say prayers at night before going to bed.

With the use of various Aura imaging machines, one can capture the movement and reflected color of a person. This imaging cannot capture the light of the Soul however, natural light surrounding the person's body can illuminate the light of the soul which are captured on the GDV machine or a sophisticated camera. Clients can also see how their thoughts and emotions are shown through the changing colors on the aura machine. Evidence of this can be empowering for the client to focus on constructive thoughts and positive emotions.

Below is an example of a positive and negative aura impression. The negative impressions can appear as dull red with grey or black layers around the red color. Positive aura will present no dark or grey layers around the aura. A negative aura also looks smaller and closer to the body compared to a positive aura that is wider and more vibrant.

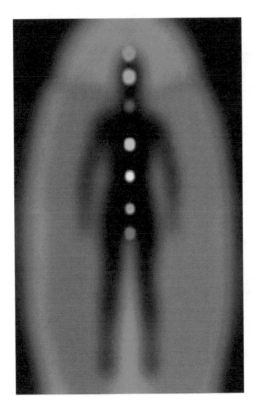

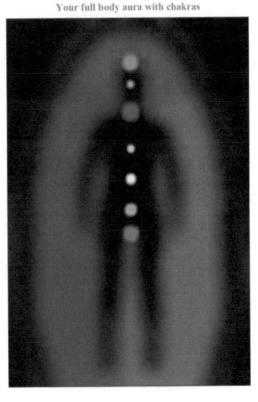

Your full body aura with chakras

Positive Aura Impression

Negative Aura Impression

Clients seek me out for aura cleansing and chakra balancing, and the GDV machines can provide proof of change in their aura. Clients can have spiritual experiences during the energy healing session which I always make sure to discuss after the session. Clients have experienced seeing colors with their eyes closed, electrical feelings, energy coursing through their bodies, visions, messages from their inner self, feeling floating, and more at ease. A few people described feeling more in their bodies, grounded, free of negative thoughts, and having clarity and optimism. I usually follow-up with clients weeks later and most report that there has been consistency in positive changes in their overall wellbeing.

Figure 2 Before and after energy healing.

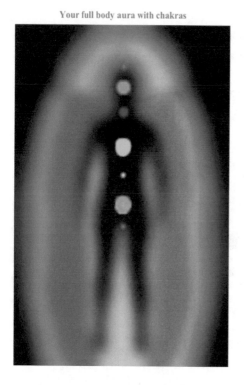

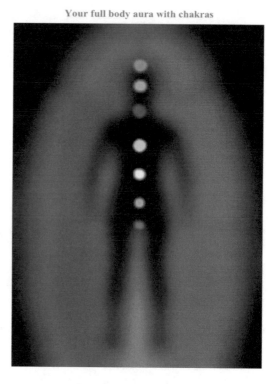

Before Energy Healing   After Energy Healing

Figure 2 captures a before and after energy healing with a client. Prior to energy healing, the client reported health issues related to digestion. She had a gallbladder taken out, extreme sensitivities to certain foods, chronic constipation, and an unusual obsession with sex. She had just ended a romantic relationship and was grieving the loss of the relationship. These difficulties can be observed in the first picture, where her sacral and heart chakras have expanded owing to misuse. The after-energy healing picture shows a more balanced chakra system.

Hypnotherapy and Past-Life Regression

For the last decade, I have used hypnotherapy and past life regression in my psychotherapy practice to heal issues ranging from anxiety, depression, phobias, weight loss and addiction and by grace have received enormous success. Still yet, I have had potential clients call it the work of the devil and that their Christian pastors told them not to engage in it. I usually counter this by asking them if they felt the same way while under anesthesia or zoned out during their football game or when stung-out on alcohol? If they felt nothing wrong with hypnotic suggestions during their halftime football game where advertisers program the minds of television viewers why then would they feel it wrong to use this same technique for healing?

A hypnotherapist can guide clients into this deep state of focus and relaxation with verbal cues, repetition and imagery. When under hypnosis, this intense level of concentration and focus allows the client to ignore ordinary distractions and be more open to guided suggestions to improve their health. Hypnotherapy can be an amazing tool for teaching the client meditation, relaxation and breathwork.

Hypnosis is simply a conscious state where our mind becomes receptive and open to suggestions. We go through this state of mind daily, for instance, when daydreaming, watching a movie, or when we fall asleep while reading a book. Hypnotherapy, on the other hand, is a therapy form whereby a hypnotherapist and the client both apply the hypnosis technique to try and identify false beliefs with the intention of changing them so that we may move on in life.

To help explain this idea, think of a garden. Hypnosis is like sowing a seed and watering it so that it can germinate and grow into a healthy plant. Hypnotherapy, on the other hand, is like weeding the garden so that we can remove any unwanted plants the weeds. In hypnotherapy, practitioners help individuals relax and focus their minds, putting them in a state that makes them more receptive to suggestions from a practitioner (American Psychological Association, 2016).

Conditions are treated by psychotherapists successfully with hypnosis. Milton Erickson, a leader in hypnosis practice and theory, thought of hypnosis as communication (self-communication) and a way to concentrate on personal thoughts, memories, and beliefs (NYSEPH, 2016). Erickson found that the trance state is active unconscious learning with a shift of attention from the external to the internal reality, with highly focused attention directed toward one experience at a time (NYSEPH, 2016).

Hypnotherapy is successful treatment for drug and alcohol addiction, anxiety or behavior problems in part because it produces quick results for changing habits. Thus, treatment outcomes may be more long-term than with other treatments due to the assistance of automatic behavior change.

CHAPTER 13

Intuitive Guidance
& Discerning True Causes

We live inside an anti-realm. A place where base matter is convincing, and the spirit is confined. Inside this construct, the truth is always perpetuated as fictions. This is the realm of the liar where the exact opposite of the truth is consistently uttered to make it true. But in the dungeon of the demiurge, the oversoul has provided a way to use the rules of this construct to reach the individualized souls trapped inside the body.

In this construct, the soul is encouraged to speak those things that are not as if they are and act as if it is so it will be. To those lost in this darkness, this secret is absolute foolishness. Those souls that are lost, focus on what is as opposed to what can be.

The truth is that a problem should never be the focus of awareness instead as co-creators, we must do the exact opposite. We must act as if the solution already exists, and our physical body must act as if what is wanted is already possessed. My focus in life has been to realize truth, wisdom, and knowledge. The truth of my being, although not known does not mean that it cannot be found. When I delve into my spiritual practice,

I do so with the belief that no matter the limitations of my circumstances, I am not limited in my ability to find the deep truths in the most mundane things before me. I know that through concentration and contemplation, I will receive the insights that others may find of value.

By adopting this mindset, I know that the result is already secure. Therefore, the methods I employ to find the results are no longer guided by me which has limitations but guided by intuition and imagination. In turn my intuition is empowered and guided by my oversoul. So, when we adopt this idea as a guiding principle, that the end is secure, then we can know for certain that all steps leading up to this result are secure as well.

The thought that great effort is required to accomplish a desired end only ensures that great effort is required. The informed field of the individual broadcasts the conditions expected into the neutral field of the construct. This fields begins to move all the pieces that are already in the field into position to fulfill the upload. If you hold that certain conditions must be met before fulfillment, then what you want will be kept from you until those conditions are met.

We must imagine the end result as if it is already a set of conditions that already exists. The idea that you are the cause and builder of your future will hinder your efforts. The idea that GOD will give you what you want has not worked for hundreds of millions of people who are still praying for change. Remember, the prayer of desperation admits a situation for what it is and thus continues it. Both positions deny a key fundamental which has everything to do with how the oversoul sees us as individuals. To be a co-creator means this is a shared experience and implies that we are engaged in a relationship with it.

The dynamic is simple. The individualized soul projects a set of conditions and experiences it wants to bring into personal reality and the oversoul only brings to pass the conditions in accordance with the measure of energy broadcast into it. This is because it is restricted in a relationship set by the individualized soul. The parameters of the relationship between the individualized soul and the oversoul is dictated by the amount of trust the soul has in the oversoul. This is what true faith is. That the soul trusts that it is worthy and places his faith in itself (the oversoul). Trust is absolutely required in every relationship. It is from this faith and trust that the oversoul will build for you the world you want. Your ability to dictate your world and your future is 100 percent dependent on your relationship with the oversoul and this relationship is completely dependent upon you.

The first part of our lives is spent growing, learning, and adapting to the world. We live in a reactive mindset, and this continues all the way into the twenties and thirties. During this time, we are living in a reality built by others. In our forties, you are now responsible for the conditions of our world and our realities, and these conditions came through living in other people's realities and accepting the world through the lenses of other peoples' beliefs. But now, we are actively creating our own world and contributing to the construct which provides worlds for others.

In time, the more advanced souls wake up to their relationship to their oversoul and begin building fantastic lives. Most awaken in their fifties and sixties. The transformation in their lives is real, and genuine as they strengthen their relationship with the oversoul. Some of us have awakened after a lifetime of experiences that have shown the patterns of mistakes and victories.

In your mind, take a picture of the future, a snapshot of all the beautiful conditions you want to experience. Thank the oversoul for receiving this picture from you. Feel gratitude that this is now who you are and let your activities infer that you already possess everything in this snapshot.

I once had a dream of a paradise world, a beautiful world, filled with people of wisdom, power, strength, love, and genuine kindness. Everyone in it was a contributor of love and generosity. The colors were more alive than I have ever seen in my entire life. Glowing golden lights that sang the most harmonious melodies, and the sun never sets. I know this place exists and, in my mind, I will walk and act like I already live in this world. I thank my oversoul for she has made it so.

When it comes to psychic awareness, people may cringe or feel that they are not psychic. They perhaps think of a gypsy with a crystal ball or a shaman with a rattle who sees into the spirit realms and can talk to the dearly departed. The truth is that psychic awareness is about tuning into our oversoul and getting its perspective on what is truly going on in the external world of a person.

Intuition and psychic awareness connect to higher consciousness just as the lower consciousness connects with the ego mind. The body controls our cognitive mind and ego. We can talk about wanting to do better and become self-realized or successful. When we say these things, we are speaking from the ideal self and our ego will. The body acts based on our desire to make something happen. Our unconscious, intuitive, and psychic mind is the domain of our Soul. Our Soul incarnates into our body to develop its consciousness; before entering the body, it was unconscious at birth. As mentioned in previous chapters, some Souls possess more consciousness than others, depending on the level of maturity of the Soul and its ability to incorporate past life lessons.

I once had a middle-aged man referred for psychotherapy by his doctors. He was having severe anxiety and panic attacks and the doctors felt it was his mental health. The client experienced a horrific hospital trauma after contracting a virus and was subsequently intubated and placed on a breathing tube for eight weeks. During the community wide lockdown, his wife was allowed to visit him in the hospital once. Prior to this illness, the client referred to himself as a healthy man. He was retired from the military after spending twenty years of active service and several tours of duty. He never visited a mental health clinic before. The client considered himself a family man and spent his retired days tending to household chores and minor projects around the house. He had a good recollection of his childhood and described it as normal. When pressed about his religious/spiritual life, the client recalled that he was sexually abused by a priest at the age of nine and since then, cynical about religion in general.

He recalled difficulty breathing on the day he rushed to the hospital and subsequently intubated. The client reported an out-of-body experience, seeing everything that was happening around him. He saw his wife by his bedside crying, but his wife insisted this could not have been possible as he had been in a drug-induced coma. He recalled the nurses coming into his room to get his blood drawn and said that they looked like vampires. He saw giant rats and rodents crawling on the walls of his hospital room and heard the doctors having a conversation about a football game and were also mocking him. He had vivid experiences of being back in the warzone during his tours of duty. When pressed further, the client denied seeing heaven or Jesus or angels as many often do with out-of-body or near-death experiences. He insisted that he saw nothing of that nature. He recalled dreams of being back at war, engaging in battles and rescuing wounded soldiers. When he was revived from intubation, he did not realize how much time had passed. He felt he had been asleep only for a couple of hours.

Since most intubated patients do not survive this procedure, the client counted himself lucky and felt he had a renewed view of life. I suggested that the client make good use of his second chance. During his near-death experience, he appeared to be earthbound, maybe due to a lack of openness to greater possibilities. When we die, our mind goes to our greatest love and whatever we have focused on throughout our lives. For him, it was the military and that is why he saw himself back in a time where he felt most connected.

The client was sent to a rehab center to re-learn how to walk and perform basic functions after being bedridden for so many weeks. His body was pumped with various medications and his lungs were not functioning as normal after being fed through a breathing tube. Reassuring him of his determination to survive and get healthy, I suggested that he open his mind to spirituality to receive inner comfort. His childhood sexual abuse trauma by a priest had resulted in religious apathy, but the out-of-body experience should renew his hope in spirituality and expand his mind to possibilities beyond earthly concerns. Again, in our dreams and the afterlife, our mind always takes us to our greatest focus. We become what we have focused on, and for this reason, I encourage myself and others to focus on a love for God.

From time to time, I get a glimpse of a person's Soul especially during therapy or when I am with close acquaintances and often, I am aghast by what I see. People do not realize how their Soul becomes their focus. I once had a client who was always complaining about this or that. Nothing satisfied her. She moaned about her partner's inability to please her, her boss's lack of courtesy, and numerous family members for various reasons. She was a hypochondriac and always concerned about her health. She visited many doctors, specialists, healers and so on for various health symptoms but nobody could help her. When I glimpsed her Soul, she looked like a sick and suffering hag with sunken eyes, and she had a gapping mouth like a hungry ghost. I also saw lacerations on her upper right shoulder where she complained of pain. I then told her that that incessant dissatisfaction with life has turned her ethereal body into a greedy hungry ghost. These dissatisfactions have imprinted on her Soul and manifested as the pain on her shoulder. The client seemed taken aback and became upset by what she felt was a lack of empathy on my part. She canceled her sessions and never came back. I suspect that she went in search for another healer who perhaps will not be able to heal her.

In another case, I had a client who described herself as a healer and astrologer and presented herself to be quite knowledgeable, but she criticized others and was very judgmental. She always used abstract concepts to prove her superior intellect with fancy astrological concepts. She name-dropped authors of the books she had read and criticized her boss for not being as smart as her. When I got a glimpse of her Soul, she appeared like a mischievous grotesque looking gargoyle. I confronted her by asking her what mischief she plans to commit by criticizing others. "You are up to no good, I said to her", "You act lofty, and all knowing but you need to learn to listen to others and communicate truthfully. Contemplate what I just said to you and change your ways as your Soul appears like a mischievous gargoyle."

I once had a young client who suffered from strange episodes that can only be described as a demonic oppression. Every expert I spoke with trivialized her strange episodes and gave me watered-down explanations for why this young lady would exhibit the following behaviors: wagging her tongue, running out to the streets, taking off her clothes, reporting extreme burning sensations up her tailbone and feet, hearing voices, changing her voice, and being unable to control her body during these episodes. She had been to doctors, church, curanderos, was hospitalized in inpatient psychiatric care and provided various medications but nothing seemed to work. She came to me out of a last resort having tried everything else to no avail.

Using hypnotherapy and energy healing, her symptoms began to reduce but they did not go away. She did not have any episodes after two hypnosis/energy work sessions, but they returned by the third month and the episodes seemed to last longer to where she could not keep her job or attend college.

One day, during her one of her sessions, the client began to weep as she stated: *"I feel so helpless. My episodes seem random, and nobody in my family understands what is happening to me.*

In that instant, I became angry, livid, and heartbroken for her. I did not want to believe that something outside of us, unseen could torment us this way. These emotions were so deep that it took me into an altered state, and I found myself in the underworld.

The Underworld

The sky was red, a dry desolate place, grim and dark. There were dark entities running everywhere, and it was utter chaos. As floating heads appeared looking down at me. Perplexed as to how I got in this realm, I knew to begin to pray and call forth the light. The energy of the place was so low that I started to get tired and weak.

In that moment, my astral body began to fade as the light of God enveloped me. In an instant, all the dark entities disappeared. Now appearing as the light, I continued to the interiors of this underworld dimension. Moving swiftly through tunnels and dark holes, as the light, I knew what I was doing and who I was looking for. I then stopped by an entrance and waited. Soon enough, an unsuspecting demonic looking entity walked out and as soon as it saw me, he screamed at the sight of the light, and I lunged at it. Stripping it of its powers, I relieved him of his ability to oppress my client.

This event sent a clear message to the underworld for they have known not to usurp the will of God. Demons and evil spirits have a right to exist as with all humans and lifeforms in the universe. God has given the gift of free will to all. Everyone has a right to choose to be wicked, malicious, good or bad however, we will all play by the rules and follow the laws of God by respecting the free will of others. If someone tells us to leave them alone, we are best advised to comply.

When I came to, I was back in my office and with my client. She looked at me and smiled and we both knew she was free.

The Lessons Learned

We must be careful about becoming apathetic, indolent, and lazy during our journey to enlightenment. Many spiritual gurus on the internet do not understand that spirituality requires consistent refinement, and our work is never done. It is about using life's challenges to develop our consciousness and spiritual convictions. This experience gave me some insights; for one, enlightenment is not about sitting in bliss and only seeing love and light. It is also about supporting justice and enlightening entities in the depths of hell. Jesus went to hell to fight and defeat evil. The Buddha subdued Mara-the devil and Padmasambhava Guru Rinpoche subdued many demons.

This was another experience of the Light that changed my perception of what I am and what I am called to do- to bring darkness to light. My client would never be the same after this experience. Resolved to walk in spirit and resist all evil, she went on with her newly found spiritual realizations, stronger and more confident.

Divine Light reminds me repeatedly when I freak out about the evil things happening in the world that every challenge is an opportunity to upgrade and transfigure into the Christ consciousness.

In another experience, I had client who suffered from chaotic and abusive relationships. For some strange reason, she seemed to attract belligerent narcissists, including one that she married while he was in imprison serving time for drug related offenses. As she cried in my office about yet another badly behaving boyfriend, I asked why she kept getting entangled in bad relationships? Soon after asking, I heard the spirit of her father say to me:

Spirit of Father: *"She is looking for me. I am not any of these men."*

After I heard that, I asked the client if there was something about these men that reminded her of her father. She thought for a moment and said that it was the things they would say like – baby girl, how they will always take care of her and simple gestures that her father would make like caressing the back of neck and shoulders. Then I asked if any of these men knew about her relationship with her father. She told me that she often posted things on Facebook about her father and then it occurred to her that the current tumultuous relationship may have gotten some cues from her Facebook postings.

Spirit of Father Said: *"It's time to grow up."*

After hearing that, I asked the client if she may be coming off as desperate to these men. She said yes. The client reflected that she had returned to nursing school and not getting along with her mother, she often needed an escape and would spend time at her boyfriend's apartment.

The client inflected about how she was daddy's little girl, and he took care of her and always protected her. He was a cop and she never had to grow up, but he would tell her fondly that it's time to grow up.

Well then, I said to her, it is time to grow up. You have a way of attracting these men being good looking and appearing like a damsel in distress, but they soon realize that you are the one using them. We worked on a plan for her to go and get her own apartment and start paying bills like a grown up.

I had another client who came for her first appointment and the minute I looked at her, I felt fear and an airy feeling of an evil presence in the room. As I began conducting an initial assessment, she expressed obsessive homicidal thoughts that would not leave her mind and uncontrollable anger. As she said this, I got a vision of a little girl standing in front of the window and asked her to tell me when this issue began. She reflected that she had a traumatic childhood, growing up in the hood and seeing a lot of gang violence. I then told her that I saw her standing by a window. Eyes widen as she recalled a day when she was ten years old and saw a man shot dead and her stomach dropped. I then said to her, you have suffered a lot, but you are good, and you no longer want this pain. Are you ready to release it? and she said yes. In that moment, she felt her stomach tighten and then she let out a loud burped as an ugly grotesque looking energy flew out from behind her and out of my office.

It is not usual for me to sense the private thoughts of people either talking about me or thinking of me. Sometimes, clients' energies would walk into my office before they physically make it in and telepathically communicate their issues without realizing it. So, as soon as they physical walk in, I am responding to their issues.

There were times when it got overwhelming, especially when picking up on loud discordant shrieks of the collective unconscious. I prayed to the Holy Spirit to help me manage what felt like aggressive and abusive thoughts that people send out into the ethers and the Holy Spirit showed me a vision of a football game and I heard, play offense not defense and got the message! No longer wait for peoples' thoughts to be sent to me, but instead, I will send my thoughts to them and the entire collective.

Offensive play means being first at sending out thoughts and intentions and not seat there and wait for negative psychic attacks to be directed at you. We do not want to be at the defensive end of constant barrage of collective negative thoughts but to be proactive in sending positive thoughts as well.

Many people talk about empaths as if it were something so special when in fact, it is a code word for brownnosing. Getting into another person's feelings means to absorb and take on those feelings yourself. Children often do it out of love for their parents and they become empaths later in life. They absorb their parent's negative emotions to help the parent feel better and lessen abusive behavior. Empaths learn early on, how to read and navigate other people's emotions to determine their own safety around others. I have found many of these empaths may take on narcissist traits owing to their need to get into other people's fields for information, not because they care about the other but for to meet their own needs. Many people out there do not have a peaceful mind, so why would you care what they think unless you care so much about your image and not necessarily about others. A true empath rises above the emotional complexities of others to get to the energy behind their energy, to the core of their being, their true desires and root causes. A person can have depression or be behaving badly but be good at their core and a person can seem calm and positive on the exterior and be evil inside.

People do not understand how what they put attention and focus on becomes them. Not many people can see their true self but if and once they do, they can break their patterns and change the trajectory of their Soul. None of these clients physically look like gargoyles or hags on the contrary, they are quite good-looking people. Our physical body is a good cover for the Soul but once we cross over after death, we will become our focus. Once you understand that your physical life is a process of becoming what you will be on the other side and where you go, you will be more mindful about what you focus on. God does not send anyone to hell; people go to the place or dimension most aligned with what they have made of themselves. If you are a person hyper focused on materialism and less on your Soul, then on the other side you will appear poor and miserable because whereas your physical life was rich, your afterlife will be poor. The divine law in our physical reality is the law of choice. Every minute of each day, we are making a choice about our eternal body. This is a message the churches gave but it was not properly explained and the money making "law of attraction "teachers will not tell you that this divine law takes effect on the other side when we end up in a reality that matches our appearance. On the other side, the wicked live with the wicked in the wicked realm and the good live in a good place with good people. Once on the other side, change becomes difficult without divine intervention.

Scientists and philosophers are not likely to understand why humans are here on the planet because they deny the existence of life on the other side. A famous philosopher once called humans useless eaters but on the contrary, humans are the best this planet has to offer but there is still yet more development, and it is at the level of consciousness. You will become useless if you do not take ownership of your mind and realize this is where the next level of human development exists.

The spiritualists tell us that we will reap what we sow in physical life which is most certainly not always the case. You may get your hands burnt in the fire as a repercussion for an unwise decision, but the real reaping occurs on the other side after we die. If you look at life solely from the perspective of a scientist, then physical life will appear utterly meaningless and if you look at life solely from the perspectives of spiritualists without logic, then spirituality will become meaningless also. This is why true integration is key to furthering human evolution.

CHAPTER 14

The Art of Practice & Cultivation

Time and again, I have sought to distinguish between the concepts of practice and cultivation as two necessary and distinct features for enlightenment. By clarifying these terms, the reader can understand these two concepts and understand why we do not feel progress by prayer, meditation, or yoga practice alone.

What is Practice?

Practices are various activities religions and spiritual groups employ to clarify attention and prepare the body, mind, and energy systems. Many of us have been exposed to various spiritual practices. They include prayer, reading the Bible, going to church, singing praise and worship songs, chanting, yoga, meditation, chi gong, darshans, shamanic practices, and more. There are so many beautiful practices around the world rich in bringing attention to mind, body, and Soul. We must engage in practice daily as it is the first step for raising one's vibration and achieving order and discipline in one's life. These activities put the body and mind in a receptive mode and help maintain one's vibration.

Today, cultures are becoming a melting pot, and people can happily engage in any practice they desire so long as they understand why these practices are done and what one should expect to gain from them. I feel that practices must be lifelong, for throughout life, we must consistently prepare and cleanse our energy systems. Energetic pollutants are around us. With technology, our minds become inundated with toxic thoughts in the media and all around us. People are operating in fear and are affected when we do not get our lives in order and observe discipline through practice.

I have used different practices over the years. To me, it is like going to the gym and trying new machines to work and strengthen the muscles of the body. Similarly, practices strengthen the mind and bring about focus. Without meditation, for instance, the mind will keep collecting unpleasant rubbish from childhood to the present day. The mind is a sponge, and even things we are not cognitively aware of are collected by our subconscious mind. The mind is filled with all types of trash percolating up into one's thoughts and causing disruptions in our emotions, behaviors, and actions.

The mind collects many false beliefs and emotions, and they must be sorted through practice. The mind will weaken over time with constant use and no chance to power it down and re-boot. The body's energy system will become clogged up with energetic toxins from the environment. People wonder why they have negative thoughts that will not leave their minds, and they do not realize that it is due to toxins and energetic attachments in their vibration. Practice requires that we keep our energy system clean by washing the body, mind, and Soul and paying closer attention to our relationships, interactions, and thoughts.

I wish that when human society wakes up, it will recreate its systems to help children develop a good balance between disciplined, spontaneity and creativity. Practice must be carefully embedded in our daily lives, but it is difficult to do when life is chaotic.

What is Cultivation?

Our soul lives forever but our body is temporary; thus, our soul is the real us. We must pledge that we want to do good for our soul, like giving love and service to others as it helps our soul. When we do bad, our soul is responsible and must pay for it later. Our mind is a partial copy of our soul with the same characteristics but grows independently. Our soul can guide our mind, but our mind is in control. As we develop our consciousness, the mind communicates with the soul more.

CHAPTER 14

Every Soul incarnates on the planet for the purpose of developing its enlightenment quality. Cultivation aims directly at people's hearts to develop true spiritual convictions that will feed and develop consciousness, it is the key to an illumined mind. Cultivation includes the development of virtue (a white substance) and transformation of karma (a black substance). We all have a proportion of good and bad karma. Bad karma is about 1.5 times more important than good karma. Good and bad karma do not cancel out. Total good karma is mostly used to give you a higher quality reality or good life, so compare your life with everyone on Earth, not just those around you. Your proportion of bad karma will determine if you qualify to enter the gates of heaven. The more light you have the more likely you will graduate from earth and proceed to heaven. If people really understood this, they would not be wasting valuable time on silly material things.

Cultivation is the abandonment of evil, ordinary human desires and attachments, and the ability to forego the tough hardships to discharge bad karma and increase good karma. We get scored weekly and throughout our daily lives so I suggest we evaluate our lives and clean it up to where we can accumulate good karma. You can pretend to be performing good karma but if you are doing it for fame or recognition, it will not affect good karma but rather the opposite. As mentioned, earth is a school, and a serious one at that.

Many of us miss the mark on cultivation because, unfortunately, cultivation is purely an individual act, and it cannot be impacted or sold. It cannot be turned into a business where people go and pay for a service and automatically achieve enlightenment. It cannot be attained by reading a book and feeling good, watching a few podcasts here and there, or attending an ashram or spiritual retreat.

Cultivation is the real heart of spiritual practice. A person can meditate, or become a pastor or spiritual world leader, but without a thorough understanding of cultivation they may not achieve enlightenment in this lifetime. Their vibration will not move an inch, and they will then cross over from death and become stuck in the mental planes because, in all their spiritual practice, they did not develop true spiritual convictions or transform their suffering into unconditional love. Everybody wants to live a rich and easy life, but this will not motivate us to cultivate. We will then become lazy, and the Soul will become lethargic.

Two examples of cultivation come from two stories that many know well. One is the story of Jesus, on the cross, nailed, beaten, and accused of blasphemy. In the throes of deep suffering, he said, "Forgive them, Father, for they know not what they do." In that moment, by that response, he transformed suffering into light and achieved resurrection. Another example is the Buddha. Mara tempted the Buddha by demanding that the Buddha prove that he had achieved enlightenment, and the Buddha responded by placing his hand on the earth and said, "The earth is my witness." The ground shook, and Mara was defeated.

Daily, we are tempted, challenged, and even tormented by evil and agents of evil. Sitting in our homes and pretending it is not happening will not help us cultivate true conviction. Not speaking up for the truth and calling a spade a spade for the sake of being nice will not help us transform our bad karma. Doing good for the sake of good, loving our neighbors as ourselves (the neighbor being fellow souls not physical bodies), claiming the truth of our being in the face of fear is one way to transform bad karma and increase the quality of our enlightenment.

There are those who think that complacency, reading a good book, and watching spiritual movies are enough to achieve enlightenment but do not realize that all they are doing is adding more garbage to their mind. Many of these movies are created with negative subliminal messaging that will not promote true conviction. True conviction happens in daily life, and we must be awake, present, and ready for the test of daily life experiences. The goal is to take a deep breath and remember love in the face of fear, to feel compassion for another who is not your family, to be honest about your ancestry's involvement in evil, to acknowledge your history of victimization, and to recognize your negative thoughts, with repentance and a resolve to atone and makeup for what we have done. You cannot confess and repent and then go back to doing the same things you repented for. You cannot steal from your neighbor, and then, apologize but refuse to give back what you stole, like in the case of slavery and discrimination. You can enjoy the spoils of privilege, but it will only last in this material life. Judgement awaits us on the other side where all is equalized- thank you God!

CHAPTER 15

Sacred Space

The same year I was called to begin a conscious spiritual journey, I simultaneously decided to follow my career path toward private practice. Part of my preparation was to create a sacred space for healing. My first thought was to find an inspirational painting, one that represented my highest ideals for healing. I did not know what I was looking for, but my budget narrowed down my search at an antique store in the heart of San Antonio.

As I walked into the store, an old lady from Bhutan greeted me. She welcomed me and encouraged me to browse through the store fill with various antiques of Asian art and artifacts. As I admired her many beautiful items, I stopped in front of a painting of a Buddha. I recalled the experience of euphoria; a rush of energy went through my spine, and I had a deep recognition of the image. Back then, I knew nothing of the Buddha. The woman noticed I froze in front of the painting and asked me if I was okay, I forced my head to turn in her direction and asked, "Who is that?" She replied, "The Buddha of course. This painting was done by monks in Tibet." She looked at me intensely and said, "You will teach about the Buddha." Due to my limited budget, I requested to place the painting on layaway, but the woman insisted I take the painting and pay her the rest later. She was preparing to close the store and trusted me to return with the rest of the money. I took the painting home still mesmerized by the artwork but also concerned about owing the woman her money. I went back as promised to give her the rest of her money, but the store was empty with a "for rent" sign out front. What shocked me even more was that I went to the neighboring store to ask about the antique store that was once next to them, but they looked at me like I was crazy and said that there had never been any such place and the space had been vacant for months.

Completely confused by what had happened, I took the painting to my office and kept it by my side through every session. I experienced many strange phenomena, but all pointed to a deep yearning to know the Buddha. At a time when the internet had just been introduced to society, there was limited information on the teachings of the Buddha and how to meditate but somehow, I knew how to meditate and learned forty chants with little practice. It felt like I knew these Buddha chants instinctively. It also felt that I was being taught and showed spiritual visions and could sense client's deeply rooted issues and guide them appropriately. I became even more interested in learning about the Buddha and studied Dzogchen, Tibetan Buddhism, the eight-fold path, the four noble truths, the middle way, and the Dharma. In Buddhism, one must have a mentor/teacher while on the enlightenment journey. I did not have a physical teacher, but I knew I was taught and guided but by whom, I had no idea.

CHAPTER 15

Years later, I received the blessing and opportunity to visit Bhutan, the home of the Guru Padmasambhava. I made it up the mountain to the temple of Guru Rinpoche and as I stood atop the temple, the same strange rush of energy I had experienced at the antique store happened again. Frozen in the temple, I finally realized who my teacher was all along, the guru from afar, Guru Rinpoche.

Much needs to be learned about the importance of holding sacred space in any institution that seeks to promote the health and well-being of people. The practice of holding sacred space means the ability to keep a healing space spiritually and energetically clean. Places and spaces hold memories from the beginning of time to the present. There have been accounts of shamans and spiritual people who can walk to a site, house, or geographical location and sense all the memories stored in that space. (Noll, 1985). Keeping a space clean for a healer is not just keeping the place physically clean and using lots of anti-bacterial; it also involves clearing the space of negative emotions and entities so that the space can support the healing of clients, which is extremely important to shamans and ancient healers.

Since I do a lot of energetic clearing in my office space, I always make sure that the energy of the space is returned to harmony and that all emotions and energies are raised in their vibrations and brought to peace, which is why many of my clients have noted how peaceful my space seems.

Ancient healers understood the need to undertake their healing journeys, which take years to perfect. The art of authenticity, meditation, self-awareness, and connecting with divine light and wisdom takes years of concentration, which is why the elders in ancient times were respected and revered. They have passed through various stages of spiritual development and have perfected these approaches. They can then teach this wisdom to the younger generations. In many instances, the Soul of the person may be advanced and already self-aware from past life development and can use those skill sets at an early age. Holding sacred space requires the right attitude, right attention, and right intention. It is not about developing a methodology but more about becoming whole and developing living relationships with the Cosmos.

To be a healer requires decades of conscious work. The greatest, most essential, easiest, fullest, and fastest pathway to becoming a healer requires us to enter and explore the pathway of healing within ourselves. By doing so, we map the pathway of assisting others in their process of healing. Holding sacred space is important for healing work and I have come to see how easy it is to contaminate a temple or healing ground. If a space is shared by several practitioners, it only takes one practitioner to bring the vibration of the space down. I have worked solo for these reasons because I found many practitioners to be extremely unaware and do not know what they are doing. It takes precision and focus to maintain sacred space daily. An important beginning step is intention and dedication of the space. If a practitioner starts a healing business on the secret premise to make money, then that business will not invite the light. A decision to dedicate the practice for the sake of good is the foundation of the healing space. It is like building an alter for God. The space will always be held in higher vibration so long as the practitioner reinstates his intentions and does not deviate from it.

Healing is dependent on the practitioners' vibrational state. For healing to occur in any setting, consider the following conditions:

- The practitioner's state of mind is trained to hold the right vibrational state within themselves.
- Observer and Observed Effect: The practitioners can connect with the self beyond thinking and doing and realize their true essence.
- The right state of mind is a pure state of mind, devoid of attachment.
- The practitioner can manipulate energy through pure intention, pure will, and pure thought.

- The healer can set the correct energy flow and hold a coherent state for prolonged periods.
- The one being healed must recognize the pure vibration that comes from God.
- The healer must be the instrument. Some machines may draw physical energy. However, this energy is not pure. If the healer uses a machine, then they must possess the ability to direct energy through the machine.
- The client must have a willingness to take responsibility for healing and doing the inner work.
- The tools may include such items as drums, bells, rattles, voice, chant, tuning forks, and crystal bowls, quantum healing tools and more.

With time, we can heal ourselves by treating beyond the physical body. We can heal the emotional, mental, and energy bodies and this is true holistic healing.

Geopathic Stress

Indigenous cultures around the world were generally nomadic and understood the concept of geopathic stress. Because they lived close to nature, they understood that earth has hotspot areas that have higher concentration of radiation than others. They can be best described as portals that go from earth's core to the surface to release radiation. To cool its core, earth has mini releases and big releases like volcanic eruptions and earthquakes. We know about the big releases, but we tend to ignore the little releases that a scattered throughout the earth. Think of it like invisible portals were earth releases radiation. When people lived close to earth, they can spot certain areas where trees don't grow as well as other areas or we may notice sickly and even cancerous trees. You can detect these hotspots called Geopathic stress by certain activities and lifeforms that tend to like geopathic stress. Reptiles, swarms, insects, bees, wasps, and felines thrive in geopathic stress areas whereas humans, birds and dogs don't do well in it.

According to research, earth resonates with an electromagnetic frequency of approximately 7.83Hz, which falls within the range of human brainwaves. Underground streams, water pipes, electricity grids, tunnels, railroads can distort the natural resonance of the Earth and therefore creating geopathic stress (Creightmore, 2012).

Today, we live in homes where builders do not account for geopathic stress and if you are unfortunate to live in one and even station your bed close to one, you could be setting yourself up for health issues like insomnia, migraines, blood disorders, depression, fatigue to name a few. Geopathic stress as a causal link to ill health is usually ignored as most people are unaware of its presence however, research indicates that Geopathic stress can undermine both the body's subtle energy system (the etheric body, chakras and meridians) and the body's electrical system (brain, heart and muscles), thus delaying healing and recovery. (Freshwater, 1997)

According to Creightmore, 2012, measurable physiological effects of geopathic stress include changes in the electrical polarity of the cell membrane with impeded ionisation across the cell wall; altered spin oscillation and proton resonance of protein molecules; faulty hydrogen bonding; disturbed mesenchyme base regulation, hormone balance and pH values. The most frequently found symptoms occurring at an early stage of exposure to geopathic stress, perhaps immediately upon moving to a new house, are sleep disturbances. The siting of a patient's bed seems to be the most important factor, after which come favorite chair, desk, room in which most working time is spent, and so forth. Pathological symptoms can include restlessness, difficulty in getting to sleep, excessive dreaming, excessively heavy sleep and sleep requirements, waking unrefreshed, cold or restless feet and legs in bed, asthma and respiratory difficulties at night, fatigue and lethargy, unexplained mood changes, aggression and depression.

Sick building syndrome (SBS)

Sick building syndrome (SBS) and building-related illnesses are omnipresent in modern high-rise buildings. The SBS is a complex spectrum of ill health symptoms, such as mucous membrane irritation, asthma, neurotoxic effects, gastrointestinal disturbance, skin dryness, sensitivity to odors that may appear among occupants in office and public buildings, schools and hospitals. Studies on large office buildings from USA, UK, Sweden, Finland, Japan, Germany, Canada, China, India, Netherlands, Malaysia, Taiwan, and Thailand, substantiate the occurrence of SBS phenomena. (Nick, 2018)

The World Health Organization estimates that 30% of offices, hotels, institutions and industrial premises have SBS causing: headaches, a tension between staff, lethargy, respiratory infection, dry skin and throat, eye symptoms, loss of concentration, depression, stress and fatigue, leading to a high rate of absenteeism, increased staff turnover and lowered morale. While electro-, micro-, and radio waves, electromagnetic pollution and chemical and air pollution are undoubtedly major factors, SBS is generally rooted in the presence of Sha streams under the property. (Franklin, 2022)

Haunted Houses

Unfortunately, haunted houses are a common phenomenon with Geopathic stress. This is because electromagnetic pollutions of Geopathic Stress emit low vibrations that tend to attract negative energies. Many of my clients would open up about strange occurrences in the home like seeing earth-bound spirits and negative entities, including poltergeist activity which are invariably tied to negative earth energies. One can invite Priests and psychics to clear the home but without addressing the issues with geopathic stress, nothing will be solved, and the spirits will simply return on a later date.

Combating Geopathic Stress

One of the ways I detect client's exposure to geopathic stress is through my initial assessment of their physiological and mental health symptoms. Common signs of geopathic stress include; symptoms began soon after moving into a home, or have several family members diagnosed with strange anomalies or they seemed to have a lot of arguing in the home, people fighting, plants not surviving, home doesn't stay clean no matter how hard they try, getting easily distracted at home, unable to complete simple tasks, strange pet illness and out of control pests like roaches, stray cats, bees and wasps. I also use the Nuvision technology to scan the energy field of the home to collaborate suspicions of geopathic stress. Nuvision works to broadcast higher frequencies, affirmations, and prayers to raise the vibration of the home and make it incompatible to lower energies. I also work with simple remedies that combines prayer, holy water, essential oils, aqua de Florida, and crystals to help balance the energies of the client's home.

I have worked with many sensitive and clairvoyant children who reported seeing ghosts and entities in the home, school and around certain individuals. They often present with behavior problems, psychiatric disorders such as Enuresis (repeated passing of urine in places other than the toilet), Encopresis (repeated passing of feces in places other than the toilet), anger control, attention deficit disorders and depression. Many of these children would have seen multiple therapists and visited inpatient psychiatric care before coming to see me as a last resort. By studying their astrological chart, I can determine their level of sensitivities and since children don't always have a good vocabulary to explain what is happening to their less sensitive parents, a spiritual psychotherapist can discern from the child's natal chart if they are being affected by the spiritual realms. Sensitive children know immediately if a therapist can be trusted or not and may not reveal the real reasons for their emotional and mental health issues.

Maintaining an energetically clean space is extremely important for overall wellbeing. Balancing opposing but complementary energies increase the flow of good energy to generate health, improved relationships, luck, and prosperity. There are many simple ways to keep the energy of your home clean from air flow to cleanliness of the space, reducing the use of electronics, positioning the home to attract sunlight, bright colors, and the use of the five natural elements of water, fire, metal, earth and air in decorating are some simple ways to maintain sacred space. Natural elements must be pure, for instance, holy water, natural salt, pure oils, use of fire, are examples of elements found in nature. Such elements must be pure and have not been mixed with chemicals or diluted with unnatural things. Most important of all, is prayer, maintaining harmony within the family relationships and visualizing a protective shield around our home. There is a reason why the ancients prayed before bed, asking the angels to watch over them in their sleep and protect the home from energetic invasions. We all know to lock our doors at night, but those locks will not protect from spiritual attacks. We must also be careful who we invite into our home because whatever is attached to them will enter our home with them. When we buy a new home or rent a place, be sure to pray and cleanse the home and know that some homes may require weeks if not months to cleanse depending on geopathic stress, the overall energy of the neighborhood, and the history of the home. Maintaining a daily ritual to cleanse and keep the vibration of the home is important for our overall wellbeing.

CHAPTER 16

Voice & Sound Healing Therapies

European colonialism drastically affected the lives and cultures of Indigenous peoples the world over by forcing radical changes to Indigenous forms of governance, trade, material culture, religious practices, and identity. To present day, the shackles of colonial oppression can be seen throughout the world as vast number of indigenous cultures are forced to adopt European languages and forget their own.

Growing up in the seventies' colonial era in Nigeria, children were being acculturated to learn the English language and adopt new ways. Before attending first grade, I spoke my native dialects of Ijebu and Yoruba. These languages are primarily vowel-sounding with powerful intonations. On the other hand, the English language is vibrationally low because most English words begin and end with consonants; in other words, the English language emphasis consonants and silences the vowels, the latter being the primordial sound of God. For example, try saying or thinking of the word "Help!"

What did you feel? When you said the word, does it vibrate through you?

Now, try saying the same word in Yoruba, "E gba mi o!"

There is a difference in both. The "gba" (pronounced ba with the 'g' in the throat) in E gba carries a vibration, whereas "help" falls flat. To further illustrate the truth about the deadened English language, here are some differences in intonation and the use of vowels in my indigenous Yoruba language:

ENGLISH	YORUBA
Bless You (Be Less You)	Ibukun
Spirit	Emi
God	Olodumare, Olorun (n is silent)
Love	Ife
Joy	Ayo
Boy	Okunri
Girl	Obiri
Wife	Iyawo
Husband	Oko
Reason	Intori
Head	Ori
Neck	Orun
Heaven	Orunmila
Pray	Gbadura
Leg	Ese
Disease	Iesan
Finger	Ika
Ear	Eti

Virtually all English words fall flat not unless the word is spoken with passion and deeper tonal voice can it affect the spiritual realms. The point is to project a greater vibration, so when uttering a word, the body feels the vibration, and all the chakras awaken. When people say that they feel their prayers are not being heard, this may be partly the reason.

When I pray in Yoruba, I feel the words vibrate through my body and the dimensions respond. Remember the spiritual realms see the real you not the physical you. They see your vibration, soul color and quality. Many western spiritualists talk about raising your vibration, but they don't tell you how to do that. Your voice is your instrument that can cut through the ethers. Just like we need water, a turbine and sound to generate electricity, you need your voice to vibrate your water body and electrify you, thereby raising your vibration.

Ancient languages avoid labeling. Their focus is on description and not names. For example, there is no name for a tree in Yoruba, but rather, there is a description of mythical folklores associated with trees. So, the translation of the tree is *Igi*, or *Idi Iroko*, which symbolizes the home of spiritual entities. Trees are revered in that part of the world as the home of the ancestors.

Within the beautiful Hindu and Buddhist religions, the universal word for peace is OM, so people who practice these religions are told that they should meditate while chanting this word. When chanted, the inner ears begin to vibrate, activating their pineal gland, located in the deep center of the brain, the third eye. Consistently chanting OM opens your chakras, thus allowing the person to awaken to higher consciousness, which is what language is supposed to do for humans. (Misra, 2014).

Now, saying 'OM' consistently would be unnecessary if the language one spoke in their everyday lives carried the same vibration as OM. But if the language is flat, more must be done to vibrate the voice.

Because I love tonal language, I enjoy chanting Buddhist mantras. I take the time to study the words and meaning and absorb it into my being and chant with heart and passion. When I do this, God comes through, and the vibration of love can be extended to fill an auditorium. People I have chanted to may not understand what I am saying but they can feel the energy that comes through.

Another fundamental difference between my native tongue and English, is that English emphasizes the "I" not doing. So, an English sentence often begins with "I," and doing, or others implicated in the doing, is secondary. In my native language, the emphasis is on describing a person, place or thing. So, a person's name is the description of their Soul's journey. A place is described, for instance, a major city in Nigeria called "Abeokuta," which means under the rock. Except for those places named by colonialist rulers back in the 1800s, traditional names provide descriptions so that the name describes the person, place, or thing.

Western education system teaches linear and separate concepts. For instance, math is taught separately and apart from science. We are then given abstract concepts and fake problems to solve as opposed to indigenous learning that engages the child within his or her environment. Learning how to cultivate the natural cycles of plants and animals and seeing things more from an interdependent perspective as opposed to separating life forms and not connecting how they support each other. One can look at the moon and learn the moon's math, wisdom, and history. So, learning is cyclical and useful for daily life. Children tell me in therapy that they don't like school and do not see how what they are learning will be useful for their future nor could it help them navigate life correctly. I cannot disagree with them but to encourage them to engage a healthy curiosity for learning for themselves by connecting more with nature.

Possibly, the English language increased ego complexes by the emphasis on the "I" statement. I am not knowledgeable about other ancient languages. Still, I can speak intimately about my personal experience as one who was adept in the ancient language and because I was keenly interested in finding commonality.

The moment I would say the word "I," things would appear separate from me, and my chest tightens. You may not notice this feeling if you were born into the language or culture of English, and you may not notice how the English language makes the vowel sounds inconspicuous and flattens them.

CHAPTER 16

Since most of us speak English around the world, efforts must be made to emphasize the vowels and to speak with passion and authenticity. You may also notice that there is a certain decorum to which English cultures require you to speak. Mainly, they want you to speak without passion, emotion, or intentionality behind the words. They love you to be this way in corporate America and even Asian cultures avoid show of emotionality in words. Without passion and intentionality behind your words, you are disconnected from the spirit realms. We are the word of God – the word is the activity of God and so words, and language are intricate to connecting to God and to your spiritual growth.

When I pray in English, I must admit that the process of connecting and manifesting takes a while longer than if I spoke in a language that has a tone that is either nasal, guttural, or vibrating through my inner ear, throat, or stomach. Many people do not know that it is the sound used while expressing a prayer that carries the power because our voice is vibration, and the vowels, along with intention, can cut through the dimensions.

Nearly all African languages are tonal and therefore their spiritual life is that much richer. Every time they speak, they send out a vibration, like telecommunication, to things unseen. Thus, communication with the inner world is easier, and response is quicker and clearer. And if you think about it, animals, children, and even people alike respond to the "tone" of your voice rather than what you've said. That undercurrent, that vibration, conveys what you mean without even saying the direct words.

With the explosion of western spiritual teachers, who are now claiming to be the experts on spirituality when their physical mechanisms are yet to be aligned. In order words, their vibration is not matching their clever and intellectual words. You can see there is a disconnect in other arenas of western society because, quite literally because people do not use their voice unless it has a judgment and their words do not match their feelings, thoughts, or intentions. It is virtually impossible to trust a person like that and it is for this very reasons people complain of communication issues in the relationships.

In my role as a psychotherapist, I have attempted to encourage clients to chant and use their voices, but people seem shy about this and feel their voices do not sound nice enough or they feel self-conscious. This is not about sounding like a famous musician; this is about using your natural voice to connect with God. It is about the feeling and sounds more so than the meaning. A person can say "bless you" but use a tone that means " F...you." Many Buddhist chants don't have meaning, but a sense and feeling is known about the vowel sounds like OM being recited. When we chant ancient mantras, you can feel an out of body experience, a sense of euphoria and loss of boundaries. You feel more connected to the people and the world around you and when this happens, something new can take place in the psyche, vibration, and body of a person.

Trauma specialists often allude to a loss of voice when speaking about the effects of traumas, but seldom is anything done to help the client regain their voice. I often encourage my clients to project their voice and words because it points to their self-confidence and empowerment. When we speak our truth, our voice reflects it.

Some of us are fortunate to be born in places where the vibration of the language we speak resonates high throughout the realms, making us more spiritual and granting us more access to unknown things unbeknownst to us. Note my emphasis is on sound rather than actual words.

Instead of doing psychedelic drugs, consider chanting as it also stimulates the emission of certain chemicals in the brain, such as endorphins, which give rise to heightened states of awareness, blissful calm, and other deep meditative states. Chanting is a far more sustainable method of brain stimulation and wellbeing than drugs and medications.

Authenticity is born when we use our voice to draw energy deep within us without directing it toward maintaining the current paradigms of control and alienation. We are not cognitively processing the words but focusing on the sound and intention behind them. This concept is difficult to explain to people whose only language is English because of the emphasis on meaning as opposed to the intention and feeling behind it. My native language, Ijebu, does not have as much vocabulary as the English language, and one word can mean multiple things, but people will know what you mean by the feelings you accompany with the word. For instance, in Yoruba, the word *Ajah*, means dog but also means path, and Jah means fight. Aja also belongs to a Yoruba Pantheon in the Orisa religion.

European colonialism drastically affected the lives and cultures of Indigenous peoples the world over. Today the legacy of colonialism can be seen in the abysmally low numbers of native speakers of various Indigenous languages. With the growing movement of technology and global connectedness, it is important that Indigenous groups continue to work to revive and save their languages and recognize the importance of language preservation.

Healing with Sound Therapies

We live in an age of technological and scientific advancement and with these so-called advancements, there an ever-increasing global pandemic of poor mental, physical, and emotional health. The discoveries of cutting-edge treatments have given rise to a myriad of terrible side-effects which has in turn reduced our lifespan and created new diseases, but despite this, the global population continues to hail science as the answer to all our problems. They say that sound healing is a pseudoscience, but science does not deny that the body responds to sound.

We can react negatively to certain sounds and respond positively to others. The question becomes, can sound heal diseases and better still prevent it?

The protons in our bodies have a positive charge, neutrons have a neutral charge, and electrons have a negative charge, and our atoms can carry a positive or a negative charge. The flow of electrons between atoms is what we call electricity. Since our bodies are huge masses of atoms, we can generate electricity. Scientific evidence shows that our nervous system sends "signals" to the brain, or synapses "firing," (Evans, 2022). Which is the brain telling our hands to contract around a door handle, for example. This is electricity carrying messages between point A and point B. With the advent of technological advancements, we have increasingly low frequencies sound and waves in the environment which interfaces with our own electrical system causing a nervous system fluctuation. More people are experiencing anxiety and depression and other health issues as a result. I am not saying to completely disengage from technology, but we have to raise our vibration to control and limit the health effects of electromagnetic emissions from technology.

Our physical body contains about 100 trillion cells and all cells are constantly emitting electricity and magnetic energy. (Ellinger, 2014) Like all matter around us, we are electromagnetic. Our brain emits electromagnetic waves. We have all types of machines, such as biofeedback machines, which can capture thermal conductivity and measure heart rate variability and other frequencies. We can identify inharmonious frequencies in the body and restore them to homeostasis. Our brain and heart energy can be detected through EEG and magnetocncephalography (MEG) devices.

Today, technological advancements have brought about subtle energy machines such as the Bio-Well and Aura imaging that can scan for thermal conductivity, measure heart rate variability and other frequencies and help measure signals of inharmonious frequencies in the body (Kent, 2020).

We can then treat these disharmonious frequencies by feeding in the proper vibrational signals to restore the system to homeostasis. Since ancient times, one method of vibrational healing has to do with the use of sound. Sound healing tools are used to vibrate the body to altered states. The healer is trained to use sacred instruments with pure intention to heal. The principles of sound, vibration, and energy flow as healing modalities have been taught in both the East and West.

Every wisdom tradition throughout the ages has used the tenets of vibration for healing and heightened states of consciousness. From Hermetic philosophers, Chinese acupuncturists, Hindu sages, Jewish cantors, Catholic mystics, shamans, and Buddhist monks, these spiritual leaders knew the profoundly powerful effects of vibration on the nervous system, whether human voice chanting specific words (mantras) or instruments creating resonant sounds. Sound is used in many ways:

- The use of mantra to entrain (draw along) and become attune.
- Talking with drums to move clients into a deep theta state before hypnosis.
- The use of a rattle, an ancient instrument, to neutralize energy. This instrument is used in African and Indigenous cultures around the world. By focusing on the sound of the rattle, it can serve to stop one's thoughts and bring mental energy to peace.
- Connecting sound frequencies to the body.
- The power of intentional voice in contacting and working with no ordinary reality

As a psychotherapist, I understand that emotion is a vibration. Trauma is the interference of vibration that blocks and keeps a client stuck, preventing the flow of energy. Sound can be used to heal and can also destroy. The intention must be clear. Practitioners must work on themselves and clear their blocks to maintain vibration powerful enough to shift the resonance of another.

CHAPTER 17

Case Studies

Case Study 1: Holistic Healing from Drug Addiction

L.C was a twenty-nine-year-old female, recently divorced, with two young children. She worked as a bartender and reported having experimented with methamphetamines since the age of eighteen. When the study began, L.C reported drinking an average of five beers daily for the last five years. She was also experiencing legal difficulties after a driving while intoxicated arrest. She denied being addicted to methamphetamine despite testing positive for the drug during legal proceedings. Because of the latter, she was referred to Kuadra Counseling, my practice, for the abuse and neglect of her children.

L.C presented herself with a depressed mood, even when she described her life as going well by following a daily routine, caring for her children, and maintaining a full-time job. She regularly suffered from feelings of sadness. She also reported feelings of guilt over the temporal loss of her children and her inability to maintain a steady income. She felt others did not understand her and were unsympathetic to her situation. She also blamed herself and had worries. During her sad periods, L.C felt useless, empty-headed, and drained and expressed that she felt like she did not want to get out of bed. She also, at times, expressed feelings of extreme anger toward herself. She felt overwhelmed, experienced racing thoughts, and slept four hours or less nightly.

L.C said she had a normal, full-term birth and was of average weight at birth. There were no hospitalizations, complications, or medical issues at the time of her birth; she was an only child born to a military family. She described her relationship with her father as often confrontational. L.C reported that her father was quick-tempered and often yelled, showed little to no emotion toward her, and never said, "I love you."

L.C reported feeling like she was always "walking on eggshells." She reported feeling scared most of the time. She felt emotionally neglected by her father, who deployed several times during her teenage years. However, L.C had a bonded relationship with her mother, who was more emotionally available and encouraged education, religion, and ethical values. She recalled a good relationship with her mother.

L.C reported no other significant relationships. She also did not recall any significant early childhood hurts, traumas, or early medical or developmental issues, except for being frequently teased in elementary school for her hair color.

L.C does recall feeling withdrawn and extremely shy, with difficulty concentrating and completing tasks. She was raised in the Methodist faith, and that, along with the military culture, meant she had an environment with high expectations of religious faith and values. At the time of her assessment, L.C reported no current religious affiliations but had an interest in incorporating a balanced spiritual life. L.C also denied having a past diagnosis or psychiatric history, a history of hospitalizations, suicidal attempts, and a family history of psychiatric disorders. She also reported no adult traumas.

Session 1: Initial Visit and Consultation

At the first visit, I completed a psychological evaluation and an initial mental health assessment. L.C consented to explore holistic treatment using Reiki, hypnotherapy, and the aura imaging biofeedback WinAura Star machine. The first aura reading was taken, and the following aura color impressions were noted: deep red aura and a gray-colored mass over the outer aura. (See Figure 1 below). Her Reiki chakras indicated no movement or activation. L.C's reading was high on the emotional meter without any movement in the meridian points. Based on the case presentation, the treatment plan included developing a system to reduce racing thoughts, depression, feelings of guilt, and lack of sleep while promoting healthy coping skills.

The deep red with gray aura colors with inactivated chakras correlated with L.Cs' periodic feelings of imbalance, out of sorts, and stress. She may have been holding onto anger and experiencing emotional turmoil. It also indicated a lack of sleep and common psychological symptoms of an unbalanced root chakra: loneliness, insecurities, feeling ungrounded, unconfident, abandoned, indecisive, depressed, anxious, and having addictions, phobias, or obsessions.

L.C expressed shock and dismay at the appearance of her aura. Per the aura machine guidelines, she was consulted on how the root chakra and red aura are often associated with the connection to the earth, survival, health, abundance, family, passion, and moving forward in life. When the root (base) chakra becomes unbalanced, a person may feel stuck. The individual may feel unable to move forward in life and ungrounded with a depleting sense of self. There may have been an association between the aura/chakra reading and the major events in L.C's life, such as legal problems from driving while intoxicated, family problems that resulted in her children being removed from her care, and a recent divorce. The blockage in the root chakra prevents the release of grief, guilt, and sadness. It contributes to the inability to move forward, preventing her from following her destiny.

L.C was consulted on the use of Reiki healing and hypnotherapy, along with ongoing care for balancing, opening, and maintaining the root/base chakra.

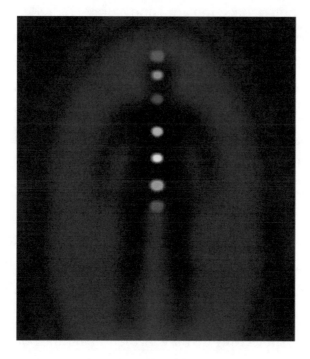

Figure 1. L.C's biofeedback WinAura Star reading during the first session.

Session 2: Hypnotherapy and Reiki healing

The second session took place one full week after the first. L.C reported that she had felt immense guilt in the past week, which may have contributed to her feelings of depression. As the practitioner, I developed a treatment goal with my client that included identifying healthy coping skills, improving her general well-being, and maintaining a positive outlook on life. L.C wanted to be mentally stronger, eliminate unhealthy behaviors, and stop irrational thinking.

After developing her treatment plan, L.C requested to begin her healing process by addressing her issue of guilt, releasing any energetic blocks, cleansing her aura, and activating her chakras. Hypnotherapy and Reiki modalities were used. After hypnosis, we discussed meditation exercises to reduce negative self-talk and improve self-confidence.

An aura reading was conducted after the healing session. (See Figure 2 below). L.C's aura appeared different from the first reading. Her colors changed from a muddy red color with a gray outline to a bright ruby red. The reading also showed that her chakras were activated which indicated a large surge of energy in her root, solar plexus, throat, and crown chakras.

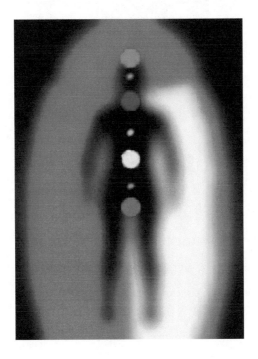

Figure 2. L.C's biofeedback WinAura Star reading after the second session.

Session 3: Additional Healing Modalities Used

During the third session, one week later, L.C noted a decline in negative self-talk, worry, and depression since her previous session. She reported optimism about the future. Another biofeedback WinAura Star reading was conducted. (See Figure 3 below). L.C expressed happiness in seeing her aura colors brighten to an orange/yellow color. The reading showed that her chakras had opened significantly. L.C was encouraged to use forgiveness mantras to help open her heart chakra and further her treatment.

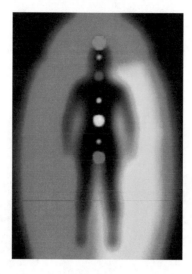

Figure 3. L.C's biofeedback WinAura Star reading after the third session.

Session 4: Talk Therapy and Power Animal Totems

During this session, L.C reported spending more time doing the things she used to enjoy, such as taking long walks, picking up trash in the park, and being in nature. After seeing a deer, she reported feeling connected to it. Because of that experience it was an opportunity to explore the significance of power animal totems, particularly the deer totem.

According to Andrews (2002), all things are connected and have significance in life, particularly nature. Totems are any natural objects that a person feels connected to through a phenomenon or energy (Andrews, 2002). Each plant, insect, and animal have its own wisdom, attributes, and instincts to help humans in times of need (Andrews, 2002). L.C shared how she also noticed feeling connected to people around her, and it brought her to tears when she realized the connectedness of all humans.

Since her third session, L.C reported a positive outlook regarding her financial situation and a loss of interest in associating with old friends who still consume alcohol. In addition, L.C stated she lost the urge to consume alcohol.

For her treatment, we discussed her continuing to find a healthy balance for enjoying life, which included continuing self-love and forgiveness work using the Ho'oponopono mantra. Ho'oponopono is an ancient Hawaiian practice of reconciliation and forgiveness. By using the phrases "I love you, I am sorry, please forgive me, thank you," one can find the divine within oneself, which helps one release and remove stress and problems in one's life (Vogel et al., 2005).

L.C was encouraged to continue exploring her feelings of connectedness to her spirituality. She stated past feelings of connectedness to earth spirits as a child, including having regular play with an imaginary friend.

When examining the power animal totem further with her, the porcupine animal was revealed in a guided meditation exercise, which suggested a need for her to reconnect with her innocence and creativity. A discussion of ways to do so ensued, where she revealed behaviors that indicated she had already begun doing so. At this point in the session, L.C reported feeling at peace and excited to begin her journey of self-discovery and stated a desire to continue therapy, which she felt helped her enormously.

At the end of the session, a biofeedback WinAura Star machine reading was taken. Her aura was a golden orange color, which expressed her cheerfulness, friendliness, and warmth for the world. The color shades expressed in her solar plexus showed a more creative and intellectually stimulating personality, suggesting L.C's energy and willingness to enjoy the sensual pleasures of life. See Figure 4 below.

Figure 4. L.C's WinAura Star reading after the fourth session.

Session 5: Psychotherapy for Relapse

L.C received a fifth session one full week later. During this session, the issue of relapse was explored. She reported running into an ex-boyfriend and having a few beers with him. L.C reported that this was the first time she consumed alcohol since her treatment began. She also reported continued use of the Ho'oponopono mantra and meditation despite the relapse. The biofeedback aura machine was used and revealed a change in her aura back to the deep red with a gray mass seen during her initial aura reading in session one. After the reading, L.C reported seeing the connection between her aura and her alcohol consumption.

L.C agreed to another hypnotherapy session with Reiki. L.C was led through a deep breathing exercise and progressive body relaxation, using drums to induce a deep hypnotic state. Through hypnosis, the practitioner introduced new suggestions focused on well-being and the elimination of alcohol consumption. L.C was then de-hypnotized, and L.C's experience was explored.

During the hypnotized state, L.C reported feeling light and deeply relaxed to the point of inability to move or feel her hands and seeing a light blue color. She recalled dreaming of being in a forest. She felt multiple people in the room even though L.C was alone with the practitioner during the session. The guilt was explored again, and L.C was encouraged to let go of any actions or regrets from the past and cultivate an attitude of forgiveness.

A second reading from the biofeedback aura machine was taken to explore L.C's aura changes after the session. Her aura color had changed from deep red to golden orange. See Figures 5a and 5b.

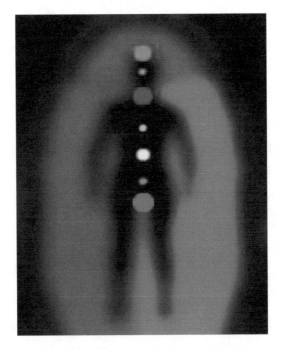

Figure 5a. L.C's WinAura Star reading before the fifth session.

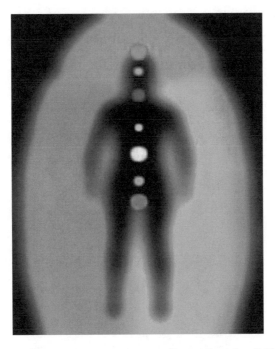

Figure 5b. L.C's WinAura Star reading after the fifth session.

Session 6: Quest for Deep Meaning

L.C was seen for her sixth session one full week later. She reported that she continued to work on her Ho'oponopono meditations and requested to have her spirit guide revealed to her. She reported experiencing moments of levity and feeling her heart chakra opening, indicated by her feeling a deep sense of self-acceptance. When asked what she had done differently since the last session, she reported feeling more in a good mood, being drawn to trees, and doing more things to care for herself, such as taking salt baths. She also reported feeling a deep need to change her job and thought seriously about becoming an eco-therapist. The remainder of the session was used to explore practical ways of achieving her goals.

An aura reading was conducted using the biofeedback machine. L.C's aura showed a yellow color on her left side and orange on her right. Her colors were explored using the biofeedback WinAura Star imaging manual (2016). According to the manual, the yellow represents joy, freedom, non-attachment, or freeing or releasing vital forces. The orange aura is uplifting and absorbing, inspiring, and/or a sign of power. When the orange becomes a strong point, it usually contributes to a yellow halo, which then becomes gold, indicating her thoughts are focused on spirituality. See Figure 6 below.

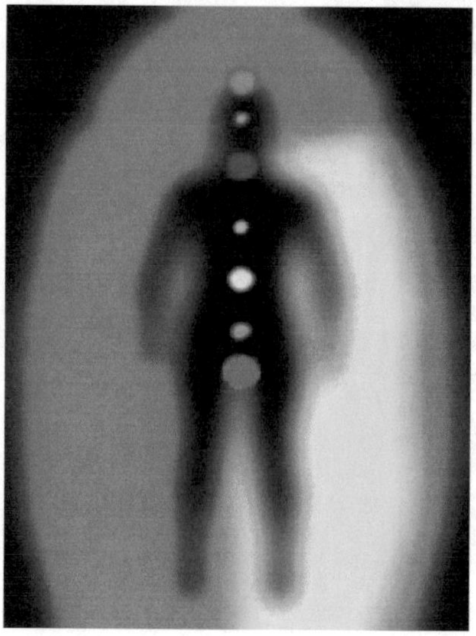

Figure 6. L.C's WinAura Star reading after the sixth session.

Session 7: Reality Reshaping Itself

L.C arrived for her session on time and reported that she had great news to share. During the last week, she reported that the state had recommended returning her kids. She also reported that she enrolled in a psychology program at a local community college and hoped to minor in eco-education. L.C reported that she has also begun making beaded jewelry again, something she used to enjoy doing. She reported that she has continued to meditate and feels positive about life. We explored her relationships and how she may best positively engage her family. She felt more accepting of others because she felt more acceptance of herself.

An aura reading was conducted, and her aura resonated a gold color, which, according to the WinAura Star manual (2016), symbolizes warmth, optimism, humor, and natural joy that inspires all those encountered. L.C expressed her excitement at the aura color, confirming that she felt hopeful and confident. See Figure 7 below.

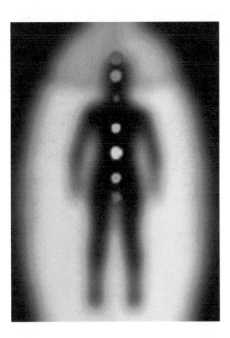

Figure 7. L.C's WinAura Star reading after the seventh session.

Session 8: Summary and Recap

For the final session, L.C was asked to complete a post-psychological assessment Symptom Checklist-90-SQL-90. L.C reported that she had not felt depressed or felt guilt during the last month. She reported feeling grateful for the sad events before being referred for psychotherapy, as it provided the catalyst for making meaningful changes in her life. She reported realizing that she could change her life by changing her thought process and identifying ways of caring for her mind, body, and spirit through meditation and positive thinking.

She reported realizing that since she meditated regularly, she no longer felt empty-headed and drained and slept an average of eight hours each night. She reported that she no longer felt angry with herself and had, most importantly, lost complete interest in alcohol and methamphetamine drug use.

She was encouraged to schedule monthly therapy sessions and engage in an Alcoholics Anonymous support group. An aura reading was conducted and showed a yellow color. (See Figure 8 below). According to the WinAura Star manual (2016), yellow auras represent happiness, confidence, and a sense of excitement and joy for the approaching future.

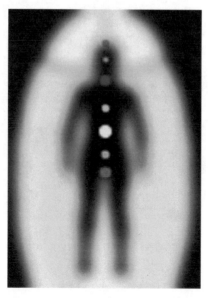

Figure 8. L.C's WinAura Star reading after the eight sessions

Discussion

Before the initial session and treatment, L.C experienced emotional abuse and neglect from one parent and felt victimized in all aspects of her life. She could not form positive, lasting relationships as an adult because of a lack of positive bonding or attachment with her parents.

When she was referred for treatment, L.C had not developed healthy coping skills and instead resorted to methamphetamine use since the age of eighteen and the consumption of five or more alcoholic beverages per day. L.C also initially minimized the extent of her drug use until seeing the biofeedback WinAura Star machine image reading of her aura and chakras. It was then that L.C became determined to improve her physical, spiritual, and mental health, which provided a healthier and more positive lifestyle.

The biofeedback WinAura Star machine is not necessarily a new tool for determining a person's emotional and mental state. Its application to digital energetics is groundbreaking for the natural health and wellness industries. However, this is a unique system that is employed as a multi-media-driven natural health tool for clients.

The aura imaging system uses a proprietary hand biosensor to compute an individual's temperature and electro-dermal details, the data of which is processed and then shown on a screen. The patented software creates aura images as a way of depicting a person's overall well-being and health. The readings include graphs and images to show characteristics of a person's mental, emotional, and physical energetic health, information can that provide solutions and data that can be monitored over time and help clients and practitioners develop a deeper understanding of a client's progress.

Visually understanding the metaphysical state of the body may also add to the healing experience and efficiency of treatments for clients. The biofeedback WinAura Star machine transforms the client's aura into a print or digital reading based on human energy, which can be extremely effective for validating aura data visually—specifically for chakra and aura changes to help those who are unable to see energy channels.

Aura devices may visually validate profound information for both clients and practitioners since they can track the nature of healing sessions over time. Both real-time and dynamic programs offer intense insight into the health and strength of auras and chakras. Clients can benefit from aura machines that display useful, easily interpreted data be tracked over time.

Using clinical intake information, psychological evaluation, talk therapy, Reiki healing, hypnotherapy, and the biofeedback WinAura Star imaging machine, practitioners can examine all facets of a client's situation. Together, this information may provide a holistic approach to treatment for addiction and mental health disorders. Future research is needed to explore Reiki, hypnotherapy, and other modalities, along with the use of a biofeedback aura imaging machine to explore changes in chakras and auras as participants progress through addiction treatment. Aura images provide visual self-feedback that may help drug and alcohol addicts recover and prevent relapses after treatment.

Case Study 2: Ghostly Illness

J.M., is a twenty-two-year-old female who was self-referred due to seven years of battling major depressive episodes and severe migraines. She had ended a romantic relationship with her boyfriend of two and half years and was devastated. Within the same month, her father had kicked her and her mother and two sisters out of the grandmother's home, and she had recently moved into an apartment with them. She worked as a cake decorator at a local grocery store.

At the time of her initial visit, J.M. reported that her depression had gotten worse and that she would be crying constantly. She had been experiencing severe headaches for seven years and felt nervous and shaky. Her presenting symptoms checklist on the SCL-90 were as follows:

She has trouble remembering things, has extremely low energy, has poor appetite, has pain in her lower back, worries too much about things, feels fearful, feels that people are unfriendly and unsympathetic, has trouble concentrating, feels hopeless about the future, suffers from gas nausea, and an upset stomach.

History

J.M. reported that her birth was normal with no pre-term complications. She had a normal bond with her parents and described herself as a "daddy's girl." Her family problems began when her family moved from Chicago to San Antonio and moved in with her paternal grandmother. At the time, J.M. was a happy and well-adjusted child. The home was a special gathering place for all her cousins and extended family. They would share holidays, birthdays, and celebrations in the home, but at the same time, disturbing things were happening in the home. Grandmother had a lengthy list of health problems ranging from eye problems to high blood pressure, severe allergies, irritable bowel, and diabetes.

Strange occurrences were happening in the home. On several occasions, she would hear footsteps upstairs even when nobody was there. Family members reported hearing footsteps as well. Sometimes, she would see a shadow of a man standing in the hallway. One day, she was talking to her mother, and suddenly, a wind rushed past them, pushed the door open, and went in the direction of her bedroom. She reported getting sick months later. She reported seeing the image of a male and female ghost in the mirror as she woke up one morning. The female ghost dressed in a cloak. The female presence stood in the middle of the room, watching her. As a twelve-year-old, she reported feeling scared for no reason. Sometimes, when she would have her back to the dining room, she would hear metal, like someone eating, and she would turn, but no one was there.

Other things would happen, like stuff falling over, things moving, and the sound of running footsteps. There was nothing violent, but it was uncomfortable. J.M. reported having dreams about the female ghost. The ghost became such a feature in the household that they would call her "Margaret." She did not know why she gave her that name, but the family later found out that a couple had died in the home, and the wife's name was Margaret. Sometimes, in the morning before school, she would hear whispers and screams in her ear to wake up.

One time, her little sister, aged four years old, asked if demons were real and started crying. Her sister reported seeing a black figure sitting in the room, and she would often talk to herself. Her other younger sister, aged two, reported seeing two men in her bedroom. Her mother believed it was the ghost of her grandfather.

Shortly after the family moved into the grandmother's home, her father was diagnosed with Lupus, and J.M. was diagnosed with encephalitis when she was twelve. Encephalitis is inflammation of the active tissues of the brain caused by an infection or an autoimmune response. The inflammation caused her brain to swell, causing severe headaches, stiff neck, sensitivity to light, and mental confusion. She reported that she was not able to maintain her balance, became dizzy, experienced loss of hand coordination, and eventually could not walk. None of the doctors she saw could ascertain the cause of the inflammation.

She went to see her regular doctor, and her vitals were normal. The only issue they found wrong was that her blood test indicated that she had low blood sugar. Her doctor recommended that she drink shakes and eat snacks to keep up her blood sugar, but nothing helped. Her mother then took her to an ear/nose and throat Doctor, and after a series of tests, all results came back normal. J.M. was taken to a neurologist, and he finally saw the problem. An EKG was done, and they found tumors. A spinal tap found the encephalitis. She was admitted to intensive care for one week and given steroids to reduce the swelling. She was told that since the swelling was caught early enough, there appeared to be no injuries to the brain. She continued to see her neurologist monthly, received physical therapy to walk again, was tested for speech therapy, and was given exam accommodations at her middle school. She also received lesson notes scince she could not write fast enough after the illness. J.M. reported developing migraines and severe allergies. Her neurologist thought that she was depressed and prescribed antidepressants. J.M. refused antidepressants and opted instead to attend counseling sessions but felt that the therapist did not pay attention to her.

J.M. reported that her migraines continued, and she started seeing an allergist. She took shots due to sensitivity and became allergic to a lot of stuff, including cats, mold, beef, soy, and a extensive list of other things. Prior to her illness, she had no sensitivities or allergies. Her allergies got better only a year ago, but the migraines have continued. She was able to walk and talk after physical therapy.

J.M. reported gaining weight from the steroids and experienced bullying as a result. She lost her friends due to illness. She finished her round of steroids and then lost weight. She resumed testing accommodations at school.

Family Health

As previously stated, her father was diagnosed with lupus a year after moving into Grandma's home, and she contracted encephalitis a few months after. She was in 7th grade at the time. Her younger sister had a mass on her thyroid and had surgery to remove it. She was just 13 years old. J.M. stated that her mother had a persistent case of eczema after moving into the house. Her younger sibling was later diagnosed with scoliosis at the age of ten. She complained of back discomfort, stomach pain, and gluteal burning. She was also diagnosed with irritable bowel syndrome, then one day it just stopped.

Social Life

J.M. reported feeling left out in high school and not feeling close to her friends. She joined her high school spirit squad but did not feel understood. She felt people did not want her around and never was invited to birthday parties.

She began dating right at the end of high school and dated her boyfriend for two and a half years. However, her boyfriend broke up with her when she was nineteen.

Religion

Her religion is Catholic.

Initial Diagnosis and Assessment: Diagnosis- Major Depressive Disorder residual effects from her encephalitis

Numerology: Numerology is calculated by adding a person's birth date until it rounds up to a single digit. For instance, a person born on 2/22/2002 will be calculated as 2+2+2+2+0+0+2+2=12 (3).

J.M. is in life path number eight. Also, her north node is in the twelfth house in Leo. Both eight Lifepath and Leo in the twelfth house are indications of a need to become empowered and assume a leadership role for herself and others in healing, facing her unconscious fears and the hidden realms, and accessing her spiritual healing abilities. To do this, she must gain a better understanding of the extent of her sensitivities and how the greater whole affects her spiritual path. She must develop inner strength in this lifetime. She may experience feelings of loneliness because of circumstances she must face alone. Her south node conjuncts her Uranus and Neptune, which indicates sensitivity to spiritual activities in her daily life and a past life that involved karmic imbalances in health and relationships. Her Chiron is in an anorectic node in Scorpio in the third house, indicating spiritual wounds from a past life with her community. Her Pluto is in the fourth house of Sagittarius, indicating hidden agendas and traumas in childhood. Her childhood indicates isolation and confusion. She must first face the truth that lies in her past, and the traumas of her ancestry and family of origin are the underlying causes of her illness.

Session 1: NuVision.

Question: What is the root cause of J.M.'s migraines and encephalitis, and what remedies and frequencies will heal her?

My client is negatively affected by Electromagnetic Interferences (J.M. confirmed that her family lived next to large electric towers).

J.M. is also negatively affected by Geopathic Stress. Geopathic stress is a disturbance in the earth's natural energies and magnetic field. These instabilities can either occur naturally, or actions of people can create them. It is a general term for energies coming from and surrounding the earth that can have an impact on people's health. It is argued that geopathic stress can undermine both the body's subtle energy system (the etheric body, chakras, and meridians) and the body's electrical system (brain, heart, and muscles), thus delaying healing and recovery (Freshwater, 1997).

Allergies can sometimes be rooted in stuck or unresolved emotions. Emotional Unsafety. Not feeling safe in life. Feeling attacked. A person may be negatively affected by a witchcraft spell from a past life. The NuVision holographic scaling system can scan the quantum field of a person and see what may be affecting the person.

- Anxiety-panic - weakness
- Cardiovascular stress due to Potassium deficiency
- Cardiovascular stress due to chocolate
- Mold - Aspergillus Versicolor

- Cardiovascular stress due to allergies
- Cardiovascular stress due to diet aids
- Lymph System Imbalance
- Hyperactive - Excess, inflamed, over-energy condition, reactive.

Solutions.

- Focus on diet (J.M. confirmed that she had a poor diet and consumed a lot of sugar).
- Use Q-Link (Q-Link is a device that helps to balance a person's energy field).
- Detox from heavy metal.
- Take Epsom salt baths.
- GG numbers: Grabovoi healing numbers.

Grabovoi codes, attributed to Grigori Grabovoi, are a unique and intriguing concept in numerology and energy healing. These codes encompass a combination of numbers believed to hold certain vibrational frequencies that can impact various aspects of life. By focusing on these number sequences, individuals claim to attract abundance, improved well-being, and even self-healing (Grabovoi, 2006).

Food Allergy 2841482, Heal Migraine 4851485, Heal Depression 514218857, Healing Energy 514891, Welfare, Joy 5148123

Session 2: Bio-Well.

J.M. stated that she did not feel any different but was hopeful that she was finally getting the help she needed. She reported using the GG numbers and purchased the Q-Link device. She reported that she realized that she may be extremely sensitive to her environment. Her mood and energy shifts depending on where she is. I asked her how she was currently feeling in my office, and she reported always feeling calm and peaceful, but that her feelings change when she leaves. Her Bio-well reading looks like my impressions, indicating she may be adopting the energy of others because of her inability to maintain a strong aura.

Session 3:

J.M. talked with her boyfriend, and they came to a resolution. They agreed to be friends, and she felt good about that. She noticed improvements in her relationship and resolutions to family conflicts.

Treatments.

J.M. started listening to GG numbers to improve her memory. The last few days, the client was doing the exercise the night before work and feeling better, not feeling cluttered in memory. She did not have to write stuff down. She was feeling more energy. She started wearing a Q-Link (a device that blocks electromagnetic influences on the energy field of a person. Q-Link has been the front-runner in the research and development of resonating frequency technologies and the scientific and popular discussion and discovery of subtle energy uses and applications for more than thirty years. The founders came of age as scientists attempted to understand and model the strange world of the quantum universe, which contained observations of natural phenomena that defied common sense - including probability clouds and the virtual emptiness of all matter).

J.M. reported feeling clearer in her head and not feeling cluttered or discordant in her thoughts. She continued going to bed late and had not noticed a change in her sleep patterns. Usually, when she woke up, she felt tired. I recommended that she explore wearing a Q-Link to sleep and research the use of fulvic acid, fish oil, daily vitamins, and probiotics. Her headaches improved within two weeks of following these recommendations. When she was at her grandmother's, she would wake up with migraines daily. At the time of the first visit, she was getting migraines about twice a week. At the first visit, she came in with a headache that persist for two days. She started listening to GG numbers for migraines and put the number under her pillow. She had not had any migraines doing this.

It was noted in this session that J.M.'s efforts to let go of her trauma become easier; she started journaling about it. Communication improved with her former boyfriend, and they both begun to talk about their sexual traumas openly. Her boyfriend revealed that his older sister sexually molested him. Therapy explored memories of physical violence in the home and how it affected her anxiety levels. She recalled lying on the couch with her dad, and he had his hands in her panties. He would constantly pat her and her sisters on the butt. She yelled at him to stop hitting her butt, but he would shrug it off as if it were her problem.

We explored ancestral traumas. J.M.'s grandparents were from Mexico, and there may have been involvement in brujería and witchcraft. She had been looking at her spirituality. She felt that she had been contacted by spirit guides in the past. She believed that they were positive. Her boyfriend had run away and was living under a bridge. She asked her guides to watch over him and give him clarity. She cried and explained that he was the only one she could talk to about her mental health. They had a trauma bond.

Treatments

- Multivitamins, Fulvic Acid, D3 5000, magnesium for better sleep and less anxiety.
- Take space away from boyfriend while you heal.
- Continue GG numbers.

Session 4:

The client reported a decrease in sensitivity to food. Before, anything she ate gave her an upset stomach. She was able to eat vegan-based food and felt no reaction. Previously, she would get an itchy throat, but when she got the Q-Link, she began to feel calm. Sometimes, she still felt clutter in her head and became easily distracted. She had not cried since the last session but had cried easily before therapy. She noticed that when she did not have the Q-Link, she felt burned out. When she wore it, she felt better. The depression had reduced. Her sleep remains the same. She reported migraines since the last session. She was still using the GG numbers. She reported strange premonition dreams. In the last week, my client had no dreams. She felt happier. During the session, we focused on distractions using hypnotherapy.

Hypnotherapy.

During hypnotherapy, J.M. saw a light that was yellow and orange. The light moved into her heart area. At the start of my background music, she immediately started seeing a mint green color in her mind. She continued seeing shades of green that looked like paint brushstrokes against a black canvas. She saw flashes of light and palm leaves waving in the wind. She felt calm and focused on her breathing.

J.M. expressed, "When you told me to imagine the color of healing, the green started to fade away into black & this purple/ indigo color began to rise until that was all I could see. I didn't see brush strokes or leaves as I did in the green, but more like blobs slowly floating through space, almost like a jellyfish."

"As you told me to imagine the color surrounding me, I felt like someone was comforting me I love. I felt like I was being held, and I felt peaceful. As you told me to imagine the color caressing the back of my neck, it felt like I was having my hair played with, which is something comforting/ soothing to me. I know my eyes were closed, but it felt like they were open, and I could look down at my feet and see the color surrounding me. You told me to make the color grow, and I could see my arms stretched to my sides (in my mind) as I let the color expand and I felt powerful and happy. Your voice started sounding further and further away as I imagined the color surrounding me. I heard you say that I didn't have to listen to the words you were saying, and I could let my mind wander because my subconscious would take in the information and that made me feel better. The first time we tried hypnosis, I was trying very hard to focus on everything that you said. As my mind wandered, I just continued to see the blobs of that purple color and feel peace."

"I began to feel like I couldn't move, but it wasn't a heavy feeling like when you're falling asleep; it was a feeling of weightlessness like I was floating in space and nothing else mattered. I heard you tell me to imagine myself sitting by a stream of water, and I began to imagine it, but I couldn't see the water as if it was in front of me, but I saw it like I was watching a video of myself. I saw myself sitting in an open field in a forest. Wildflowers were blooming, bees and butterflies everywhere. I sat in front of this stream of water wearing a white dress and a flower crown and I turned to look at myself. I was happy, my hair was long again, and I turned back to the stream of water. It didn't look exactly like me, but I knew that it was me. I felt like I was floating still, and I could feel myself slowly tipping backward, but when I opened my eyes, I was lying completely flat. I didn't see the bright orb of white light like I did the first session, but on Tuesday or Wednesday, I was lying on the floor in my living room just scrolling on my phone and on the right side of my face, I saw a bright flash and I could tell that it was in my mind's eye and I thought to myself 'Oh there's the light again. Then I saw another flash and thought well maybe my sister is behind me taking pictures, so I turned around and she wasn't there. The only other person in the room with me was my mom, who was sitting in front of me to my left."

Session 5:

J.M. reported feeling more energized, focused, and confident. Despite increasing demands at work, she had been able to stay focused, a sharp contrast from the past when she would get consistent migraines, feel overwhelmed, and be unable to remember things. She reported rekindling her relationship with her ex-boyfriend but insisted that she maintain boundaries and not lose sight of her self-healing. Her father developed skin cancer, and she felt able to detach from the myriad of problems that seemed to percolate in her former home. When asked what she would like to focus on, J.M. reported having a strange dream. She had a recurring theme about being in a car and driving fast or out of control. In this dream, she was driving, and the car started to make a strange sound, so she slowed down and got off the road. The car started falling, breaking into pieces, and its parts flew into the air. Due to these dreams, she had anxiety about driving when awake.

My intuition and experience with dream interpretation tells me that to the Soul, a car is a container and medium of movement, so it makes sense that a car in a dream would symbolize the physical body. We then engaged her Soul through muscle testing her body to get resolutions to the dream. To do this, we began aligning the energies of the body by crossing the left leg over the right leg, crossing the right hand over the left, putting the tongue in the ridge of the mouth, and taking deep breaths. I used my dowser to indicate when the energy was aligned, which took about one minute. Then I asked J.M. to stand underneath a selenite wand, which ensured that there would be no unhelpful energetic interference. I then asked J.M. to ask her body to give her a yes response. Her body then moved backward, and then her body moved forward for no.

I then asked her to repeat, "It is in my best and highest interest to treat my traumas today." Her body responded by saying yes.

We then asked her body the following questions: May I know the meaning of the car dream?

Body replied: Yes.

Was this a good dream?

Body replied: No.

Was this a bad dream?

Body replied: Yes.

Was the dream about my fears?

Body replied: Yes.

Was I afraid of something during the day?

Body replied: No.

Was it about releasing fear?

Body replied: Yes.

Does the car represent the physical body?

Body replied: Yes.

Does the car part flying away represent the body breaking down due to fear?

Body replied: Yes.

Can she replace fear with confidence using the affirmations and GG numbers?

Body replied: Yes.

Discussion

The client sought my services after a series of health issues that included migraines, encephalitis, relationship problems and childhood traumas. After receiving several therapy sessions that included hypnotherapy, quantum healing and talk therapy, her migraines had significantly improved. I was concerned about issues with geopathic stress as it prevented health improvements and an attractor for ghosts. Her parents had separated and moved into another home, which aided her recovery from the home environment. She reported feeling better in the new home and had not sensed the ghost.

Case Study 3: Clairvoyant Autistic

P.G. is an eighteen-year-old female who came in with her mother for individual therapy. She appeared quite shy and withdrawn on her first visit. Mom seemed to speak for her the entire time. The mother reported that P.G. has been nonverbal with strangers her entire life. She is a recluse and avoids being in crowds or interacting with people in general. P.G. is reported as having extremely poor social skills. She did not make friends in elementary, middle, or high school. She did have one friend who ended up becoming abusive and controlling. P.G. got poor grades but never tested by the school for learning disorders. She was quiet, and teachers liked her that way. She avoided making eye contact and reported symptoms of depression and anxiety.

P.G. had a previous diagnosis of major depressive disorder and was taking antidepressants. She reported little to no improvements with the medications and stopped. In speaking with P.G. privately without her mother, P.G. described having auditory and visual hallucinations. When asked, she described seeing ghosts who had frequently tormented her since she was five years old. They were constantly in her ear, and she had difficulty focusing when people were talking to her. They would tell her not to listen, to kill herself, and often say that she was worthless. She reported fearing her closet and felt it looked like a door to a dark place. P.G. described seeing dark shadows in her home and around family members. They would whisper in her ear and make her agitated, angry, or depressed. She had difficulty falling or staying asleep, and when she slept, she had recurring nightmares of being tormented by monsters, chasing and sometimes killing her.

When asked about her diet, P.G. remarked she has always had an unhealthy diet. She consistently had sugar cravings, and being from a poor environment, her parents could not afford healthy, organic-based meals. Considering that her personality changed from the age of five, which is usually the age autism is first detected, I can see the correlation between childhood vaccinations and poor diet and its effects on her personality and mental capacity.

To pass time throughout her day, P.G. spent an unconscionable amount of time on video games. She seemed more agitated when she was not on them. She reported making friends on the games but would quickly regress into a mental breakdown, resulting in psychiatric hospitalization the moment there was a perceived sense of rejection by her friends. By her first visit, P.G. had been hospitalized a dozen times throughout her teen years. She had received various diagnoses of depression, anxiety, split personality disorder, and schizophrenia. Each hospitalization earned her a new drug or new dosage. Some of the medications caused additional symptoms like increased suicidal ideations, paranoia, migraines, extreme fatigue, and even worsening symptoms.

Despite reporting these complaints to her prescribers, they ignored them and offered increased dosages and a solution. The psychiatric care units were not all bad. There were other reasons P.G. would opt for inpatient care. In one session, P.G. revealed that she did not mind being admitted to inpatient psychiatric care because it felt more like a getaway. With improved amenities, swimming pools, games, and making new friends, P.G. felt there were advantages to being there. She did not have to deal with life, and she could devote more time to her feelings. Most importantly, she could have a better meal than the ones she received at home. When asked if the voices were present when she is inpatient, she reported yes, but they seem more pleased about her admission and tended to torment her less when admitted.

The human brain is very delicate, and nature has made incredible efforts via the construction of the skull to guard it. Scientists still do not fully understand the brain or the mechanisms of the mind. I suspected that P.G. might have pathogens and toxins in the brain, which can be due to various forms of vaccinations, poor diet, toxic foods, and psychotropic medications that may be affecting personality, thinking, and focus. Autism, schizophrenia, depression, and obsessive-compulsive disorder are either partially induced or worsened by foreign matters that make their way past the blood-brain barrier.

Traditional and naturopathic healthcare systems in the United States are now understanding the need for patients to detox heavy metals and parasites for general wellness.

At first glance, many would think that autism and detoxication have nothing to do with one another. However, it has been shown that kids with autism have impaired detoxification. Furthermore, one in six children has a neurodevelopmental disability. Elevated levels of pollution in the air, water, and land, along with increased use of chemicals, have had a detrimental effect on our children. (Kidd, 2002). Shockingly, only 1% of chemicals we use today have been safety tested (EcoWatch, 2015). Supporting detoxification through gentle methods can help kids with autism achieve greater health, better cognition, and improvements in behavior.

What is Detoxification?

Detoxification is the metabolic process of changing toxins into less toxic or more readily available excretable substances. Detoxification interventions are aimed at supporting the body's ability to restore balance. First, the detoxification process begins in the cell, goes to the liver, and finally, to an organ for excretion. Fat-soluble toxins enter the liver, go through two distinct phases of the liver, and exit the liver as water-soluble waste products. From here, they are eliminated from the body via the gall bladder to the bile before the stool. Similarly, toxins are sent to the kidneys to be excreted in the urine.

I suggested to P.G. that she change her diet and investigate methods of eliminating toxins and heavy metals from her body in order to start the healing process. As I spoke with P.G.'s mother about heavy metal toxins, she recounted a time when P.G. was four years old and taken in for a dental appointment. The dentist strapped her down, took out all her front teeth, and replaced them with silver metal teeth. A high majority of children suffer from ADHD due to toxic exposures. In addition to detoxification and a change in diet, P.G. received eight sessions of spiritual hypnotherapy and energy healing. By touching the acupressure points of her head and body, I could help bring balance to her energy field through the influence of my energy field.

Remember that we are electrical and energy beings, and easily influenced by our environment and other people's energies. Stronger energy always influences weaker energy. For example, a person who is strong in depression will influence those around her into depression if those around her are not strong in their vibration. Likewise, a person whose vibration is high in healing, peace, and enlightenment can influence the vibration of another person into homeostasis, which is not that easy to do. Many so-called healers have mixed light and dark, and the outcome of the session may be skewed. Only a completely high spiritual person can affect healing upon another. Because most people cannot see their spectrum of light or others, many healers claim the title but are not healing or helping and doing more harm.

Since the foundation of healthcare systems in the United States has become more profit-driven, authenticity has become more lacking. People would rather trust titles, charisma, and looks. It is from the knowledge of my energy that I can allow myself to be a doorway for healing, and it is from this that I work with P.G.

Presentation of Aura with Bio-Well Imaging at the initial visit

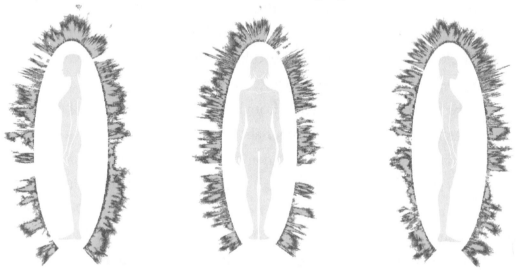

Assessment

P.G. presented with the autism spectrum even though she went through early school years undiagnosed. Children who do not behave disruptively and who do not perform below grade level appear to represent a large number of those who are not selected for additional testing. P.G. also presents with symptoms of schizophrenia, but it is not unusual for autistic children to be clairaudient and clairvoyant. The reason is that their aura fields—an invisible shell around us that individuates and protects us from outside elements and other people's thoughts are either broken or weak—exposes them to hearing subtle energy and discordant thoughts of people.

Treatment

I administered eight sessions of psychotherapy, hypnotherapy, and energy healing. Auditory noises slowly began to decrease by the first session, and P.G. reported experiencing more confidence in herself. In the second session, we explored her basic ego personality via her natal astrological chart, and there were several key findings. P.G. presented with strong conjuncts with Neptune, the moon, and Chiron in her fourth house, which was an indication that she tended toward being withdrawn, extremely distrustful of her emotions, and preferring to overthink things. Her home does not feel secure, and the subtle, ethereal realms tend to be heightened in her home environment, which is coupled with the chronic effects in the fourth house, making her insecure in groups. Having experienced the first trauma with a friend, she projects her fears of rejection toward her online friends and family members.

Given that her north node is in the sixth house of Pisces, this is where I will steer P.G. to focus on rationality, learn responsibility, and reduce her desire to escape into fantasy. She will learn to become grounded in realism and balance her idealism. The goal is for her to have discipline in her daily life and balance her sensitivities with other people's energies.

P.G. has a stellium in the tenth house in Leo, which can present as a need for approval and recognition and, on a shadow level, can present with anxieties over fears of what people think. The need for other people's approval and the fear of rejection is a source of anxiety and depression. Her chart shows that she demands positive attention from others, and the slightest inclination that someone is not being friendly sends her into a full-blown panic attack at school, resulting in her multiple hospitalizations. We explored the need for her to develop ways to build herself up emotionally by engaging in enjoyable activities, positive self-talk, and becoming more emotionally independent.

Her north node concerns guided subsequent sessions as we explored rationality, becoming grounded, and practicality. Hypnotherapy sessions provided inductions for relaxation, well-being suggestions, confidence, and stress management. As we developed her ego strength, the attachments and voices that caused disturbances in her thinking began to reduce. By this time, P.G. and her mother had decided to taper off her psychotropic medications. They had introduced a clean diet and detox remedies such as green vegetable juices, fewer carbohydrates, and a healthy protein diet.

We used the Aura with Bio-well after eight hypnotherapy and energy healing sessions.

Presentation of Aura with Bio-Well Imaging after 8 sessions

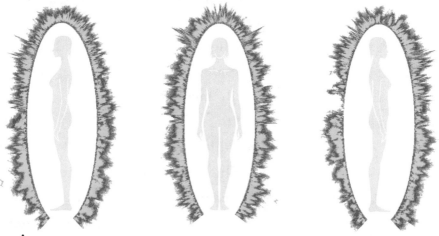

Discussion

I administered twelve sessions over eight months, continued to check in, and built P.G.'s personality and confidence. She reported that she no longer had intrusive thoughts or panic attacks. She reported having a more positive outlook and began making friends in daily life as opposed to just online friends. P.G. noticed she had more energy during the day, was sleeping throughout the night, and forbade any nightmares.

Case Study 4: Participant G.R.

G.R. is a thirty-nine-year-old single female. She is an active military personnel and has engaged in multiple tours of duty throughout her twenty-year military career. G.R. has had a series of mental health and chronic health issues for three years with no resolution prior to seeking services. She self-reported multiple diagnoses that include high blood pressure, executive dysfunction, polycystic ovarian syndrome, chronic pain, fibromyalgia, pre-diabetes, high cholesterol, depression, anxiety disorder, ADHD, carpal tunnel, and sciatica. G.R. was on twelve different pills for the various diagnoses but reported no improvements in her symptoms. Her symptoms included migraine headaches, blurred vision, fatigue, insomnia, poor memory, brain fog, and digestive issues.

G.R. denied a history of drugs or alcohol. However, she had a traumatic childhood, growing up in a very violent city in the United States. She has had to care for her mentally ill mother and schizophrenic sister since the age of eleven and reported living through multiple crises and traumatic situations with family and at work. G.R. reported traumatic experiences of racism and discrimination in the workplace, which has increased her stress levels and ability to heal in a toxic work environment. I offered her IMAET treatment sessions, and she agreed to try them.

Initial Impressions

G.R. has the negative personality of a martyr, which sabotages her healing process. Her energy and vitality are low due to her giving her energy away and not having healthy boundaries with others. She is an empath and affected by other people's pain. She learned at an early age to absorb other people's traumas into her energy field. She developed a behavior pattern of absorbing other people's issues—the main root cause of her own health issues.

Her NuVision scan (previously described) showed she had issues with low iron and thyroid hormone. Still, she refuted any medical diagnosis that pointed to her having thyroid issues, which were affecting her energy levels and sleep issues. Two months later, she found out from test results that she did, indeed, have thyroid issues.

Session 1

G.R. received information and education about how the IMAET worked. Although not intended to diagnose, it provides information about what resonated in her energy field and provided biofeedback to harmonize these issues. A harness was placed on G.R.'s forehead to scan her energy field. The first impressions on the scan were issues with hemoglobin, cholesterol, candida (yeast), and mold toxicity. She also received vitamin B brain balance as part of the SHOW method protocol. G.R. confirmed that she had been working in a mold-infested building and had a series of yeast infections. She also had a fungus overgrowth on her toe.

I put G.R. in a zero-gravity recliner chair with healing sounds during her feedback and encouraged her to relax and engage in meditation during her feedback session. I encouraged her to pay attention to any physiological changes that may occur after the feedback and throughout the week and be ready to report for the next week. I encourage participants to track their recovery and confirm if the IMAET sessions are working for them.

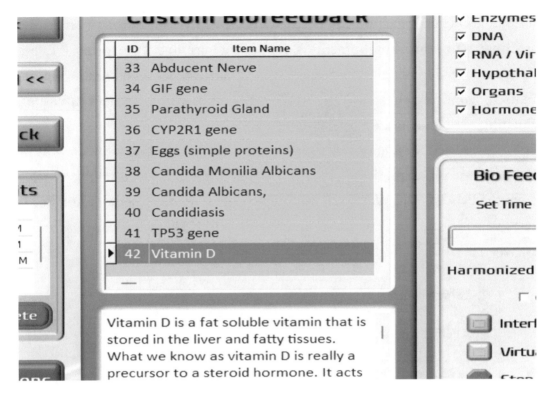

Figure 1. G.R.'s biofeedback IMAET reading during the first session.

Session 2

I saw G.R. a week later for her second session. I asked her if she experienced any issues or changes after the last biofeedback session. G.R. reported having a Herxheimer reaction. Specifically, she reported having body aches, headaches, increased hypertension, nausea, and feeling exhausted. Dhakal & Sbar (2023) define Jarisch Herxheimer reaction (JHR) as a transient clinical phenomenon that occurs in patients infected by spirochetes who undergo antibiotic treatment. It is simply an immune-system reaction to the endotoxins released when substantial amounts of pathogens are being killed off, and the body does not eliminate the toxins quickly enough. The symptoms do not indicate failure of the treatment; in fact, it is usually just the opposite. It indicates that parasites, fungi, viruses, bacteria, or other pathogens are killed off. The reaction can occur within twenty-four hours of antibiotic treatment for spirochete infections, including syphilis, leptospirosis, Lyme disease, and relapsing fever. HR usually manifests as fever, chills, rigors, nausea, vomiting, headache, tachycardia, hypotension, hyperventilation, flushing, myalgia, and exacerbation of skin lesions.

I conducted another IMAET session, including detoxification support of detox genes, inflammation, and lymphatic stimulation. Additional protocols from the IMAET SHOW method were included in the treatment basket. Feedback was repeated until all items in the treatment basket were harmonized to between 80-100%.

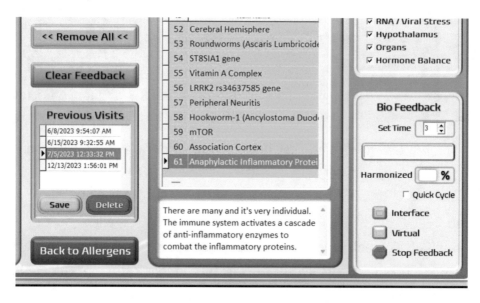

Figure 2. G.R.'s biofeedback IMAET reading during the second session.

Session 3

I saw G.R. a week later for her third session. I asked if she experienced any issues or changes after the last biofeedback session. G.R. reported that her blood pressure reduced to 103/69, the first time in years that her blood pressure was normalized. She also reported that her weight had reduced from 233 to 226 pounds. G.R. reported increased bowel movements from once a day to three times a day. She reported feeling more energy and motivation and has been more productive. When prompted about any negative symptoms, G.R. reported increased itchiness around the rectum and various parts of her skin. She stated, "I am sold on this treatment! I have not felt more energized or felt better until I began the IMAET treatment." G.R. received her third IMAET session, this time focusing on the lymphatic system. I encouraged her to pay attention to any emotional or physiological changes and report back at the next session.

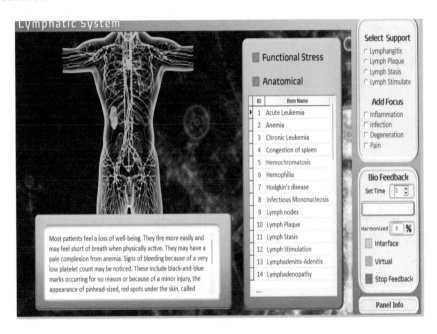

Figure 3. G.R.'s biofeedback IMAET reading during the third session.

Session 4

I saw G.R. a week later for her fourth session. I asked her if she experienced any issues or changes after the last biofeedback session. G.R. reported having migraines and spine and nerve issues. She reported that she had stopped taking her anti-depressant, ADHD medication, and sleep medication, which she was not advised to do. She felt she might be having withdrawal symptoms from stopping her medication. I advised her to always check with her doctor before making such a medical decision.

I gave G.R. another treatment of the IMAET and received a frequency sweep for a herniated disk and sympathetic and parasympathetic stim. These panels do not scan for problems but for feedback features. Muscle testing the client helps to determine if an item is too high or too low and what areas of the panel to focus on.

Session 5

I saw G.R. a week later for her fifth session. I asked if she experienced any issues or changes after the last biofeedback session. G.R. reported increased weight loss and more energy. She remained off her prescribed medication and confirmed that she had spoken to her doctor about not taking her medication. She informed them that she would prefer to go the alternative medicine route and would maintain her biofeedback sessions. G.R. requested to focus on her lymphatic system. She also received a detox foot bath.

Sessions 6-9

G.R. received weekly lymphatic system support to release the effects of inflammation, infection, lymph plaque, lymph stasis, lymph stimulation, congestion of the spleen, and lymphedema. She also received an ionic foot detox in conjunction with the IMAET treatment.

Figure 4. Before and After Photos of G.R. She had lost thirty-eight pounds by the end of the ninth session.

Discussion

G.R, came to therapy due to several health issues that included mental health and chronic pain. She received holistic therapies with the IMAET, talk therapy and quantum healing. G.R made significant improvements with maintaining stronger boundaries, managing stress levels, and no longer having back pains, increased energy and motivation and lost thirty-eight pounds.

Case Study 5: Participant C.S.

C.S., is a sixteen-year-old female with a history of anxiety, depression, and social skills problems. She was hospitalized for psychiatric care on multiple occasions due to attempted suicide and suicidal ideations and was subsequently diagnosed with schizophrenia. C.S.'s mother reported that C.S. was extremely paranoid, antisocial, and refused to interact with her peers at school. She had multiple personalities and alters.

C.S. was on a cocktail of six different medications but reported that she had noticed no improvement. She still had homicidal and suicidal thoughts. C.S. was failing in school and unable to concentrate or complete a semester without ending up in psychiatric care. On occasions C.S. would dress up like a five-year-old and regress in her behavior. At our first meeting, she never made eye contact and seemed easily agitated.

Due to the medications that she was taking, C.S. was diagnosed with kidney and liver issues and gained forty pounds. Although the medications were not helping and causing more problems, C.S.'s mother said she couldn't stop giving her the medications as the doctors threatened her that they would call child services if she stopped the medications.

The initial diagnostic impression was autism. C.S. may have been incorrectly misdiagnosed, which is why none of her meds or previous therapies have worked. Several counselors dismissed her from treatment because they couldn't get her to say anything. Since there were little to no treatments available to sixteen-year-old autistic patients, I offered to assist with utilizing the IMAET biofeedback sessions. The mother agreed, and I provided a treatment plan that would incorporate hypnotherapy, energy healing, and the IMAET biofeedback.

Initial NuVision impressions indicated medical malpractice, polarity imbalance, hereditary parasite information stress, pituitary imbalance, low bile production, Epstein-Barr virus, VCA antibody, and gut infection.

Assessment

From her astrological chart, C.S. had a past life experience of alienation owing to her south note in Virgo in the twelfth house. She has a Jupiter in Scorpio in the first house, making her deeply focused on herself and needing attention from others. Her charts also make her very introverted, intuitive, and prone to escapism. She feels intense insecurity around groups and reacts negatively to perceived forms of rejection. C.S. reported having an innate distrust of emotions and reported not being able to express her feelings. A major spiritual lesson for her would be to let go of the desire to escape into fantasy and develop a productive life.

C.S. received three sessions of hypnotherapy and three Reiki healing sessions. Healing focused on general well-being, cognitive restructuring, self-confidence, and releasing trapped emotions. Energy healing focused on clearing her energy field and restoring her auric field.

IMAET Biofeedback Sessions

C.S. received brain harmonic balance brain wave tuning.

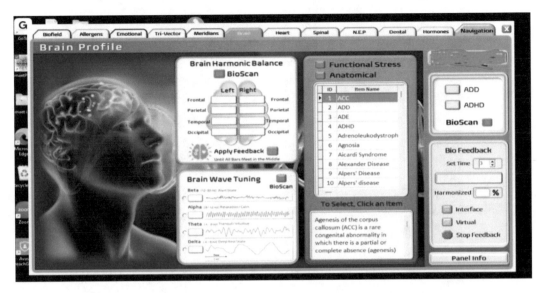

Figure 1: Emotional Panel scan and clearing of the energy field

Discussion

In total, C.S. received twenty-eight sessions that included psycho-therapy, energy, Reiki healing, hypnotherapy, and biofeedback therapies. By the end of her sessions, she had lost fifty pounds and was completely off her medications. She was not hospitalized for suicidal ideations or attempts during her therapy and treatment at Kuadra Counseling. C.S. became more social. She was expressing herself and making new friends. She even attended a school prom and formed close relationships. C.S. will be graduating high school plans to attend a nearby college to become a veterinarian.

C.S Before Treatment   After Treatment

Feedback from the Parent of C.S

"There are so many illnesses in this world. Many have treatment plans with long successful rates that all doctors agree to use. However, in the mental health realm, there are so many factors that intertwine that need to be attended to that makes it hard to cure someone struggling with mental health, in my opinion. The mind can be like Pandora's box. You need to really find a treatment that deeply investigates what's going on inside All of You.

"My daughter started seriously struggling with anxiety, paranoia, and depression when she was fourteen years old. She was taken into mental hospitals seven times in one year. The most she could do in school was three hours before I would get a call to pick her up. Several doctors/psychiatrists evaluated her throughout the two years. Each doctor had his opinion on the diagnosis, but oddly, my daughter's medication stayed the same from the beginning, even if there was no significant progress. The only things the medicines really did for my child was keep her zoned-out, gain weight, and cause fatty liver, and diabetes, among other things. Each time I spoke up, my opinion didn't count. I was devastated because I didn't want her to suffer now or later from the side effects. There seemed to be no light at the end of the tunnel until I found Kuadra Consulting and Counseling Service, LLC, near my daughter's third year of struggling.

"Here, a refreshing treatment plan was put in place. My daughter was introduced to a new form of therapy that involved an interesting machine. It's based on IMAET Technology, where a person's body is evaluated from the inside to assist a licensed therapist/doctor in better counseling on your overall health. I am a true believer that the mind, body, and spirit need to be healthy and in sync. Each session consists of addressing issues my daughter speaks about and what the IMAET Technology machine points out she needs help with. The machine has correctly pointed out physical health issues my daughter had/has and is being treated. She has significantly progressed and feels more comfortable in her body and mind. Her feeling of being zoned-out and depressed has faded. She even speaks more in therapy. She has more inner strength to fight for her mental stability and has shown doctors that she doesn't need to be categorized and be heavily medicated. She shocked/impressed her psychiatrist and primary doctor with her overall health progress. She hasn't been taken to a mental hospital in over a year. She will definitely continue to benefit from IMAET technology.

"She is now a strong seventeen-year-old girl soon to go to college!"

Other Comments from Clients

"IMAET treatment has been different than any other treatment that I have received because it looks closely at what's going on inside my body. It's like having a super personalized guide that exactly shows what's not working right. This special attention helps fix not just the things that bother me but also the reasons behind them." – G.R

"IMAET understands that my body, mind, and feelings are all connected. It's like having a plan that makes sure everything is in harmony. For the first time in my life, I feel like my whole self is being taken care of." – M.T

"I have had a long history of taking medication and have had horrible side effects. But with IMAET, it's different; it only works where it's needed, and for me, that means no more feeling horrible from unnecessary medication—just feeling better without any problems on the side." – A.C

"IMAET has given me hope. It has looked at the things causing the trouble and helped manage them better. It's like having a friend who knows exactly how to handle the tough stuff so I can focus on being happy." – S.B

CHAPTER 18

Conclusion

They dress the wounds of my people as though it were not serious. Peace, peace, peace, they say, when there is no peace. That is, the false prophets and lying priests, who pretended to be physicians, and to heal the sickly and distempered state of the people; and they did do it, in their way, but not thoroughly; they did not search the wound to the bottom; they drew a skin over it, and made a scar of it, and called it a cure; they made light of the hurt or wound.

Jeremiah 6:14

As with many indigenous people around the world that were colonized and assimilated into western religions and beliefs, we have learned to keep an open mind to the endless possibilities in other people's ideas.

No Indigenous person will hear of the love of Christ and not accept it because the Spirit of Christianity was already embedded in the hearts of Indigenous people. We would not discount the teachings of Prophet Mohammed because it brings about the foundations of brotherhood, discipline, and chastity. Indigen will also not discount the Buddha teachings because it brings forth wisdom and compassion. We don't claim one is bad and another is good. We open our minds to dig deeper into other peoples' points of view because we know that the deeper, we dig, the more likely we will contact hidden meanings of spiritual and heavenly representations.

Indigenous peoples never refuted the concept of God or Christ or Holy Spirit or the Buddha because, we know how to cultivate relationships with the true essence of these Spirits.

God means many things to many people. To some, it is just a word and to others, there is a deeper relationship and still, yet others will have direct experiences and unite with the source of all creation.

Indigen will not discount science because everything logical and plausible is also spiritual and spirituality is logic. In the mind of an Indigen, everything is connected, everything is important, and nothing operates by itself – A basic tenet of Buddhism.

The life of Indigen is rich because daily life is pregnant with meaning no matter how mundane or eventful because all experiences including the traumatic ones are opportunities to deepen in spiritual growth. This attitude allows Indigen to integrate ideas and widen the field of possibilities for creativity, innovation, and growth.

My message is not for the world but for the earnest seekers of the light. It is not for individuals who would not be caught dead in a negative light by the world, or who placate the misery of others while basking in their meaningless baubles and colorful phrases that conceal their evil egos.

God's children will be redeemed. They require no fake sympathies or evil recognition for all the evil atrocities committed against them worldwide. Our justice is by the recompense of God, and that time has come.

The journey of the wounded healer requires that we no longer hide our wounds but bring them to the light of day through confession, admission, and surrendering to the light. It is about getting to the core of wounds with intuition, innovation, creativity, a reverence for divine light as the healer, and the willingness of the practitioner to be a conduit for healing.

The objective is not about finding history because the truth is right in front of us. We will have to be honest with ourselves and accept what we truly are as children of God or a child of the world. After we have answered that question, true healing can begin.

I have shared an intimate journey to self-discovery and healing in hopes that others who have experienced extreme forms of trauma can find and embrace their own experiences as an opportunity for truth telling and self-discovery. My childhood trauma in no way was meant as a victim story or to expose my oppressors but to thank them for re-directing me toward the unique connection I can establish with God and to inform others that traumas have the same goal. This goal is an indefinable decision to take the journey to the divine.

As we journey from past life, karmic influences, pre-birth circumstances, and all the various synchronicities of our current lives, each must be carefully contemplated and are all distinct clues that pave the way to God.

How much trauma do we need in life to realize our divine mission? What will it take to decide to fight our way out of the myriad of distractions that take our energy and consistently distract us from our birthright? What would it take to realize that humans have no other purpose except the function given by the laws of God? What would it take to realize we hurt only ourselves?

As a child exposed to many religions, I realized by the age of eight that all religions hold the key to the whole puzzle. By dismissing any one doctrine and even any one person, you miss opportunity to gain wisdom and insight about the path to God. The path is not solely an intellectual one; it is of a different quality, a fine art, a cosmic and romantic dance with synchronicity and a deep desire to receive insights within every encounter with nature, people, and the subtle realms. Nothing can be ignored as foolery, and everything is a clue or puzzle piece to achieving wholeness in the mind. That wholeness is the enlightened mind.

It is time that we begin to delve beyond the norm and consider holistic approaches to healing body, mind, and spirit. As a practitioner, I knew that I needed to heal from my traumas before I could even consider healing others. Healers must heal themselves and then map the path for others to follow. Considering creativity in the psychotherapy process allows us to use our intuitive perceptions to understand what is occurring in the other realms and how it is affecting us individually. The process of getting to know ourselves is a lifelong journey worth undertaking for the sake of our ascension to the afterlife. Deep contemplation is a necessary part of the spiritual path, and a healed psychotherapist can lend much to others in the way of understanding their daily life experiences. Humanity has a lot healing work to do; we must undo all the lies and preconceptions and teach our children the right way so that they have a strong physical and spiritual foundation. We must train ourselves to see beyond the physical and use all our senses to interact with the world.

Spiritual psychotherapy gives us this fine dance. It allows us to be able to sit with one another and experience divine flow as we express our traumas and find the wisdom and insights that give way to expanding our consciousness. It explores beyond the known by mapping the clues to our past, present, and future.

I am daring to take the risk for true healing unabated by controlling institutions. I share the possibilities that may exist for healing when we blend psychology and spiritual healing. Considering the differing world views related to mental health and spiritual health from different countries, spiritual psychotherapy offers a blend of Eastern and Western philosophies. It gives the practitioner creative and intuitive impulses to support client healing. This type of approach may certainly be more palatable to countries in Africa, Asia, and South America. It would truly be amazing to see more explorations and research into how spiritual psychotherapy can further be developed.

Before the initial sessions and prior to treatment, all participants had experienced various mental health and chronic disease issues and had been in the care of medical professionals and specialists for their various conditions for more than two years. They all reported not getting better even with treatment, and some reported adverse effects from treatment. All the participants had agreed to try the holistic approach of the IMAET biofeedback treatment along with holistic modalities offered at my practice. My approach to healing is often described as holistic, intuitive, and creative. It incorporates methods that explore the spiritual, psychological, and physical aspects of a person to find true energetic causes and bring harmony and balance to the individual. All the participants received multiple IMAET feedback sessions, hypnotherapy, energy healing, and other alternative approaches and reported getting and staying better.

Given the sweeping declining health and wellness in the United States, it would be beneficial for healthcare systems to consider other noninvasive tools that can promote wellness and restore the health of individuals. The IMAET is an epigenetic and bioenergetic healing tool, Hypnotherapy heals subconscious programming, Astrology provides a map into a person's personality and energy healing is explores the restoration of Prana in Hindu culture, and in Chinese traditional culture, called Qi.

My approach to healing using the IMAET and more merges traditional wisdom with modern scientific knowledge of body biochemistry and epigenetics and allows us to enter a new universe of understanding health and disease. We are entering the cyberspace of the body. Gaining this new understanding becomes a matter of information analysis. It has been called decoding the human biofield by Peter Fraser in "Interacting Fields of Energy and Information that Surround Living Systems" by the NIH.

The healthcare system of specialists and subspecialists has created a nightmare for individuals seeking wellness, and it has become more difficult to navigate an increasingly disintegrated system. As the system disintegrates, so do the individuals, as they are left to piece together the various treatments and medications given to them by multiple specialists. The mechanisms for holistic wellness require the joining of hands of the spiritual, emotional, and behavioral in such a way that the individual is getting a holistic view of his or her problems, and solutions appear less complicated than the medical system makes them out to be.

In my practice, I incorporate quantum healing and intuitive models with emerging interactive technology to encourage a new phase of research and implementation of biofeedback. Future biofeedback interventions offer a great deal of promise because they harness the power of epigenetic quantum tools to help people regulate their overall health in a way that feels engaging, personal, and meaningful.

References

Abd-Ru-Shin. (1995). *In the light of truth: The grail message.* Grail Foundation Press.

Abe, M., & Abe, M. (1997). Emptiness. Zen and Comparative Studies: Part two of a two-volume sequel to Zen and Western Thought, 42-53.

African Shamanism / Shaman Portal. www.shamanportal.org/shamanism_african. php Retrieved May 12, 2020

Alabdali, A., Al-Ayadhi, L., & El-Ansary, A. (2014). *A key role for an impaired detoxification mechanism in the etiology and severity of autism spectrum disorders. Behavioral and Brain Functions,* 10, 1-11. https://link.springer.com/article/10.1186/1744-9081-10-14

Albanese, C. L. (2000). *The aura of wellness: Subtle-energy healing and new age religion. Religion and American Culture,* 10(1), 29-55. https://www.jstor.org/stable/1123890

Alizamar, A., Ifdil, I., Fadli, R. P., Erwinda, L., Zola, N., Churnia, E., Bariyah, K., Refnadi, R., & Rangka, I. B. (2018). *The effectiveness of hypnotherapy in reducing stress levels. Addictive Disorders & Their Treatment,* 17(4), 191-195.

American Psychiatric Association. (2013). *Diagnostic and statistical manual of mental disorders: DSM-5* (5th ed.).

American Psychological Association. (2016). *Hypnosis today: Looking beyond the media portrayal.* https://www.apa.org/topics/psychotherapy/hypnosis

Andrews, T. (2002). *Animal speak: The spiritual & magical powers of creatures great and small.* Llewellyn.

Arafat, S.M.Y., Menon, V., Varadharajan, N., & Kar, S.K, (2022). Psychological autopsy studies of suicide in South East Asia. *Indian Journal of Psychological Medicine,* 44(1), 4–9. https://pubmed.ncbi.nlm.nih.gov/35509662/

Arafat, S.M.Y., Saleem, T., Menon, V., Ali, S.A., Baminiwatta, A., Kar, S.K., Akter, H., & Singh, R. (2022). *Depression and suicidal behavior in South Asia: A systematic review and meta-analysis. Global Mental Health,* 9, 181-192. https://pubmed.ncbi.nlm.nih. gov/36618741/

The AstroTwins. (n.d.). *History of astrology: A timeline.* Astrostyle. https://astrostyle.com/astrology/history/

Baigent, M., Campion, N., & Harvey, C. (1992). *Mundane astrology: An introduction to the astrology of nations and groups.* Thorsons Publications.

Bailly, F., & Longo, G. (2009). Biological organization and anti-entropy. Journal of Biological Systems, 17(01), 63-96.

Baldwin, A. L., & Trent, N. L. (2017). An integrative review of scientific evidence for reconnective healing. *Journal of Alternative and Complementary Medicine,* 23(8), 590-598. https://pubmed.ncbi.nlm.nih.gov/28654301/

Barnhart, J. E. (1972). Freud's pleasure principle and the death urge. *The Southwestern Journal of Philosophy,* 3(1), 113-120. https://www.jstor.org/stable/43154869

Batalla, A., Bhattacharyya, S., Yücel, M., Fusar-Poli, P., Crippa, J. A., Nogué, S., Torrens, M., Pujol, J., Farré, M., & Martin-Santos, R. (2013). Structural and functional imaging studies in chronic cannabis users: a systematic review of adolescent and adult findings. PLOS ONE, 8(2), 1-18. https://pubmed.ncbi.nlm.nih.gov/23390554/

Bateman, A., & Holmes, J. (1999). *Introduction to psychoanalysis: Contemporary theory and practice.* Routledge.

Bishwajit G., O'Leary, D.P., Ghosh, S., Yaya, S., Shangfeng, T. & Feng, Z. (2017). Physical inactivity and self-reported depression among middle-and older-aged population in South Asia: World health survey. *BMC Geriatrics,* 17(100), 1-8. https://pubmed.ncbi.nlm.nih.gov/28454520/

Black, D. W., & Grant, J. E. (2014). *DSM-5 guidebook: The essential companion to the diagnostic and statistical manual of mental disorders* (5th ed.). American Psychiatric Association Publishing.

Body Soul Rhythms (https://www.mwfbodySoulrhythms.org/).

Braithwaite, J. J., & David, A. S. (2016). Out of body, out of mind? An examination of out-of-body experiences and dissociative disorders. Cognitive Neuropsychiatry, 21(5), 373-376.

Brennan, I. B. Talk on Theology and Energy Healing ACT Post Conference Circle of Inquiry on Energy Healing-2002 by Robert Sears, SJ, Ph. D. I. Barbara Brennan In her book, Hands of Light, Barbara Brennan speaks of her childhood on a farm in.

Brink, N. E. (2017). *Ecstatic soul retrieval: Shamanism and psychotherapy.* Simon and Schuster.

Campion, N. (2018). *Astrology in ancient Greek and Roman culture* (P. Read et al., Ed).

REFERENCES

Oxford Research Encyclopedia of Planetary Science. https://doi.org/10.1093/acrefore/9780190647926.013.46

Cappuccio, F. P., & Miller, M. A. (2006). Energy cannot be created nor destroyed. Nutrition, Metabolism and Cardiovascular Diseases, 16(7), e11.

Castaneda, C., & Moreno, L. (1993). *The art of dreaming* (p. 272). New York: Harper-Collins.

Catlin, A. & Taylor-Ford, R. L. (2011). *Investigation of standard care versus sham Reiki placebo versus actual Reiki therapy to enhance comfort and well-being in a chemotherapy infusion center.* Oncology Nursing Forum, 38(3), E212-E220. https://pubmed.ncbi.nlm.nih.gov/21531671/

Corballis, M. C. (2014). Left brain, right brain: facts and fantasies. PLoS Biol, 12 (1), e1001767.

Chrysopoeia Astrology. (2022, March 5). *What is psychological astrology? A brief history.* Medium. https://medium.com/@chrysopoeia.astrology/what-is-psychological-astrology-a-brief-history-735e34370980#:~:text=The%20origins%20of%20psychological%20astrology,and%20humanistic%20psychology%20with%20astrology

Clinton, A. N. (2009). *Advanced Integrative Therapy: The Basics.*

Crockford, S. (2011). Shamanisms and the authenticity of religious experience. *Pomegranate: International Journal of Pagan Studies,* 12(2), 139-158. https://journal.equinoxpub.com/POM/article/view/3184

Creightmore, R. (2012). Geopathic stress. The Geomancy Group, available http://www. geomancygroup. org/geopathic% 20stress/richard_gs_01. htm (accessed 06 November 2012). https://www.safespace.net.nz/pdf/GEOPATHIC%20STRESS%20by%20Richard%20Creightmore.pdf

Das, L. S. (2010). Natural radiance: Awakening to your great perfection. ReadHowYouWant. com.

Dhakal, A., & Sbar, E. (2023). *Jarisch herxheimer reaction.* StatPearls Publishing. https://www.ncbi.nlm.nih.gov/books/NBK557820/

Dharmadhikari, N. P., Meshram, D. C., Kulkarni, S. D., Kharat, A. G., & Pimplikar, S. S. (2011). Effect of geopathic stress zone on human body voltage and skin resistance. *Journal of Engineering and Technology Research,* 3(8), 255-63. https://www.semanticscholar.org/paper/Geopathic-stress%3A-a-study-to-understand-its-nature-Dharmadhikari-Meshram/49bb8796acffa5caa2e41c05c758ec0e31c6e762

DiNucci, E. M. (2005). Energy healing: a complementary treatment for orthopedic and other conditions. *Orthopedic Nursing*, 24(4), 259-269. https://pubmed.ncbi.nlm.nih.gov/16056170/

Dorahy, M. J., Brand, B. L., Şar, V., Krüger, C., Stavropoulos, P., Martínez-Taboas, A., Lewis-Fernández, R., & Middleton, W. (2014). Dissociative identity disorder: An empirical overview. *The Australian & New Zealand Journal of Psychiatry*, 48(5), 402-417. https://pubmed.ncbi.nlm.nih.gov/24788904/

Dressen, L. J. & Singg, S. (1998). Effects of reiki on pain and selected affective and personality variables of chronically ill patients. *Subtle Energies & Energy Medicine*, 9(1), 51-82. https://journals.sfu.ca/seemj/index.php/seemj/article/view/247

EcoWatch. (2015, July 6). 84,000 *Chemicals on the market, only 1% have been tested for safety.* https://www.ecowatch.com/84-000-chemicals-on-the-market-only-1-have-been-tested-for-safety-1882062458.html

Elhauge, I. (2010). *The fragmentation of U.S. health care: Causes and solutions.* Oxford University Press.

Ellinger, I., & Ellinger, A. (2014). Smallest unit of life: cell biology. Comparative medicine: Anatomy and physiology, 19-33.

Evans-Martin, F. (2022). The nervous system. Infobase Holdings, Inc.

Evans, T.S., Berkman, N., Brown, C., Gaynes, B., Weber, P. W. (2016). *Disparities within serious mental illness* (Report No. 16-EHC027-EF). Agency for Healthcare Research and Quality. https://www.ncbi.nlm.nih.gov/books/NBK368427/

EXPLORE, 4(3). pp. 201-209. ISSN 1550-8307, https://doi.org/10.1016/j.explore.2008.02.005.

Fernandez, G. (2021). *The intersection of mental health and chronic disease.* Johns Hopkins Bloomberg School of Public Health. https://publichealth.jhu.edu/2021/the-intersection-of-mental-health-and-chronic-disease

Filbey, F. M., Aslan, S., Calhoun, V. D., Spence, J. S., Damaraju, E., Caprihan, A., & Segall, J. (2014). Long-term effects of marijuana use on the brain. *Proceedings of the National Academy of Sciences, 111*(47), 16913-16918. https://pubmed.ncbi.nlm.nih.gov/25385625/

Forscutt, G. (n.d.). *Galactic astrology.* Galactic Astrology Academy. Retrieved January 15, 2024, from https://galacticastrologyacademy.com/

Fowler, K. (2022). *The ultimate guide to energy healing: The beginner's guide to healing your chakras, aura, and energy body* (Vol. 14). Fair Winds Press.

Franklin, H. (2022) Geopathic Stress. https://www.hollandfranklin.com/geopathic-stress-the-ultimate-guide/ Retrieved April 30, 2024

REFERENCES

Fraser, P.H., Massey, H., Wilcox, H.P. (2008). *Decoding the Human Body-Field: The New Science of Information as Medicine.* Healing Arts Press.

Friedman, H. (2014). Finding meaning through transpersonal approaches in clinical psychology: Assessments and psychotherapies. Journal of Existential Psychology and Psychotherapy, 45, 49.

Freshwater, D. (1997). *Geopathic stress. Complementary Therapies in Nursing and Midwifery,* 3(6), 160-162. https://pubmed.ncbi.nlm.nih.gov/9511645/

Frinta, W. J. (2018). *Energy healing: A surprising form of medicine.* iUniverse.

Glaser, B. G. & Strauss, A. L. (1967). *The discovery of grounded theory: strategies for qualitative research.* Aldine Publishing Company.

Hall, J. A. (1983). *Jungian dream interpretation: A handbook of theory and practice* (Vol. 13). Inner City Books.

Jarvis, C. (n.d.). *The halls of Amenti.* Official Charles Jarvis Website. http://www.charlesjajarvis.com/GreatWhiteLodge/HallsOfAmenti.pdf

Jung, Carl Gustov (1955) Jung on Astrology. https://www.jungiancenter.org/jung-on-astrology

Jung, Carl Gustov (1950) Jung on Astrology. https://www.jungiancenter.org/jung-on-astrology

Grabovoi, G. (2006). *Program of training the teaching of Grigori Grabovoi* [Course]. Grigori Grabovoi. https://www.grigori-grabovoi.world/index.php/educational-program/introductory-course-of-educational-program-of-training-the-teachings-of-grigori-grabovoi

Gray, M (2015). Psychological astrology: A therapeutic tool on our journey of individuation. *Inside Out Journal.* https://iahip.org/page-1075925

Greene, L., and Sasportas, H. (1987). *The development of the personality: Seminars in psychological astrology* (Vol. 1). Weiser Books.

Greene, L., and Sasportas, H. (1988). *Dynamics of the unconscious: Seminars in psychological astrology* (Vol. 2). Weiser Books.

HAIR (1967) Rado, James, & Ragni, Gerome. Broadway Musical Home https://broadwaymusicalhome.com/shows/hair.htm#gsc.tab=0

Harvey, G., & Wallis, R. J. (2010). *The A to Z of Shamanism* (Vol. 173). Scarecrow Press.

Hodges RE, Minich DM. Modulation of Metabolic Detoxification Pathways Using Foods and Food-Derived Components: A Scientific Review with Clinical Application. J Nutr Metab. https://www.ncbi.nlm.nih.gov/pmc/articles/PMC4488002/2015;2015:760689. doi: 10.1155/2015/760689. Epub 2015 Jun 16.

PMID: 26167297; PMCID: PMC4488002.

Hollis, J. (2002). *Creating a life: Finding your individual path.* Inner City Books.

Hollis, J. (2003). *On this journey we call our life: Living the questions.* Inner City Books.

Hunter, C. R., & Eimer, B. N. (2012). *The art of hypnotic regression therapy: A clinical guide.* Crown House Publishing.

International Association of Reiki Professionals. (2016). Reiki in the clinical setting. http://iarp.org/reiki-clinical-setting/

International Society for the Study of Trauma and Dissociation. (2011). Guidelines for treating dissociative identity disorder in adults, third revision. *Journal of Trauma & Dissociation, 12*(2), 115-187. https://pubmed.ncbi.nlm.nih.gov/21391104/

Jain S, Hammerschlag R, Mills P, Cohen L, Krieger R, Vieten C, Lutgendorf S. Clinical Studies of Biofield Therapies: Summary, Methodological Challenges, and Recommendations. Glob Adv Health Med. 2015 Nov;4(Suppl):58-66. doi: 10.7453/gahmj.2015.034.suppl. Epub 2015 Nov 1. PMID: 26665043; PMCID: PMC4654788. https://pubmed.ncbi.nlm.nih.gov/26665043/

Jungian Center for the Spiritual Sciences. (n.d.). Jung on astrology. https://www.jungiancenter.org/jung-on-astrology

Kent JB, Jin L, Li XJ. Quantifying Biofield Therapy through Biophoton Emission in a Cellular Model. J Sci Explor. 2020 Fall;34(3):434-454. doi: 10.31275/20201691. Epub 2020 Sep 15. PMID: 33223611; PMCID: PMC7676814.

Keyes, R. & Feldman, S. M. (2015, April 8). *Reiki in the operating room: Breast cancer & beyond* [Special Event Presentation]. Spirituality Mind Body Institute of the Columbia University Teachers College, Clinical Psychology Program, New York, NY, United States.

Kidd, P. M. (2002). Autism, an extreme challenge to integrative medicine. Part 1: The knowledge base. Alternative medicine review, 7(4), 292-316.

Korotkov, K. (2011). Measuring human energy field: Revolutionary instrument to reveal energy fields of human and nature. *International Union of Medical and Applied Bioelectrography,* 1-15. https://korotkov.co/archive/wp-content/uploads/2014/04/2011-Human-Energy-Field.pdf

Korotkov, K. Dr. Ekaterina Yakovleva Dr. Konstantin Korotkov.

Korotkov, K., Shelkov, O., Shevtsov, A., Mohov, D., Paoletti, S., Mirosnichenko, D., Labkovskaya, E., & Robertson, L. (2012). Stress reduction with osteopathy assessed with GDV electrophotonic imaging: Effects of osteopathy treatment. *The Journal of Alternative and Complementary Medicine, 18*(3), 251-257.

REFERENCES

Kostyuk, N., Cole, P., Meghanathan, N., Isokpehi, R.D., & Cohly, H.H. (2011). Gas discharge visualization: An imaging and modeling tool for medical biometrics. *International Journal of Biomedical Imaging*. https://www.ncbi.nlm.nih.gov/pmc/articles/PMC3124241/

Kuman, M. (2022). Scientific explanation of the biofeedback method of healing. *Journal of MAR Case Reports*, 6(4). https://www.medicalandresearch.com/assets/articles/documents/DOCUMENT_20230208164839.pdf

Levin, J., & Mead, L. (2008). Bioenergy healing: a theoretical model and case series. *Explore*, 4(3), 201-209. https://pubmed.ncbi.nlm.nih.gov/18466852/

Laufer, C. E. (2016). *Hell's Destruction: An Exploration of Christ's Descent to the Dead.* Routledge.

Linsley, A. C. (2020, December 19). *Yebu, ijebu, jebusite.* Biblical Anthropology. https://biblicalanthropology.blogspot.com/2020/12/yebu-ijebu-jebusite.html?m=1

Lajoie, D. H. & Shapiro, S. I. "Definitions of transpersonal psychology: The first twenty-three years". Journal of Transpersonal Psychology, Vol. 24, 1992

Luzac's Semitic Text and Translation Series, 2007. Xonfcon : LUZAC AND CO. 1902. https://ia601302.us.archive.org/32/items/seventabletsofcr02kinguoft/seventabletsofcr02kinguoft.pdf

Mageau, M. (2014). *Our chakra system: A portal to inter-dimensional consciousness.* DoctorZed Publishing.

Mandela, N. (1994) Inaugural Speech [Speech Transcript]. University of Pennsylvania African Studies Center. https://www.africa.upenn.edu/Articles_Gen/Inaugural_Speech_17984.html

Merriam-Webster Dictionary. https://www.merriam-webster.com/dictionary/pseudoscience

McKusick, E. D. (2021). *Tuning the human biofield: Healing with vibrational sound therapy.* Healing Arts Press.

McInturff, Brian. (2006). The Electroherbalism Frequency Lists

Misra, S., & Shastri, I. (2014). Rumination of Music on Buddhism and Hinduism. International Journal of Human Movement and Sports Science, 2(3), 33-40.

Moss, Robert (2012). *Dreaming the Soul back home: Shamanic dreaming for healing and becoming whole.* New World Library.

Monroe, R. A. (1996). *The ultimate journey.* Harmony.

Mulligan, A. (2021). *Muscle testing: What it is and how it helps with treatment.* Psychreg. https://www.psychreg.org/muscle-testing/

Munson, R. (2018). *Tesla: Inventor of the modern.* WW Norton & Company.

National Institute on Drug Abuse. (2023, April 17). What are marijuana's long-term effects on the brain? https://nida.nih.gov/publications/research-reports/marijuana/what-are-marijuanas-long-term-effect brain#:~:text=Some%20studies%20suggest%20regular%20marijuana,people%20who%20do%20not%20use.

New York Milton H. Erickson Society for Psychotherapy and Hypnosis. (2016). *What is hypnosis?* NYSEPH. http://nyseph.org/what-is-hypnosis/

Nag PK. Sick Building Syndrome and Other Building-Related Illnesses. Office Buildings. 2018 Aug 18:53–103. doi: 10.1007/978-981-13-2577-9_3. PMCID: PMC7153445.

Nield-Anderson, L. (2000, April). The empowering nature of reiki as a complementary therapy. *Holistic Nursing Practice,* 14(3), 21-29. https://pubmed.ncbi.nlm.nih.gov/12119625/

Noll, R., Achterberg, J., Bourguignon, E., George, L., Harner, M., Honko, L., ... & Winkelman, M. (1985). Mental imagery cultivation as a cultural phenomenon: The role of visions in shamanism [and comments and reply]. Current anthropology, 26(4), 443-461.

O'Neil, J. A. (2009). Dissociative multiplicity in psychoanalysis. In P. F. Dell & J. A. O'Neil (Eds.), *Dissociation and the dissociative disorders:* DSM-V and beyond (pp. 287–325). Routledge/Taylor & Francis Group.

Öztürk, E., & Sar, V. (2016). Formation and functions of alter personalities in dissociative identity disorder: A theoretical and clinical elaboration. *Journal of Psychology and Clinical Psychiatry*, 6(6), 00385.

Parekh MA, Majeed H, Khan TR, Khan AB, Khalid S, Khwaja NM, Khalid R, Khan MA, Rizqui IM, Jehan I. Ego defense mechanisms in Pakistani medical students: a cross sectional analysis. BMC Psychiatry. 2010 Jan 29;10:12. doi: 10.1186/1471-244X-10-12. PMID: 20109240; PMCID: PMC2836996.

Perry, G. (n.d.). *What is astropsychology? Astropsychology* Services. https://aaperry.com/what-is-astropsychology/

Petrarca, R. (2023). Chapter 22: The history of astronomy [lecture]. *In Basics of Astronomy.* Study. https://study.com/learn/lesson/astrology-overview-history.html#:~:text=History%20of%20Astrology,-Astrology%20is%20older&text=Western%20astrology%20began%20with%20the,astrologers%2 0in%20history%20was%20Nostradamus

Pica, M. (1999). The evolution of alter personality states in dissociative identity disorder. *Psychotherapy: Theory, Research, Practice, Training*, 36(4), 404-415.

Poulin, P. A., & West, W. (2005). Holistic healing, paradigm shift, and the new age. In R. Moodley & W. West (Eds.), *Integrating traditional healing practices into counseling and psychotherapy* (pp. 257-269). Sage Publications.

Powell, A. E. (Ed.) (1928). *The causal body and the ego.* Kessinger Publishing.

Prescott, R. C. (2014). VAJRASATTVA. Author House.

Ramana Maharshi (2006). The Collected Works of Ramana Maharshi. Sophia Perennis et Universalis.

Rinpoche, S. (2009). *The Tibetan book of living and dying.* HarperOne.

Rudd, Richard. (2013). *The gene keys: Embracing your higher purpose.* Watkins Publishing.

Ruiz, D. J. (2019). *The wisdom of the shamans: What the ancient masters can teach us about love and life.* Hierophant Publishing.

Publication: Scientific American Publisher: SCIENTIFIC AMERICAN, a Division of Springer Nature America, Inc. https://www.scientificamerican.com/article/are-virtual-particles-rea/

Date: Oct 9, 2006

Sands, S. H. (2010). On the royal road together: The analytic function of dreams in activating dissociative unconscious communication. Psychoanalytic Dialogues, 20(4), 357-373.

Scudder, J. D. (1996). Electron and ion temperature gradients and suprathermal tail strengths at Parker's solar wind sonic critical point. Journal of Geophysical Research: Space Physics, 101(A5), 11039-11053.

Sharma, N. (n.d.). What is Human Aura? BioField Global Research, Inc. http://www.biofieldglobal.org/what-is-human-aura.html

Singg, S. (2009). Reiki: an alternative and complementary healing therapy. In C. M. Davis (Ed.), *Complementary therapies in rehabilitation.* SLACK, Inc.

Singh, J. P. (2013). Physics, consciousness and health in relation with aura energy field. *International Journal of Engineering Research and Development*, 6(11), 84-87.

Stavish, M. (2018). *Egregores: The occult entities that watch over human destiny* (2nd ed). Inner Traditions.

Steiner, R. (2024). Human and cosmic thought. Rudolf Steiner Press.

Straile, B. (2022). *The show method guidebook: For epigenetic energy balancing treatments.*

Straile, B. (n.d.). Imaet pro. IMAET. https://www.imaet.com/imaet-pro IMAET INC, 1326 New Seneca Tnpk Skaneateles, NY 13152

Strachey, J., Freud, A., Strachey, A. & Tyson, A. (1955). *The standard edition of the complete psychological works of Sigmund Freud, volume xviii (1920-1922): Beyond the pleasure principle, group psychology and other works.* London the Hogarth Press.

NSDUH. (2021). *2021 National survey on drug use and health release.* Substance Abuse and Mental Health Services Administration. https://www.samhsa.gov/data/release/2021-national-survey-drug-use-and-health-nsduh-releases

Sumbal A, Sumbal R. Mystical and mythological believes not only limited to psychiatric diseases? A dynamic overview of medicine. Ann Med Surg (Lond). 2023 Feb 17;85(2):311-312. doi: 10.1097/MS9.0000000000000108. PMID: 36845757; PMCID: PMC9949817.

Sun, H., & Sun, D. (2013). Color Your Life: How to Use the Right Colors to Achieve Balance, Health, and Happiness. TarcherPerigee.

Swanson, C. (2011). *Life force, the scientific basis: Breakthrough physics of energy medicine, healing, chi and quantum consciousness* (Vol.2). Poseidia Press.

NASA. (2012). Hidden portals in Earth's magnetic field. https://www.sciencedaily.com/releases/2012/07/120703140559.htm
https://phys.org/news/2012-07-hidden-portals-earth-magnetic-field.html

Tart, C. T. (Ed.). (1992). *Transpersonal psychologies: Perspectives on the mind from seven great spiritual traditions.* HarperCollins Publishers.

Tonsager, S. R. (2017). *Intention based field resonance testing: The magnification of the whisper.* Dog Ear Publishing.

Traumadissociation.com (2024, Jan 14). Alters in Dissociative Identity Disorder and OSDD/P-DID. http://traumadissociation.com/alters.

Tsang, K. L., Carlson, L. E., & Olson, K. (2007). Pilot crossover trial of Reiki versus rest for treating cancer-related fatigue. *Integrative Cancer Therapies*, 6(1), 25-35. https://pubmed.ncbi.nlm.nih.gov/17351024/

Upanishad, M. The Astral and Causal Bodies. https://www.simonheather.co.uk/pages/articles/the_astral_body.pdf

UNESCO. *Did you know? The influence of astrology on the science of astronomy along the Silk Road.* https://en.unesco.org/silkroad/content/did-you-know-influence-astrology-science-astronomy-along-silk-roads

Valverde, M. (1998). *Diseases of the will: Alcohol and the dilemmas of freedom.* Cambridge University Press.

Villoldo, A. (2016). *One spirit medicine: Ancient ways to ultimate wellness.* Hay House.

Vogel, J. H. K., Bolling, S. F., Costello, R. B., Guarneri, E. M., Krucoff, M. W., Longhurst, J. C., Olshansky, B., Pelletier, K. R., Tracy, C. M., Vogel, R.A., Abrams, J., Anderson, J. L., Bates, E. R., Brodie, B. R., Grines, C. L., Danias, P. G., Gregoratos, G., Hlatky, M. A., Hochman, J. S., & Winters, W. L. (2005). Integrating complementary medicine into cardiovascular medicine: A report of the American College of Cardiology Foundation task force on clinical expert consensus documents. *Journal of the American College of Cardiology,* 46(1), 184-221. https://www.jacc.org/doi/10.1016/j.jacc.2005.05.031

Walsh, B. (2016). Utilization sobriety: Incorporating the essence of mind-body communication for brief individualized substance abuse treatment. The Milton H. Erickson Institute of Portland. https://www.researchgate.net/profile/Bart_Walsh/publication/268328248_UTILIZATION_SOBRIETY_INCORPORATING_THE_ESSENCE_OF_BODYMIND_COMMUNICATION_FOR_BRIEF_SUBSTANCE_ABUSE_TREATMENT/links/548bbb370cf214269f1dd7a8.pd

Walsh, R. & Vaughan, F. (1993). On transpersonal definitions. *The Journal of Transpersonal Psychology,* 25(2) 125-182. https://www.atpweb.org/jtparchive/trps-25-93-02-199.pdf

Webster, L. C., Holden, J. M., Ray, D. C., Price, E., & Hastings, T. M. (2020). The impact of psychotherapeutic reiki on anxiety. *Journal of Creativity in Mental Health,* 15(3), 311-326. https://www.tandfonline.com/doi/full/10.1080/15401383.2019.1688214#:~:text=Preliminary%20medical%20research%20has%20demonstrated,as%20well%20as%20enhance%20mood

What Are the Five Major Types of Anxiety Disorders? Health and Human Services. Accessed 12/22/2023. https://www.cdc.gov/chronicdisease/index.htm

Willis, R., & Curry, P. (2020). *Astrology, science and culture: Pulling down the moon.* Routledge. https://doi.org/10.4324/9781003084723

Williams, R. M. (2009). Introduction to SCIO (frequency healing technology). *Townsend Letter,* (307-308), 59-63. https://www.thefreelibrary.com/Introduction+to+SCIO+(frequency+healing+technology).-a0194825339

Woollacott, M. H., Kason, Y., & Park, R. D. (2021). Investigation of the phenomenology, physiology and impact of spiritually transformative experiences–kundalini awakening. Explore, 17(6), 525-534.

World Health Organization. (1992). *The ICD-10 Classification of Mental and Behavioural Disorders.* Version: 2015. http://traumadissociation.com/alters

World Health Organization. (2014). *International Classification of Diseases,* 10th ed. Retrieved November 16, 2014, from http://www.who.int/classifications/icd/revision/en/

About The Author

Khadijat Quadri, nee Omobolanle Khadijat Alatise, was born in the native Ijebu-Ode tribe of Nigeria. She grew up in Lagos and migrated to the United States at the age of twenty-two. Quadri is a Board Certified Licensed Professional Counselor (LPC) with decades of experience in Clinical Mental Health, Holistic Healing Methods, Development, and Implementation of Community Based Mental Health and Education Programs. Her education includes multiple Advanced Degrees in Mental Health Counseling, International Development from St Mary's University, and Mastery in Global Mental Health Trauma and Recovery from Harvard University.

She received additional training in Contemplative Group Therapy, Transpersonal Psychology, Clinical Hypnotherapy, Reiki Energy Healing, Astrological Psychology, Advanced GDV Assessment, Advanced Integrative Therapy, Energy Psychology, Biofeedback Modalities, and Sound Frequency Healing.

Her past experiences range from developing programs for Refugee Communities, Infant Mortality, and developing Education Programs for low-income Communities. She currently operates a Transpersonal and Intuitive Counseling Private Practice in San Antonio, Texas, and has a wide range of practical experience in trauma and mental health recovery. She has routinely treated mental health issues ranging from Personality Disorders to Depression, Anxiety, Grief, Attention Deficit Disorders, Sexual Abuse, Mood Disorders and Post Traumatic Stress Disorders.

Providing services to more than thirty thousand clients over a span of twenty-five years, she has conducted thousands of energy healing sessions, hypnotherapy, and holistic therapies to clients in various communities around the world. Khadijat has worked with individuals on their spiritual journeys, abused and neglected children, autism disorders and provided counseling to couples and families. Khadijat is a multifaceted educator whose global work and educational offerings have extended beyond traditional counseling to assisting countless lives in spiritual awakening and consciousness transformation.

Growing up within the Islamic faith and attending Christian Colleges, Khadijat developed an intimate understanding of both religions and spiritual practices and engaged in decades of consistent meditation and contemplative practice later in life. She undertook a more intimate spiritual journey where she practiced Dzogchen meditation, Zen Philosophy, and the noble eightfold path of the Buddhist Contemplations. She enjoys chanting, shamanic healing, sound healing therapies and is versed in over a hundred spiritual chants and mantras from across religions. Khadijat's international travels extend beyond multiculturalism to providing education, research studies, mental health development projects while immersing herself in the beauty and wisdom all faiths and cultures have to offer.

Her practice has a 95% retention rate because of a creative and transpersonal approach that provides a full spectrum of the client's cognitive, transcendental, and spiritual life paths. Through her intimate dance with spirit, she can weave gentle, creative models that are insightful for clients' journeys.